FRAGMENTS OF INEQUALITY

FRAGMENTS OF INEQUALITY

SOCIAL, SPATIAL, AND EVOLUTIONARY ANALYSES OF INCOME DISTRIBUTION

SANJOY CHAKRAVORTY

Routledge
Taylor & Francis Group

New York   London

Published in 2006 by
Routledge
Taylor & Francis Group
270 Madison Avenue
New York, NY 10016

Published in Great Britain by
Routledge
Taylor & Francis Group
2 Park Square
Milton Park, Abingdon
Oxon OX14 4RN

Printed in the United States of America on acid-free paper
10 9 8 7 6 5 4 3 2 1

International Standard Book Number-10: 0-415-95295-6 (Hardcover) 0-415-95296-4 (Softcover)
International Standard Book Number-13: 978-0-415-95295-8 (Hardcover) 978-0-415-95296-5 (Softcover)
Library of Congress Card Number 2005015174

Library of Congress Cataloging-in-Publication Data

Chakravorty, Sanjoy.
  Fragments of inequality : social, spatial, and evolutionary analyses of income distribution / Sanjoy Chakravorty.
    p. cm.
  Includes bibliographical references and index.
  ISBN 0-415-95295-6 (hb : alk. paper) -- ISBN 0-415-95296-4 (pb : alk. paper)
  1. Income distribution. 2. Equality. I. Title.

HB523.C44 2005
306.3--dc22   2005015174

Taylor & Francis Group
is the Academic Division of Informa plc.

Visit the Taylor & Francis Web site at
http://www.taylorandfrancis.com

and the Routledge Web site at
http://www.routledge-ny.com

To
Basudeb and Minati Chakravorty, Baba aar Ma,
My parents, human capitalists

CONTENTS

PREFACE

This book has grown out of some scattered thinking over several years that ultimately demanded to be organized. I felt strongly that the compartmentalized approach that the academy favors and rewards can be very effective in analyzing narrow questions but provides far less satisfying answers to the bigger questions, such as the most fundamental ones on income distribution. Why are incomes distributed the way they are? And how do these distributions change? This work is therefore a conscious effort to look beyond disciplinary boundaries, to bring an interdisciplinary approach to distributional analysis. The "fragments" in the title refers not only to disciplinary fragmentation, but also to the fact that societies are fragmented into unequal groups and territories are fragmented into unequal regions. I think that we do a better job of understanding inequality when we are able to stitch these fragments together.

Philadelphia, May 2005

ACKNOWLEDGMENTS

I wish to acknowledge the individuals and institutions that have helped in this effort. Temple University provided a semester-long study leave during which the manuscript was written. Subhrobaran Das did many of the calculations of the numerical illustration in Appendix 2. Numerous individuals at Cambridge University, Jadavpur University, Temple University, Warwick University, the Center for the Study of Social Sciences (Calcutta), the Society for the Advancement of Socio-Economics, the Development Studies Association, and the Association of American Geographers commented vigorously on fragments of the argument. Two anonymous reviewers commented constructively. They cannot, however, be blamed for errors of fact or reasoning. I must claim sole responsibility for those. My son Shourjo bore my unpredictability with good humor, as always. My wife Pallabi was a fount of encouragement and a touchstone for ideas. To my family my gratefulness knows no bounds.

1

THEORY AND EXPLANATION

Consider the following facts. The richest 20 percent of Brazil's population earns about 30 times more than the poorest 20 percent. This level of inequality has continued virtually unchanged from the 1950s, when analysts began measuring income inequality in Brazil. In the Russian Federation, this ratio (of income shares of the richest and poorest 20 percent of the population) was around 12 in 1998, which is about twice as high as it had been just a decade earlier, before the collapse of the Soviet Union.[1] These are dramatic examples: one of a very high level of inequality that has remained unchanged for decades, the other of a rapid change from a low to a high level of inequality. How do we explain this diversity of experiences? There is no doubt that random events (such as Boris Yeltsin's speech atop a tank during the 1991 coup attempt in Moscow) play a large role, just as there is no doubt that the structure of inequality can be understood in terms of economic, social, and spatial structure, and inequality change can be understood in terms of changes to these underlying structures. I begin from the position that, despite the likelihood of random events that can change distribution patterns, explanation is possible.

However, the search for explanation is stymied by epistemological boundaries. Because distribution is one of the pillars of development[2] there is a large literature on inequality. Unfortunately, this literature, and therefore our understanding of inequality, is fragmented by academic discipline. The discourse on income distribution is dominated

2 • Fragments of Inequality

by economists. The discourse on classes, stratification, and power is in the domain of sociologists. And spatial inequality has traditionally been studied by geographers and regional scientists. The theoretical foundations and methodologies of these disciplinary approaches are often so far apart that it has been difficult to create a solid theoretical understanding of inequality as an outcome of economic, social, and spatial processes. This book attempts to fill some of these large gaps in interdisciplinary knowledge about the structure of inequality and processes of distributional change using a new theoretical approach combining elements of economic, sociological, and geographical theory.

This new approach is built on evolutionary foundations. I begin from the recognition that human behavior and action follow evolutionary principles (identified in fields as diverse as evolutionary psychology, sociobiology, and behavioral economics) and not some unproven assumptions about rationality and self interest. This means that individuals and groups are both important elements of social and spatial structure, and, therefore, both are relevant for theorizing structure and change in inequality. Second, we must acknowledge that evolution itself is not linear and continuous. The standard Darwinist-gradualist view of evolution has to be supplemented with the near certainty of discontinuity and nonlinearity, or what is called the punctuated equilibrium model of evolution. These ideas are detailed later in this chapter and permeate the explanatory part of the book (Chapter 4 onward).

These shifts—from linear to punctuated models, from individuals to groups, from abstract and monolithic to fragmented space —purposefully suggest a fundamental shift away from the dominant mode of inequality analysis, which, as is well known, is the economic approach. Because of the limiting assumptions used in mainstream economic theory, assumptions that infer substantially more equality (of knowledge and power) than exists in reality, economic approaches turn out to be limited in their explanatory power. Inequality, I conclude, is too important a subject to be left to economists.[3] I retain the important contributions: the theories on human capital, the interaction of demand and supply of different forms of capital, but reject the narrow specifications of the rational, self-interested actor model. The goal is to shift the discourse away from economic to social theories of inequality.

QUESTIONS AND ANSWERS

The analysis focuses on income inequality. The idea of income inequality is easily understood, relatively easily measured, universal in its manifestation, and tangible, at some level, to everyone with social awareness. Data are collected to measure income inequality with increasing frequency and sophistication. Therefore, there is a concrete empirical basis from which one can begin an examination, and to which one can turn for support or falsification. I seek answers to the four fundamental questions on income inequality:

- What explains the level of income inequality in a given nation?
- Why do income inequality levels vary so greatly worldwide?
- What causes the level of income inequality to change?
- What explains the diversity of trends in income inequality change?

I come to the answers using an approach that seems simple and obvious but has never been used. Let me begin with the obvious: the world is fragmented. It is fragmented into geographical or spatial units that differ in terms of the average life chances of their inhabitants. This gives rise to spatial inequality. The spatial units themselves are fragmented into social groups with unequal power and resources; group membership is a significant determinant of an individual's life chances. This gives rise to social inequality. I argue that income inequality in any given nation is a result of its particular combination of social inequality (which arises from social fragmentation or heterogeneity) and spatial inequality (which arises from spatial fragmentation or heterogeneity). Nations vary in their specific combinations of social and spatial fragmentation that are the outcomes of specific histories; hence, they vary in their levels of income inequality. Broadly, the more fragmentation there is, the higher is the level of income inequality. Distributional change takes place as a result of changes to social and spatial inequality. Changes in social inequality can be dramatic when there are distributional transitions, which are possible under conditions of revolution, invasion, and war; in general, though, changes in social inequality are more likely to be gradual. Changes in spatial inequality are always gradual. The diversity of trends in distributional change are explained by the fact that nations differ in the rates and directions of change in social and spatial inequality and in their specific histories, which may or may not include one or more incidents of fundamental distributional change. In general, in the last 50 to 100 years, social inequality levels have declined in most nations (especially in the more developed nations) while spatial inequality levels have increased.

To put it in another way: a nation can be thought of as a combination of a social system and a spatial system. The social system is made up of individuals who compete for scarce resources and for status or recognition. The individuals are also organized into groups that are at least class-based and usually also identity-based (using ascriptive markers of race, ethnicity, religion, or language). Systematic and durable differences exist between group average incomes. Groups with access to more productive resources and power have higher average incomes and superior life chances than groups without. Hence, every society is fragmented to some degree. A social system is historically formed through migrations, invasions, wars, revolutions, expulsions, and trade, all of which have brought people with distinct ascriptive identities into common geographical confines. The variations in these conditions or events are largely responsible for the level of heterogeneity in a social system. A spatial system is made up of urban and rural areas in the first instance, with further delineations between urban areas (big city or small city) and rural areas (valley and hill, coastal and inland). These spatial differentiations are also largely historically constructed as a result of imperialism, colonialism, and trade. The different spaces offer different average incomes and life chances for their residents. Hence, a national territory is also spatially fragmented to some degree. Combinations of these two fragmentations create the conditions of economic inequality in given nations.

The critical questions relate therefore to change—social change and spatial change—and this is where I focus. Specifically, I concentrate on two forms of distributional change: the quick distributional transition as a result of state transition and consequent fundamental social change, and the slow, gradual transformation as a result of spatial transformation. One cannot, however, get to these narratives without a clear understanding of the structures that exist and are changed, and the agents and the processes of change. As a result, the first half of the book is devoted to setting the table. I begin by presenting data on income distribution and distributional change, with next a discussion of economic theories of inequality followed by a discussion on why and how economic theory must be and can be supplemented with social and spatial theory to create a true picture of the structure of inequality. Finally, in the later chapters (5 and 6), I am able to focus on the question of change.

THREE GENERAL PRINCIPLES

The setting would not be complete without a discussion of the principles that are foundational for this work. Some of these will become obvious from the brief arguments outlined in the following section. Nevertheless, it is necessary and useful to have a clear understanding of what it means to try to build theory using basic principles from the economic and social sciences. This distinction is important. At several points in the book, particularly in Chapters 3, 4 and 5, I refer to the idea that there are two fundamentally different ways of understanding human action and interaction: in simple terms, we can call these the economic perspective and the social perspective. I argue that it is not possible to build theories that make sense when these two perspectives are kept in separate boxes, rather, it is necessary to find ways to integrate them. Let us consider (briefly, since these ideas are spelled out in greater detail in other chapters) the principal building blocks of such an integrated theory.

First, we need to resolve a fundamental question in a non-judgmental way: What is the basic unit of a society? In the economic perspective, this is the individual. Individuals compete in a world of scarce resources to attain their primary goals of survival first and growth second, where survival and growth both have intergenerational dimensions. This means that people are primarily self-interested beings. (There are complications about the meaning of self-interest; these are taken up in Chapter 4.) The social perspective does not deny the importance of self-interest, but suggests that it is moderated by the interests of the groups to which the individual belongs. Hence, in the social perspective, the basic unit of a society is the group. Groups compete in a world of scarce resources to attain their primary goals of survival first and growth second, where survival and growth both have intergenerational dimensions. This means that groups are primarily self-interested entities (and basic group interests are established as norms, more on which soon). Virtually every statement we can make about individuals we can also make about groups: they compete, they are self-interested, they seek domination over others, they can engage in violence when threatened, they are interested in intergenerational continuity. It stands to reason, therefore, that individuals are motivated by both individual and group interests, and often the two cannot be identical. What happens when individual interests clash with group interests? Again, it stands to reason that the latter generally prevails, but, and this is a very important idea, it is possible for individuals to persuade groups to change or modify their interests. This, often, is the source of social change.

Therefore, to build sensible theory, we must recognize the coexistence of individual and group interests. In defining groups, however, we run into the problem of plurality, because individuals, more and more, are members of multiple groups. They are members of racial, ethnic, religious, and linguistic groups, and, without exception, they are members of economic groups or classes. This problem of plurality is usually partially resolved because the groups substantially overlap; that is, ethnicity, race, and class intersect. The problem can be tackled even more definitively if we recognize the existence of another type of group, one that is based on geography or location. At small geographical scales, groups are more easily delineated and it is possible to identify paired oppositions.

Individuals are organized into groups and groups are organized into territorial units. Therefore, we have another level of competition. Almost anything we can say about individuals and groups we can repeat about territorial units: they compete for scarce resources, they seek domination over others, etc. The world, I repeat, is fragmented. Individuals compete with other individuals, groups compete with other groups, and territories compete with other territories. Individuals often have to act, not in their individual interest, but in the interest of the group or the territory. On the positive side, it follows that individuals cooperate and have reciprocal relationships with members of their group and their territory. A good understanding of the social world must begin from recognizing this tripartite division of interests and the potential for inter-unit conflict and intra-unit cooperation and competition.

Second, economic and social interactions are characterized by "increasing returns" and "norms." Increasing returns are also called "cumulative causation" processes (they are not identical phenomena, as the latter includes the problem of vicious cycles) or "positive feedbacks" in which the "payoff to taking an action (increases with) the number of people taking the same action … or the payoff to engaging in a collective action depends on the number of participants" (Bowles 2004, 12). Norms include two overlapping classes of features: *ideologies,* which are sets of beliefs and desires, and *habits,* which are routine and standardized responses to a variety of situations. The existence of these features is usually well known by agents when they take decisions; as a result, they often turn into self-fulfilling prophecies or self-reinforcing actions. Let me explain:

Formal economic models of production are based on the assumption of constant returns to scale and diminishing returns to capital. These two assumptions drive (among other things) the preoccupation with convergence and equilibrium that are the mainstays of economic thought. Later we will see, for instance, that income convergence between territorial units is supposed to be the long-term outcome. Yet common sense suggests that many critical aspects of economic and social life are the way they are because of increasing returns, or at least the existence of the general belief that there are increasing returns. Cities, for instance, would not exist without scale economies and increasing returns. If it were equally easy for an entrepreneur to locate a factory or office anywhere, why would she locate it where rents are high? Either there really are benefits to locating where many other similar enterprises exist (that is, there really are increasing returns to the density of interactions), or it is a habit, a decision taken without much conscious thought because one presumes that others who have taken similar decisions must have given it much thought. Hence, increasing returns and habits result in the growth of cities, and consequently, there is spatial heterogeneity. Increasing returns are not limited to geography, but are common in other significant areas. As far as income distribution is concerned, the most important of these are intergenerational increasing returns, which result in the concentration of property ownership and widening disparities in human capital acquisition.

The existence of norms (ideologies and habits) simultaneously constrains and simplifies decision-making. Such norms also seriously damage the "rationality" and "perfect information" assumptions of mainstream economic theory. Individuals, groups, institutions, and states all have ideologies and habits. They constrain decision-making because when the number of options considered is limited, it is possible that better options than the ones chosen are not even considered. At the same time, since fewer options are considered, the cost of making decisions is minimized. One can think of norm-based vs. rational behavior as analogous to the thought processes of chess champion Garry Kasparov vs. the chess computer Deep Blue. From almost any given situation in a chess game there are millions of possible moves and paths. Kasparov ignores almost all of them because he thinks they lead to nowhere good; sometimes he misses the best possible move. Deep Blue, on the other hand, has to compute the outcome of each path, including the obviously pointless ones, before making a move.

This analogy is useful but incomplete because it makes no reference to the relationship between norms and power. Norms are inscribed with the relations of power in a society—among genders, classes, social groups, and between the state and its subjects or citizens. Norms prescribe and proscribe behaviors that uphold the social order. They are the most direct expressions of group interests, and the interesting aspect is that this happens without constant collective action. To understand the structure of income distribution in a society it is vitally important that we know about its norms. To understand the processes of distributional change, it is necessary to know how norms change.

Third, we must have a clear understanding of change in general. Specifically, we must incorporate the possibility of discontinuities in evolutionary change. Theories in mainstream economics are built upon the understanding that social and economic systems resemble models in physics—more accurately, Newtonian physics. Objects (agents) follow physical laws (economic principles) that tend to keep a universe of objects (the economic system) in equilibrium. Any perturbation (shock) to this universe sets forth forces (economic actions) that restore equilibrium. This physical metaphor makes many logical problems analytically tractable, but it bears little resemblance to the universe of real people. Many social and economic theorists prefer to use biological and evolutionary metaphors. In these views, equilibrium does not and cannot exist because organisms (agents) continually seek to perpetuate (grow) their genes that have the possibility, but not certainty, of undergoing spontaneous mutation (change). In a world of genetic competition, only those organisms survive whose genetic mutations give them the capacity to better adapt to their environments. The Darwinian view of evolution is that it is a gradual process, incremental genetic changes being compiled over millions of years to produce the still evolving organic forms we see today. The post-Darwinian view is that there are discontinuities (punctuations) or sudden sharp transitions in evolution rather than (or in addition to) continual minute adaptations. Stephen Jay Gould, the primary proponent of the punctuated equilibrium thesis, draws his metaphors from the social science of history (Gould 2002). History, he says, is marked by quick transitions separated by long equilibria; so is evolution.

There are obvious problems in basing analysis on metaphor. Robert Nisbet (1969, 6) points out that: "to build rigorous propositions of scientific analysis upon ... metaphor, mistaking attributes of analogy for attributes of reality, can be ... profoundly limiting and distorting." Nisbet also argues that change is not natural or normal, lacks direction, is not immanent or endogenous, is non-cumulative and non-patterned, and is neither necessary nor completely explainable. This is a serious attack on both the evolutionary and mechanical views of social change. Nisbet was a political conservative. He would probably be shocked at his intellectual cohort today, made up as it is of post-structuralist, post-modern, post-grand narrative scholars, but as far as I am concerned, his critique has excellent intellectual credentials.[4] Individual actions are indeed unpredictable. Social groupings are often shifting and their identities often amorphous. Grand theories are over-inclusive and not very good for prediction. Nonetheless, when there are patterns and trends (as there are in income distributions) good social scientists must begin from the position that there are general explanations. This book is, in the tradition of liberal modernism, a search for explanations for change beginning from the principle that some changes are regular and some unpredictable.

THE SPECIFIC ARGUMENTS

The general principles discussed above form the foundation on which are constructed the detailed arguments of this book. Let us now consider the specific arguments that are detailed in the coming chapters.

Inequality levels and trends over the last five to seven decades are diverse and variable but identifiable. Income inequality levels vary from very high in many Latin American nations to moderate in most developing and south Asian nations to very low in most northern European and several central European nations. Inequality trends are also variable. In evolutionary terms, the trends show evidence of both *Darwinian gradualism* and *punctuated equilibria*. That is, there is evidence that income inequality levels usually change very slowly, often not at all; these are instances of gradualism. There are also instances where income inequality levels change very substantially in very short periods; these are punctuations. Every nation has the potential to undergo both forms of change. Most nations, including obvious examples like Russia and China and less obvious ones like the U.S. and India, have undergone both; some others, such as Scandinavian nations, have undergone only the gradualist form of change in the modern period. These realities, along with an important list of cautions on income distribution data comparability over time and space, are established in Chapter 2 (Patterns and Trends).

In Chapter 3 (Economic Theory and Income Distribution) I present a summary of economic theories on inequality and suggest that on the whole they provide incomplete and narrow explanations. *Functional theories* of distribution (also known as factor theories), where the determinants of inequality are the demand-and-supply conditions for the factors of production (land, labor, and capital), are abstract and unrelated to political and social reality; in fact, this approach is discounted even by economists who specialize in income distribution. *Theories of personal income distribution*, which are based on conceptualizing how luck, inheritance, ability, education, age, and policy influence the earning capabilities of individuals, are highly contested. However, these theories, especially human capital theories, are foundational for understanding how individuals are rewarded in market societies. *Theories of distribution change*, which identify variables such as growth, trade, technological change, etc., as the key reasons for change, are deterministic or particularistic and unable to provide general explanation. The Kuznets hypothesis (which suggests an inverted-U relationship between growth and inequality) and its obverse, the endogenous growth theory that initial equality leads to better growth performance, are both seen to be too linear, simplistic, and non-historical; more to the point, they are empirically unverified. The trade-based (Stolper-Samuelson) and technological change-based arguments are better theorized but are nonetheless simplistic abstractions of social and political reality. Many of the empirical tests of these theses are marred by the use of regression models, which are based on a linear evolutionary understanding of change.

The right way to analyze the structure of income distribution must begin from the fundamentals of human behavior. The rationality and self-interest assumptions of economic theory have to be reformulated with new theories of knowledge and action derived from behavioral economics, sociobiology, evolutionary psychology, social psychology, and more traditional sociological theory. This reformulation suggests that people act as individuals as well as members of groups. Their knowledge is perceptual and socially embedded and their actions habitual and largely conformist. Hence, social theory on institutions, groups, and power relations embedded in specific spatial (which are also historical) contexts, must be combined with economic theories of demand and supply of capital and skills to create a sound explanatory framework. These positions can be summarized in four arguments:

1. Individual knowledge and action rules are informed and constrained by cultural and institutional contexts.
2. Self-interest is often subsumed by group-interest, whereby societies are characterized by in-group cooperation and out-group competition.
3. The concentration of power, in the market or in non-market institutions, influences the distribution of resources and income.
4. The appropriate geographical scale for understanding income generation and distribution processes is the local scale.

These arguments are fleshed out in Chapter 4 (Social Theory and Income Distribution) and lead to the conclusion that the level of inequality in a society is a function of social fragmentation (expressed through inter-group bias and within-group solidarity) and spatial fragmentation (significant and systematic differences between geographical units). Income inequality can, as a result, be disaggregated into specific combinations of *social inequality* (that is, inequality within, but more importantly, between groups) at a local level and *spatial inequality* (that is, inequality between sub-national territorial units). At the end of Chapter 4, I set up and discuss a numerical illustration with different combinations of within-group, between-group, and between-region inequality, and show that social inequality (between-group inequality) at the local scale, and between-region inequality are the two primary components of variation in society-wide or national inequality.

Next, in Chapter 5 (Punctuated Equilibria and Social Inequality), I turn to questions on the composition of and changes to social inequality. This, I argue, is best accomplished by understanding the laws and norms that influence distribution. Institutions make laws and society has norms that create the conditions that determine the returns to inheritance and human capital, that is, the specific market rules of specific societies. Laws (or institutional settings) are changeable, and when there are significant state transitions, laws can and often do change. Norms are more durable. The most important norms that sustain durable social inequalities are marriage norms (homogamy, which dictates that marriages take place between status equals) and inheritance norms. In Chapter 5 I use these principles to construct a theoretical framework in which transition agents, who can be endogenous (insiders) or exogenous (outsiders), change the laws and norms of a society by mutation, adaptation, or invasion, based on an ideology of surplus expropriation, redistribution, or reinvestment. Insiders are reformers who change norms and laws at the margin; outsiders are revolutionaries who radically transform inter-group relations and laws. Hence, change agents and their ideologies are at the center of distributional change arising from social change.

Punctuated equilibrium models of inequality change can be explained using this theoretical framework, where the equilibria are "initial conditions" and the punctuations are "institutional transitions." I will show that there are many examples of distributional punctuations. Some are progressive, others are regressive. For instance, several distributional transitions in the early to mid twentieth century have been progressive, all at the end of the century have been regressive. Case studies of colonialism and nationalism from Latin America (Brazil and Mexico) and Asia (India and Indonesia), socialism and post-socialism (in the Soviet Union / Russia, China, Poland), non-socialist revolutions in Bolivia and Iran, postwar reconstructions in Taiwan, South Korea, and Japan, etc., repeatedly show that outsiders have wrought serious and rapid distributional change whereas insiders have worked toward gradual change. This theory is also used to show how social inequalities are reconstructed in many significant institutional transitions, and how pluralistic democracies may make such transitions impossible; hence gradualism may, over time, become the only model of distributional change.

I take up a detailed discussion of spatial fragmentation in Chapter 6 (Gradualism and Spatial Inequality). Spatial inequalities are created through trade and market exchange mediated by power, and "cumulative causation" and "increasing returns" are the key features of spatial divergence. State ideology (expropriation, redistribution, or reinvestment) is able to significantly influence the spatial distribution of economic activity, and market processes usually reinforce the tendency toward geographical clustering of more productive activity. Largely because state ideologies are episodic, changes in spatial inequality are also episodic. Nevertheless, the last two hundred years have featured significant geographical divergence, especially in developing nations. This tendency toward income concentration in leading regions or interregional divergence is manifested at all spatial scales, and is especially pronounced when smaller geographical units are compared.

Changes in spatial inequality are relatively slow. Certainly they do not have the speed of fundamental social change, but they are probably faster than gradual social change. Hence, changes in spatial inequality represent the major form of *gradualist models* of inequality change. Case studies from Brazil and Mexico, India and Indonesia, Russia and China, Japan, the U.S., and Europe illustrate the arguments. A remarkable aspect of the current period of globalization (post-1980) is the universal tendency toward increasing spatial inequality, including in developed nations where, during the middle third of the last century, spatial inequalities had declined substantially.

In the final chapter (Where We Stand) I consider the consequences of these arguments. I show that distributional change, the phenomenon that is at the heart of this analysis, depends on the joint outcome of changes to social inequality and spatial inequality. In the gradualist mode, when both change in the same direction, income inequality changes in that direction. That is, when both social and spatial inequality decline, income inequality declines, when both increase, income inequality increases. In the middle third of the twentieth century, social and spatial inequality declined in the more developed nations (and later in China); their income inequality levels declined as a result. The most common combination, however, pairs declining social inequality with rising spatial inequality. This leads either to distributional stasis or gradual, very slow change in one direction.

The most pressing distributional question of our time—how does globalization affect income inequality?—can be understood in terms of how globalization affects social and spatial inequality. The effect of globalization on social inequality is indeterminate. Certainly there is little scope for punctuations or fundamental change under democracies. On the other hand, the long-term prospects for social change should be progressive, especially in situations where the historically dominant groups are also numerical minorities. However, spatial inequalities have increased and will continue to increase almost everywhere and at every scale. I suggest that increasingly segregated urban structures and regional variance arising from differential engagement with globalization will increase spatial inequalities at all geographical scales, from the neighborhood to the international system. Hence, we can expect globalization to lead to less social fragmentation and more spatial fragmentation, possibly with the net effect of gradual increases in income inequality in most nations. The answers are not clear cut, but there are reasons to believe that movement toward income equalization within individual nations may not be possible in the foreseeable future.

2

PATTERNS AND TRENDS

What do the long-term data on income distribution reveal about the patterns of inequality and its trends? It is possible to answer this question only after providing a brief background on some methodological issues pertinent to inequality measurement. Before we begin that discussion it is useful to note two points. First, inequality measurement is a vibrant and active sub-field in economics. There are dozens, possibly well over one hundred measures of inequality.[1] However, only a handful of measures are used in practice; as a result, the choice is not as difficult as it could be. Second, the quality and availability of income distribution data vary widely over time and space. Much of the usable data cover only the last two to three decades; hence, historic data of the kind necessary to establish long-term trends are simply not available. Moreover, data for some countries are more reliable and consistent than for others; therefore, for many countries, particularly in Africa, it is virtually impossible to identify patterns or trends.

The first section of this chapter focuses on inequality measurement — the desirable properties of such measures, the significance of definitions and units of measurement, etc. Much of this material is widely reported elsewhere, so I will not devote more space to it than is necessary to understand the data that are reported in the second section. This discussion, however, leads to a critical look at the problems in inequality measurement; I show why it is essential that inequality data be studied with careful attention to the details of measurement methods.

Next, I report data from developing and developed nations, using one major source, theWorld Institute for Development Economics Research database (WIDER), supplemented by some more recent and some older sources. In the final section, I summarize the patterns and trends that are identifiable from the data.

INEQUALITY MEASUREMENT

To measure inequality we must first be clear about what the term means. According to Cowell (1998, 1):

> The problem is that "inequality" itself ... is not self-defining, and the definitions applied may be derived from sometimes sharply contrasted intellectual positions. Inequality measurement is an attempt to give meaning to comparisons of income distributions in terms of criteria which may be derived from ethical principles, appealing mathematical constructs or simple intuition.

But what is an income distribution? Perhaps the best description of the term is the one provided by Jan Pen (1971) and his parade dwarfs and a few giants. Let us say that it was possible to arrange a parade of income earners where each person's height is proportional to his or her income; that is, an average income earner would be of average height, say about five and a half feet. If such a parade were to last for one hour, starting with the lowest-income earner and ending with the highest, one would "see" the income distribution of a given territorial space in dramatic light. The parade would begin with individuals walking on their hands, representing negative income earners. Using 1978–79 data for the U.K., Atkinson (1983, 14–15) summarizes the rest of the parade.

> Next come old age pensioners (with) the height of the pensioners not much over a foot. After them come low paid workers, with ... the rule of women first for each occupation.... The slowness with which the height increases is one of the striking features of the parade.... It is only when we pass the average income (with twenty-four minutes to go) that events begin to speed up, but even when we enter the last quarter hour (the top 25 percent), the height of marchers is only some 7'. But then they begin to shoot up. Police superintendents are 11' tall. The average doctor or dentist is some 14'. Around 20' come senior civil servants, admirals and generals. The chairman of a medium sized company may be 35' and for larger companies his height could be 35 yards. Indeed, the highest paid directors are ... over 70 yards tall. They are not, however, the

last, since the final part of the parade is made up of people of whom Pen says 'their heads disappear into the clouds and probably they themselves do not even know how tall they are'.

Note that this parade takes place at a time when the distribution of income in the U.K. was significantly more evenly distributed than it is now (the details are discussed later in this chapter). A parade with current data would show more disparity—average income earners would come later in the parade, the early marchers would be shorter and the marchers in the final minute or two would be much taller. So how would one capture the level of "inequality" in these two distributions: the parade with Atkinson's data, and a parade with more recent data? How can we determine which of these distributions has less "equality"?

Properties and Values of Inequality Measures

The process of comparing different income distributions begins with making a choice between two alternatives. First, one must choose whether to include the complete distribution (including all income earners) or whether to compare just the top and the bottom of the distribution. For instance, one can calculate decile or quintile ratios of income shares. The income-earning population is sorted by income, divided into five or ten equal population groups, and the share of income of the top group (the richest decile when there are ten groups, the richest quintile if there are five groups) can be compared with that of the bottom or any other group. This method is useful for investigating changes at the extremes of a given distribution, and its use suggests that the investigator is interested in studying income polarization. This method of reporting income-distribution data is quite common but rarely used in isolation; typically we see some measure of inequality in the full distribution reported along with decile or quintile ratios.

If the full distribution is to be used, certain measurement properties are considered desirable. Discussions on these properties are available at many sources, the most accessible of which is on the World Bank's website.[2] The following paragraph is based on material from this website. In general, there are five key axioms that inequality measures should follow:

1. The *Pigou-Dalton transfer principle* whereby an income transfer from a richer to a poorer person should lower (or at least not raise) inequality, and an income transfer from a poorer to a richer person should raise (or at least not lower) measured inequality.

2. The axiom of *income scale independence* whereby uniformly proportional changes to income shares should leave the inequality levels unchanged. In other words, if each individual's income share changes by the same proportion, the level of inequality should not change.

3. The principle of *population*, following which there should be no change in inequality if two identical populations are merged.

4. The axiom of *anonymity* or symmetry whereby the inequality measure is independent of any characteristics of individuals other than their incomes.

5. The principle of *decomposability* whereby changes in the inequality level of a given population should be consistent with the inequality changes in subgroups of the population. If the inequality levels in all population subgroups increase, the overall inequality of the full population must also increase.

These axioms are not, however, value-free. Consider the second axiom of income scale independence: if every individual's income increases by the same proportion (say everyone receives a five percent increase in income), a proper inequality measure should not change. However, it is easy to see that this is a *status quo* condition that can also be considered regressive. Richer individuals will receive higher absolute income increases than poorer individuals. If we believe in the utilitarian argument that each successive marginal income increase produces less utility or welfare (since the 101st income unit is valued more highly than say the 1001st income unit), then an equal proportional increase in all incomes produces less overall utility or welfare than when the same total income increase is distributed more heavily among the lower-income groups (see Sen 1973).

Partly in response to such normative anomalies in supposedly value-free inequality measures, explicitly normative or welfarist measures have been proposed. The pioneering work in this arena has been done by Kolm (1969) and Atkinson (1970). The argument, in the words of Dalton (1920, 349) is that "... the economist is primarily interested not in the distribution of income as such, but in the effects of the distribution of income upon the distribution and total amount of economic welfare which may be derived from income." Atkinson's measure based on explicit choices of "inequality aversion" is the best known of these measures, where the level of inequality depends on the weight given by society (or the researcher) to inequality in a distribution; a weight of zero suggests that society is indifferent to inequality, a weight of infinity suggests that society is concerned only with the position of the lowest income group. Intuitively, the Atkinson measures calculate the welfare gain from redistribution, based on the utilitarian principle of diminishing marginal utility of income.[3]

The explicitly normative measures are not commonly used. In spite of the existence of a very large number of inequality measures, just a handful are used repeatedly. Table 2.1 summarizes the properties of

TABLE 2.1 Measures of Inequality and their Properties

	Gini	Theil	Relative Mean Deviation
Formula	$\dfrac{1}{2m}\dfrac{1}{n^2}\displaystyle\sum_{i=1}^{n}\sum_{j=1}^{n}|y_i - y_j|$	$\dfrac{1}{n}\displaystyle\sum \log \dfrac{1/n}{Y_i/n}$	$\dfrac{1}{2m}\dfrac{1}{n}\displaystyle\sum_{i=1}^{n}|y_i - m|$
Compares person's income to:	Other persons' income	His share in population	Mean
Features	Mean-normalized measure. Shows percentage difference between incomes of two randomly selected individuals.	Compares relative incomes of all individuals (either population weighted or income weighted)	Mean-normalized measure.
Intuitive explanation	Gini of 30 means that the expected difference in income between two randomly selected persons is 60% of overall mean income.		Shows percentage of total income that should be transferred so that all incomes are the same.
Income-scale independence	Yes	Yes	Yes
Absolute increase of all incomes reduces inequality	Yes	Yes	Yes
Population size independence	Yes	Yes	Yes

(Continued)

TABLE 2.1   Measures of Inequality and Their Properties *(Continued)*

	Gini	Theil	Relative Mean Deviation
The Pigou-Dalton transfer principle	Yes	Yes	Not if both individuals have incomes greater (or lower) than the mean.
Symmetrical	Yes	Yes	Yes
Measure varies between 0 and 1	Yes	Not bounded from above	Yes
Decomposability	Yes, between income sources No, between recipients	Yes (both)	No
Sensitivity to transfers	Greatest at the mode (varies as density function of the distribution)		Insensitive if transfers take place between two individuals with income above or below the mean.

Source: Adapted from http://www.worldbank.org/research/inequality/inequalitycourse/sess2—slides.doc

three of these popular measures: the Gini coefficient, the Theil Index, and the Relative Mean Deviation. Of these, the Gini coefficient is surely the most widely used summary measure of inequality. It is a bounded measure (unlike the Theil Index), taking values between 0 and 1, where 0 is the minimum and 1 the maximum possible inequality. More recently, the Gini coefficient has been expressed in percentage terms, between 0 and 100. The Gini coefficient has an effective visual analog in the Lorenz Curve. The latter plots the cumulative distribution of population against the cumulative distribution of income; the line of equality is a diagonal straight line, in which all persons have equal shares of income. Real distributions sag away from the diagonal, and the further these lines sag, the higher the level of inequality. The Gini coefficient is the ratio of the area between the line of equality and a given distribution to the total area between the line of equality and the measurement axes. (There are many graphic examples of the Lorenz curve on the web. Readers can find these easily.)

The Theil Index has been widely used in situations where inequality decompositions have been necessary. In Chapter 6 I will discuss the inequality decomposition idea more thoroughly. For now, it may be adequate to understand that inequalities can be broken into within-group and between-group components; in a situation where the population can be divided into groups, say black and white, it is often useful to consider how the population inequality can be decomposed into a within-group component (inequality within the black and white populations separately) and a between-group component (inequality between the black and white groups). "An inequality measure is said to be additively decomposable if it can be expressed as a weighted sum of the inequality values calculated for population sub-groups plus a contribution arising from differences between subpopulation means" (Sastry and Kelkar 1994, 584). In the early days of inequality studies, the Theil Index was the only available decomposable measure. Its popularity stems from that initial advantage. The Atkinson measure was also designed to be decomposable. Now there are several decomposable measures; the Gini coefficient, too, can be decomposed in some limited ways.

In this chapter, and in much of the book, the Gini coefficient is often the only measure of inequality used. This is not because the Gini is a superior measure to all others, but because it is easily understood and widely used. Through much of this book I use inequality data reported by others, and with few exceptions these secondary sources report only Gini coefficients. A few words on understanding the Gini may be useful. First, all five principles identified earlier hold for the measure (see Fields 2001). Second, it is worth noting that the Gini is most sensitive to transfers at the middle of a distribution—that is, transfers from middle-income earners to other middle-income earners—rather than at its extremes, such as from the very rich to the very poor. Finally, to understand what a specific Gini coefficient means in terms of the shares of rank ordered groups, see Appendix 2, where there are several illustrations.

Problems of Inequality Measurement

Inequality measurement is notoriously problematic, and worse, it is rather difficult to generate measurements that are comparable over time and space (to create longitudinal or cross-sectional data sets). The problems begin from an understanding of what is being measured. Income, surely, but what is the meaning of income? Income for whom, or which income-receiving unit, for which population? It is easy to show that the measured outcome depends substantially on answers to these questions.

In discussing how these variables differ and what these differences mean for inequality measurement, I will begin from the source of income-distribution data. These are typically surveys, most often household surveys that are undertaken specifically for the purpose of estimating the condition of income distribution, or poverty, or some welfare variable such as nutrition. In the past, some nations calculated and reported inequality information based on national accounts statistics, but because these data usually cannot be reconciled with household accounts, the practice of calculating income distribution statistics from national accounts is no longer considered acceptable. The household surveys have their own problems; most notably the tendency to under-report income by the rich and over-report it by the poor, combined with an inability to survey the very rich (Nugent 1983). However, even in nations where the tax net is widespread (i.e., virtually all residents are on tax rolls, unlike most developing nations where most agriculturists usually remain untaxed) household surveys are preferred to tax accounts for estimates of income distribution.

Household income can simply be earnings, which are receipts from all sources (from labor, capital, and property) received by all household members from any economic activity. In addition, it may include imputed income (from items such as food grown for household consumption), and transfers (such as unemployment wages, pensions); together with earnings, transfers and imputed income constitute gross income. When taxes are taken out we are left with net income. Disposable income is net income less the imputed income.

What is the time period over which these incomes are being generated? Income surveys typically do not cover a full year. Good surveys derive data from income or expenditure logs maintained by respondents; it is easy to see that maintaining such logs over a full year is very difficult. Hence, income-distribution surveys provide a snapshot capturing a brief time period; in societies where a large proportion of labor derives income from the agricultural sector (in which incomes vary seasonally), the timing of the survey can be of critical importance. Plus, it is difficult to collect income data from surveys. Several nations, including some such as India and Indonesia, which have among the better time-series data on distribution, have opted instead to collect consumption or expenditure data.

Therefore, we can identify several possible variations in the definition of the key concept: income. The data can be on expenditure, which places it in a category of its own, or on income, which can be simply earnings, or earnings plus imputed income; the latter is typically considered gross income in developing nations where social security systems, and hence transfer payments, have little significance. In developed nations, gross income includes transfer payments. Net income, which is net of taxes, is usually reported in developed-nation data only. According to the WIDER report (2000, 8) accompanying the dataset to be discussed later:

> Series which adapt different income concepts or different reference units are inconsistent and cannot be combined unless data corrections and adjustments are introduced. For instance, Gini coefficients of gross incomes are roughly 5–10 points higher than Gini coefficients of net (disposable) incomes, and Gini coefficients of (net) earnings may be roughly 5 points higher than Gini coefficients of (net) expenditure. Gini coefficients of disposable incomes may also be roughly 5 points higher than Gini coefficients of expenditure.

Next, we must distinguish between sampling and enumeration units. Typically, the sampling unit is the household (though there are several examples where the sampling unit is individuals or persons), but the enumeration unit, which is the scale to which income data are disaggregated, is the individual. The principal reason for doing this is to correct the effect of household size; larger households, *ceteris paribus*, have higher incomes because there are more earning members. But larger households also have lower average incomes. Therefore, reporting distribution data at the household level provides a misleading picture of inequality. But how is household income distributed among the individuals who make up the household? Researchers use "equivalence scales" whereby household members are given weights based on their expected levels of consumption (for instance, children can be expected to consume less than adults). At the extreme, every household member could get an equal weight. More realistically, some arbitrary weights (like 1 for adult males, 0.7 for females, 0.5 for children) are assigned. It follows that the distribution generated from a household survey can be significantly shaped by equivalence scale assumptions (see Bazen and Moyes 2003).

Consider the conclusions of Szekely and Hilgert (2003, 1):

> We find: a) that the way countries rank according to inequality measured in a conventional way is to a large extent an illusion created by differences in characteristics of the data and on the particular ways data is treated; b) Our ideas about the effect of inequality on economic growth are driven by quality and coverage differences in household surveys and by the way in which the data

is treated; c) Standard household surveys in LAC [Latin American Countries] are unable to capture the incomes of the richest sectors of society; so, the inequality we are able to measure is most likely a gross underestimation.

In addition to these problems, if one considers problems with surveys in general—reasonable sample size, comparable sample size over time, appropriate randomization, the wording and ordering of questions, gender and class issues between surveyor and respondent —it is possible to ask whether income-distribution data, especially in developing nations, can be compared at all. But without comparison it is not possible to discover patterns and trends. I suggest we adopt Ahluwalia's (1976) "satisficing" approach. At the beginning of the "growth with equity" debate, faced with a direr situation of income distribution data of more dubious quality in developing nations, he argued that the subject was so important that it was necessary to work with what was available; if the data problems were not systematic then any patterns that did emerge could be considered indicative of reality.

Finally, consider the meaning of small changes in Gini coefficients. As shown above, the Gini numbers themselves should not be considered etched in stone; rather they should be considered to be indicative of some social reality. A Gini coefficient of 50 may or may not be on the mark and, for a number of reasons, may not be exactly comparable to a Gini index of 47 for the same country for a different time (this is the problem that has largely been solved in the newer data to be discussed later in this chapter), or a different country for the same time (this problem still remains, but appears to be less acute than before). Yet, a Gini index of 47 or 50 does tell us some things: first, the level of inequality in the given country is fairly high—it is much higher than in a country with a Gini index of 30, 35, or even 40. This would appear to be a self-evident point, but one that often gets lost in the debate over whether inequality has increased or decreased. Second, the numbers taken together suggest that there is little difference between the two measurements. In theory, one number is six percent smaller than the other. Even assuming that the two measurements were taken using identical methods and calculated in exactly the same way, the small difference could be explained by a poor monsoon or a fall in the price of coffee. In other words, the difference can be attributed to variations in temporal economic reality rather than secular or structural social reality, and one should not see any trend, one way or another, in such cases.

LONG-RUN INCOME INEQUALITY

It is with these cautions and caveats in mind that we should begin to look at income-distribution data over the long run. Having access to high-quality, comparable, long-run inequality data is considered a rather high priority among development analysts. So much so, that at least three significant efforts at creating such compilations have been attempted: two at the World Bank by Jain (1975) and Deininger and Squire (1996), and one at the United Nations (WIDER, 2000).[4] The WIDER effort is not only the latest such major attempt but it also has two special virtues. First, it incorporates the data reported in the two earlier collections; second, it categorizes the different inequality estimates according to the acceptability of the methodology (the Deininger and Squire dataset does that too). As a result, the WIDER dataset is by far the largest such compilation. There are more than 5,000 Gini estimates (about half of which are from Deininger and Squire), but only about 2,200 are identified as "OK" or "Reliable" estimates at the national scale. The decision on reliability has been made based on what is known about the "area and population coverages, income recipient units, income concepts used, and any survey design and sample size descriptions used in the original sources" (WIDER 2000, 9).

In the following pages I summarize and discuss the inequality data reported in the WIDER compilation, the main data source, and additional reliable data that have either been partially reported in WIDER or not reported at all.[5] I have used data that meet the following conditions:

- The estimate is "reliable" according to WIDER.
- The estimate is for nationwide coverage (not urban, rural, or otherwise limited geographically).
- There are at least twenty years of data with a minimum of four data points or estimates during that span.

The data are presented in Appendix 1, organized into the following categories: Developed nations (14 cases), Latin American nations (eight), Asian nations (13), Africa (five), and Transition nations (two). A summary of the detailed data in Appendix 1 is shown in Table 2.2. Having discussed the significance of the income concept and the sampling/enumeration unit in the previous section, I present the data (in Appendix 1) keeping these units consistent. This is a departure from how summary inequality data are typically presented elsewhere. I also present data for a single year where there are separate estimates by sampling or enumeration unit, and also when these two units are the same. When differences arise in the latter situation (same year, sampling,

TABLE 2.2 Summary Information on Long-Term Inequality Change

Country	Time covered	Current inequality level	Trend of inequality change
More Developed Nations			
Australia	1967–96	Moderately high	Increase in the late 70s, the late 80s and early 90s
Canada	1965–98	Moderately low	No change
Denmark	1963–97	Low, after taxes	No change
Finland	1966–2000	Low	Declined in the late 60s/mid 70s; no change since then
France	1956–94	Moderately low	Long-term decline
Italy	1948–2000	Moderately low	Long-term decline
Japan	1962–98	Moderately low	No change
Netherlands	1962–97	Moderately low	No change
New Zealand	1973–97	Moderate	Increase in the 80s
Norway	1962–2000	Moderately low	No change
Spain	1965–94	Moderately low	Indeterminate but little change
Sweden	1967–2000	Low	Decline in early 70s; no change since then
United Kingdom	1961–99	Moderately low	Steady decline to mid 70s; steady increase since early 80s
United States	1947–2000	Moderate	Steady decline to mid 70s; steady increase since early 80s
Latin America			
Brazil	1960–96	Very high	Some fluctuation but no long-term change
Chile	1968–96	High	Some fluctuation, probably with an increasing trend

Colombia	1964–94	Very high	Indeterminate; depends on data series chosen
El Salvador	1965–95	High	No change
Mexico	1950–98	Very high	Big swings around a steady long-run average
Panama	1969–87	High	Stable in the 70s, increase in the 80s
Peru	1961–95	Moderately high	Fluctuating; possible increase in the 90s
Venezuela	1962–98	High	No change
Asia			
Bangladesh	1963–96	Moderately low	Little change with possible increase in early 90s
China	1953–97	Moderate	Early large decline; recent steady to large increase
India	1951–97	Moderately low	No change
Indonesia	1964–96	Moderately low	No change
Malaysia	1967–97	High	Fluctuating within small range
Pakistan	1963–96	Moderately low	No change
Philippines	1956–97	High	Fluctuating with increase in the 90s
Singapore	1973–93	Moderate	Small increase in the 80s, small decrease in the early 90s
South Korea	1965–93	Moderately low	No change
Sri Lanka	1953–95	Moderate	Big fluctuations
Taiwan	1964–97	Moderately low	No change
Thailand	1962–98	Moderately high	Fluctuating; possible decrease in the 90s
Turkey	1968–94	High	Possible early decline

(Continued)

TABLE 2.2 Summary Information on Long-Term Inequality Change *(Continued)*

Country	Time covered	Current Inequality level	Trend of inequality change
Africa			
Egypt	1969–95	Moderately low	Early decline; indeterminate after that
Nigeria	1959–97	High	Indeterminate; possible increase in the 1990s
Tanzania	1964–93	Indeterminate	Indeterminate
Tunisia	1965–90	Moderately high	No change
Zambia	1959–96	High	Indeterminate early; possible increase in the 90s
Transition Economies			
Slovak Republic	1958–97	Low	Early large decline; possible increase in the mid 90s
Poland	1976–97	Moderately low	Little change early; increase in the mid 90s

and enumeration unit) it is the result of differences in calculating the measure, including, but not limited to, differences in the way equivalence scales have been used.

The descriptive terms that will be used for the Gini coefficients are as follows: very low for Gini under 20; low for Gini between 20 and 30; moderately low for Gini between 30 and 35; moderate in the 35 to 40 range, moderately high in the 40 to 45 range, high in the 45 to 55 range, and very high above 55. Again, remember the caution on interpreting Ginis that are relatively close to each other.

Developed Nations

Australia, Canada, Denmark, Finland, Japan, the Netherlands, New Zealand, Norway, Spain, Sweden, the U.K., and the U.S. are the countries that met the criteria for inclusion outlined above. Before we discuss the specifics of the trends and patterns in this data, let me show what large differences arise from choice of sampling unit, enumeration unit, and calculation method. In Appendix 1, look at the data for Sweden, especially for 1981. Five data points are reported for this year: two estimates of gross income enumerated per household (Ginis calculated at 29.3 and 34.7), one estimate of net income enumerated per family equivalent (Gini 19.1), one estimate of net income enumerated per household (Gini 29.2), and one estimate of disposable income enumerated per person (19.7). Depending on which estimate one uses, it is possible to identify Sweden as a very low inequality country in 1981, or a medium inequality country. Also, it is possible to pick an estimate, knowingly or otherwise, that is useful to make one's case, especially in a regression model (that inequality is rising or falling, or follows an inverted-U-shaped path [more on this in Chapter 3]), and be not close at all to the reality of inequality in Sweden; which is that income inequality before taxes in Sweden is moderately low, but possibly very low after taxes, reinforcing Sweden's reputation as an activist, egalitarian, welfare state.

The Australian data are difficult to interpret. Inequality of gross income per household probably increased in the late 1970s and then again in the late 1980s, from moderately low to moderately high levels. However, inequality of net income per person is in the low to moderately low range and appears to have increased by about 3 points from the early 1980s through the mid 1990s. Australia scholars argue that there was a discernible increase in inequality in the country in the 1990s (Athanasopoulos and Vahid 2002; Harding and Greenwell 2001). Longer-run data for Australia have been analyzed by Saunders (1993, 353) who concludes that "the distribution of individual income in

1989–90 is very similar to that estimated for 1942–43, and there is evidence that income inequality has been increasing during the 1980s."

In Canada and Denmark there has been no change in inequality. In Canada, taxes and transfers have moved inequality of gross income per family from the moderately low range to the low range measured in net income per person.[6] In Denmark, where the tax structure is more progressive, inequality of gross income per person stays steady in the moderate range, but the inequality of net income per person stays close to very low levels. In Finland, inequality declined from the mid 1960s to the mid 1970s, from a moderately low to a very low level, and remained at that range through the 1980s and 1990s. There may have been a recent very small rise in inequality according to the 2000 data.

In France and Italy, there were significant declines in inequality in the post-World War II period. The decline has been larger in France, where the inequality of gross income per household has fallen from high to moderately low levels; inequality of net income, for which we have data only for the last two decades, remains steady at low levels. The Italian data are slightly more volatile, often moving in a range of two to three Gini points in a period of two to three years. Nevertheless, it is clear that the long-term trend has been downward.

In Japan and the Netherlands, there has been virtually no change in inequality over a period of three decades. The Japanese data have been widely studied, and post-war Japan has long been described as a homogenous, classless or all middle-class society (data not shown here, from Mizoguchi and Takayama [1984], for the period 1953–60, show similar low inequality levels). There is little doubt that it is also a redistributive state (note the difference between inequality of gross income and disposable income). Recently, however, some scholars have begun questioning this bland, undifferentiated image of Japan, and have argued that inequality there has really not been very low, and that it has been increasing in the 1990s (Tachibanaki 1998, quoted in Shirahase 2001). The Netherlands data are less disputed. We do not have the long-term data that would allow us to identify when the inequality decline began, but there is little doubt that, from the mid 1970s, the inequality of net income has been low in the Netherlands, and remains steady.

In New Zealand, inequality appears to have increased from a borderline-low level to a borderline-high level, especially if one considers the single source (New Zealand OYN) with data from the mid 1970s to 1990. In Norway, there is no change in inequality, again if one follows a single source (the Statistical Yearbook); inequality of net income per household has steadily remained in the moderately low range. The Luxembourg Income Study (LIS) data for the late 1970s through 2000, calculated for net income per person, also shows a steady and low level of inequality throughout the period.

The Spanish inequality data are indeterminate. There may have been an increase in inequality in the early 1970s, but by the early 1990s the inequality level was at about the same level as in the mid 1960s or mid 1970s. Inequality in Spain is moderately low. The Swedish data (remarked upon earlier) show very low to low levels of inequality of net income (according to one source), at a steady level from the mid 1970s. It is very likely that inequality in Sweden underwent a decline between the late 1960s and the mid 1970s.

The U.K. and the U.S. have rather similar recent histories with inequality change. In both nations the level of inequality declined at a slow and steady pace till the early to mid 1970s, and after that have increased quite steadily.[7] In fact, these countries have among the highest levels of inequality among all developed nations. The increase has been more dramatic in the U.K., where the inequality of net income has gone from low to moderate levels, whereas in the U.S., these levels have moved from borderline low to moderate levels. This increase in inequality has not gone unnoticed. A large literature is devoted to analyzing and explaining this somewhat unexpected phenomenon. In Chapter 3 I will detail some of the arguments that have been put forward as explanations.

Inequality in Latin America

The Latin American nations that meet the criteria for inclusion here are: Brazil, Chile, Colombia, El Salvador, Mexico, Panama, Peru, and Venezuela. On average, inequality in Latin American nations is the highest among all regions worldwide. As we shall see, these are sustained inequalities that have not changed much over the last several decades. Note that the income definition in most cases is gross income; as shown earlier, the impact of taxes, and especially transfers, is not very significant.

Brazil is known to have one of the highest levels of inequality in the world. The question is: how has it changed? There is little evidence of inequality change in the last four decades in Brazil. If the inequality measurement for 1960 is correct, then it is possible that the inequality level increased sometime in the 1960s, but from 1970 has remained within a narrow range of three to four Gini points (see Fishlow 1972, Wood and Carvalho 1988). In the recession of the 1980s, the "lost decade" in Latin American development, many scholars argued that inequality in Brazil (and several other Latin American nations) had increased, and then declined again when the economies rebounded in the 1990s. Note again the earlier caution about differentiating between "temporal" and "structural" changes in inequality—i.e., changes that are temporary, related to immediate economic conditions vs. changes that are long-term, related to social and structural conditions. I discuss the effects of growth/recession in detail in Chapter 3.

Inequality in Chile for gross income per person appears to have been stable through the 1980s (ignoring the quirky figure for 1982). It is difficult to be sure about the rest of the time. There probably was some increase in inequality between the late 1960s and 1980, and probably some decline in the early 1990s (related perhaps to the recession/growth cycle discussed above). In Colombia, too, the results are indeterminate. Depending on which data series one agrees with (the gross income per household or per person series) it is possible to argue that inequality has been stable, with little change from 1970 to 1992, or has been through wild fluctuations, with a 12–15-point decline before the mid 1970s and a similar increase after that date. The data series for El Salvador does not have many points; it suggests that there has been no change in inequality from the mid 1960s to the mid 1990s.

Inequality in Mexico, as in Brazil, has been the subject of considerable analysis. The long series presented here, from 1950 to 1996, is for inequality of gross income per household. The Gini level at the beginning and end point are identical; in between there appear to have been large swings: inequality probably increased sometime during the late 1960s and early 1970s, declined into the early 1980s, and increased again by the late 1980s (probably another casualty of the continent-wide recession). Mexico is the only developing nation for which high-quality LIS data have been generated, data which, between 1984 and 1998, show some volatility with a possible upward creep in inequality of disposable income per person. The Mexican inequality levels are on par with the other Latin American countries discussed thus far, from high to very high levels. Good accounts of Mexican inequality can be found in Psacharopoulos et al. (1992) and Lustig (1995).

Inequality in Panama is high, and after staying stable through the 1970s, these levels appear to have increased into the very high levels by the late 1980s. The data for Peru are difficult to interpret. There appears to have been a significant inequality decline in the 1960s or early 1970s, and thereafter the inequality levels have remained steady, with a possible increase in the early 1990s. In Venezuela, between 1962 and 1990, the level of inequality of gross income per person remained virtually unchanged (if one downgrades the 1971 data). Inequality in Venezuela is moderately high, unlike most other Latin American nations where it is high or very high.

Inequality in Asia

In Bangladesh there has been no change in the moderate inequality from the mid 1960s to the mid 1980s (assuming that the 1969 measurement is an aberration); if the 1996 data are correct, there may have been a slight increase in the early 1990s. The Bangladesh data should be seen alongside the data for its South Asian cohorts India and Pakistan; we can see that the inequality levels and trajectories in all three nations are virtually identical.

China is one of the nations with large inequality changes. First, there was a large decline in inequality under early communism. From a high Gini in 1953, China's inequality declined to low levels by the mid 1960s. It is very likely that this level of inequality remained unchanged till 1984, six years after the Deng reforms of 1978. From that date on, inequality in China has increased steadily, to moderate, and more recently, moderately high levels. I report on inequality in all of China only up to 1992. More recent estimates are available (including ones that show that by the late 1990s the Gini of inequality at the household level had crossed into the 40s), but because I am unsure about the reliability and comparability of the data, I have not reported them here. Inequality in China is a big subject with a large literature. I will not be able to refer to the full range of the literature, but I will discuss Chinese inequality in several subsequent chapters.

As mentioned earlier, inequality in India is measured on the basis of expenditure rather than income. Expenditure inequality is typically about five Gini points lower than inequality of net income. The Indian data should be read with that caveat in mind; therefore, though the inequality figures here suggest a moderately low level, in reality they probably are at a moderate level. The data show that expenditure inequality in India has remained virtually unchanged through more than four decades. There may have been a slight decline in the late 1950s, but there was no change after that. Expenditure inequality in urban areas (generally slightly higher than in rural areas) has also followed a similar pattern—possible decline in the 1950s followed by unchanged decades. There is anecdotal evidence that inequality increased in India in the late 1990s, and the estimate for 1997 from the World Bank (also in WIDER) may indeed be confirmation of a new rising trend. However, because it is only a single data point, it should be viewed with some caution. As with China, I will discuss the Indian experience with inequality in detail in later chapters.

Indonesia's inequality experience is very similar to that of India. As in India, here too inequality is estimated for expenditure rather than income. The levels calculated are quite similar, and the absence of change is equally noteworthy. Urban inequality is higher than rural inequality, which has declined from the late 1970s. I will discuss the Indonesian case in later chapters. In Malaysia, on the other hand, inequality changes have gone through three trends: a period of increase from high to very high levels through the mid 1970s, a period of decline through the late 1980s, and a period of possible increase in the 1990s (see Fields and Soares 2002). Malaysian inequality has been the subject of some notable in-depth studies (Snodgrass 1980, van Ginneken 1982), and the ethnic dimension of inequality is generally considered very important.

In Pakistan, inequality of gross income per household has followed the same pattern as in the rest of South Asia: stable inequality through three decades at a moderately low level. It is interesting to note that there is not much difference between the Gini coefficients of gross and net incomes. The Philippine data, in contrast, can be interpreted in two ways. Following the gross income per family series we see stability up to the early 1970s, a decline after that through the mid 1990s, and a possible increase in the late 1990s. Following the gross income per household data, it is possible to discern an early increase in the 1950s, stability through the mid 1970s, and a decline after that. It is very likely that the Philippines has experienced some swings in its inequality levels over the last four decades.

In South Korea, inequality may have increased from moderate to moderately high levels in the mid to late 1970s, but by the end of the 1980s the inequality appears to have declined to its 1960s level. The data for Singapore are somewhat contradictory. Depending on the source followed, it is possible to argue that inequality held steady, or went up and then down. No such equivocation is possible with the data for Sri Lanka, where the evidence is clear that there was a dramatic decline in inequality from the 1950s into the early 1970s, followed by an equally dramatic increase through the late 1980s. The expenditure inequality data available for the mid 1990s (if extrapolated) appears to show that inequality in Sri Lanka has declined from the late 1980s high. If this is correct, the inequality experience of Sri Lanka is best compared to a roller-coaster ride.

The Taiwanese government has been collecting data on income distribution regularly since 1964. A well known analysis by Kuo, Ranis and Fei (1981) has made the case for Taiwan as a case of growth with equity. It is very likely that there was a significant inequality decline in the 1950s (comparable data are not available), and it is certain that inequality has remained virtually constant at or around low levels over the last four decades (there are some who argue that inequality in

Taiwan increased marginally in the late 1980s and early 1990s; see, for instance, Hung 1996). The story of inequality in Thailand is a little more complex. There is no doubt that inequality increased in the 1970s from moderately high to high levels (it is unclear as to when the increase began), and probably increased through the 1980s into the early 1990s. By the mid to late 1990s there may have been a small decline in inequality. The Thailand case will be discussed again in Chapter 6. The data for Turkey are spotty, and it is possible that inequality there has declined substantially from very high to moderately high levels.

Inequality in Africa and the Transition Economies

Reliable longitudinal data for inequality in the African continent is difficult to acquire. The WIDER data series provides data for only five nations that meet the conditions outlined earlier. Even among these five, it is rare to find continuous or long series data on a single income and enumeration concept. From the sparse data that can be used, we can conclude that inequality in Egypt may have marginally declined or probably did not change much from the late 1950s to the mid 1970s. Then there is a big data gap. In the mid nineties, expenditure inequality may have declined. It is difficult to draw any conclusion with the Nigerian or Tanzanian data. In Nigeria, expenditure inequality may have increased in the mid to late 1990s. It is not possible to say even that much for Tanzania. In Tunisia, inequality of net expenditure per person appears to have remained unchanged from the mid 1960s to the early 1990s. In Zambia, expenditure inequality may have increased in the 1990s. If the data are to be believed, the increase may have been quite substantial. In both Tunisia and Zambia the inequality levels are from the high to very high range (projecting expenditure inequality to income inequality).

Inequality in the transition economies of the old Soviet Union and its satellites is a subject of considerable current significance. Unfortunately, we do not have many instances of nations with data that meet the conditions stipulated earlier. In fact, the data are available for only two nations (Poland and the Slovak Republic). In Poland the transition from centrally planned to emerging market economics has led to some inequality increase, moving from low to moderately low levels. The Slovak data are particularly interesting because they include an old data point from 1958, well after its subjugation under the Soviet system but well before the turbulence of the 1980s. It would have been desirable to have more such older data points, especially some from before the transition to socialism; in later chapters I will raise this again. In the Slovak Republic, there was a significant drop in inequality between the later 1950s and the late 1980s, from moderately low to very low levels, and there has been some increase in the 1990s, to low levels.

These long-term data can be supplemented with some recent estimates of inequality in the transition economies by Branco Milanovic (1998) and the World Bank (2000) in Table 2.3. Milanovic's study of

TABLE 2.3 Inequality in the Transition Economies (Gini Indices)

Country	(1) Income per capita 1987–88	(2) Income per capita 1993–95	(3) Income per capita 1996–99	Difference (2-1)
Balkans and Poland	24	30		+6
Bulgaria	23	34	41	+11
Poland	26	28	33	+2
Romania	23	29	30*	+6
Central Europe	21	24		+3
Czech Repub.	19	27	25	+8
Hungary	21	23	25	+2
Slovakia	20	19		-1
Slovenia	22	25	25	+3
Baltics	23	34		+11
Estonia	23	35	37	+12
Latvia	23	31	32	+8
Lithuania	23	37	34	+14
Slavic Republics	24	40		+16
Belarus	23	28	28	+5
Moldova	24	36	42	+12
Russia	24	48	47	+24
Ukraine	23	47	33*	+24
Central Asia	26	39		+13
Kazakhstan	26	33	35*	+7
Kyrgyz Repub.	26	55	47	+29
Turkmenistan	26	36	45	+10
Uzbekistan	28	33		+5
All Transition	24	33		+9

*Consumption data used to calculate Gini because income data were unavailable.
Note: For most countries, the income concept in 1993–95 is disposable income; in 1987–88, gross income. Personal income taxes are small and so is the difference between disposable and gross income. Regional averages are unweighted.
Source: For columns 1 and 2: Milanovic (1998); for column 3: World Bank (2000).

the Soviet bloc countries reveals some startling results. The inequality data for two points (in 1987–88 and 1993–95) show that there has been a marked increase in inequality in the five to eight years of transition covered by the study. Although inequality levels in most of the transition economies is still low by world standards—lower on average than in Latin America certainly, and in Africa—in some countries there has been an alarming increase in inequality. In Russia, Ukraine and the Kyrgyz Republic, the Ginis have doubled (from the mid 20s to the high 40s and 50s), in the Baltic states (Estonia, Latvia, Lithuania) the Ginis have increased by more than 50 percent.[8] These data are not accepted without dispute. For example, WIDER's list of estimates for Russia for the later part of this period (1995–96) includes two rather different Ginis: 28.3 in 1995 and 37.83 in 1996 (from the Transmonee Project). In some transition economies such as Slovakia, Poland, and Hungary, the inequality increases, if any, have been minimal; in other transitions economies such as Russia and Ukraine, there have been very significant increases in inequality.

GRADUALISM AND PUNCTUATED EQUILIBRIUM

To summarize: inequality in Latin American nations is the highest worldwide (this has been well known for some time), lowest in Central European nations (even after the transition), followed by North European nations. Other Western nations (in Europe and its diaspora) and South Asian nations have moderate inequality levels, as have most East Asian nations. There is great variation in inequality levels among Southeast Asian nations.

Inequality levels within individual nations do not follow any predictable invariant path. That is, for developing nations as a group, or any collection of national economies for that matter, it is not possible to identify any clear long-term income inequality pattern or path. Rather, it is seen that inequality levels can change significantly very rapidly, or may change incrementally or gradually, or may not change at all for long periods. In other words, individual national inequality histories can be broken into phases or episodes whereby three types of inequality trends can be observed. First, there are periods of rapid inequality change, as witnessed in Eastern Europe over the last decade; Second, there are periods of gradual inequality change, as seen in China and Thailand over the last two decades; Third, and most common, there are periods during which inequality levels remain virtually static—there are numerous examples of this pattern (in South Asia and East Asia, for example). Any single nation can experience all three types of distributional change—significant, incremental, or none.

Let us borrow some terminology from evolutionary biology to suggest metaphors for this pattern of inequality change. Darwinian biology argued that species evolution takes place gradually or incrementally, through minute adaptive changes over millions of years. The position of Saltationists such as T. H. Huxley (Darwinians but non-incrementalists) never became dominant. However, post-Darwinian biologists (starting with Eldredge and Gould 1972; also see Gould 1982, 2002) argue that the evolutionary process is characterized by "punctuated equilibrium," in which adaptive changes take place rapidly over short time periods, whereas for the rest of the time there are few if any evolutionary changes. The debate has not been resolved in biology. I suggest that the debate need not be resolved in studying income distribution.

The long-term evidence on inequality suggests that distributional change can be characterized by *both* gradualism and punctuated equilibria. That is, there are examples of gradual change over time (the U.K. and the U.S, China and Thailand in recent times); there are also examples of brief periods of significant change interspersed with longer periods of no change or gradual or incremental change. In fact, in some countries (such as those in South Asia), a punctuation point (the brief period of rapid change) has not been documented in the twentieth century. In other words, there is no "inherent tendency" toward some immutable trend as far as income inequality is concerned. The tendency, if any, is toward stability, or absence of change. Yet change does happen, and in some cases drastic changes can happen.

These are the patterns and trends that I seek to understand in the remainder of the book. Why is there such variation in the patterns of inequality? Between regions, between countries within the same regions, between countries at similar levels of development, and between countries at dissimilar levels of development. Why are the trends of inequality change so different? Little change in most countries, gradual change in others, and short bursts of fundamental change in yet others, with a single country capable of demonstrating all three trends over a very long term.

APPENDIX 1

Income Distribution Data

The Gini Indices are shown (with source in parenthesis) for the following regions:

1. More Developed Nations
2. Latin America
3. Asia
4. Africa
5. Transition Economies

The vast majority of the data are from the WIDER (2000) database. These can be easily accessed at http://www.wider.unu.edu/wiid/wiid.htm. The original sources that form the basis of the WIDER compilation are also listed here. Some generic titles (such as "Statistical Yearbook" for such and such country) have not been detailed in the bibliography.

The second major single source of data is the Luxembourg Income Study. Their data are also public and can be accessed at http://www.lisproject.org. These are referenced as LIS Web in this compilation.

1. MORE DEVELOPED NATIONS

Australia

	Income-Gross; Per Person	Income-Gross; Per Household	Income-Net; Per Household	Income-Gross; Per Family	Disposable Income; Per Person
1967	32.00 (1)				
1968		33.50 (2)			
1969		32.02 (2)			
1976	34.51 (4)	34.33 (3)			
1978		38.10 (3)			
1979		39.33 (3)			
		39.96 (3)			
1981		35.11 (5)	31.07 (5)		28.10 (6)
		37.58 (3)			
1985		36.50 (5)	31.48 (5)		29.20 (6)

(Continued)

Australia (Continued)

	Income-Gross; Per Person	Income-Gross; Per Household	Income-Net; Per Household	Income-Gross; Per Family	Disposable Income; Per Person
1986		40.60 (3)			
		37.32 (3)			
1989		35.92 (5)			30.40 (6)
1990		41.72 (3)			
					31.10 (6)
1996				41.00 (3)	

Sources: 1. Paukert 1973; 2. Podder 1972; 3. Statistical Yearbook; 4. Kakwani 1986; 5. LIS database 6. LIS Web.

Canada

	Income-Gross; Per Family	Income-Gross; Per Household	Disposable Income; Per Person
1965	31.61 (1)		
1967	31.41 (1)		
1969	32.30 (1)		
1971	32.24 (1)		31.60 (4)
1973	31.60 (2)		
1975	31.62 (2)		28.90 (4)
1977	31.97 (2)		
1979	31.00 (2)		
1981	31.80 (2)		28.40 (4)
1983	32.80 (2)		
1985	32.81 (2)		
1987	32.28 (2)		28.30 (4)
1988	31.91 (2)		
1991		31.47 (3)	28.20 (4)
1994			28.40 (4)
1997			29.10 (4)
1998			30.50 (4)

Note: Between 1973 and 1987 data for every other year are shown.
Sources: 1. Statistical Yearbook; 2. IDS Canada; 3. LIS Database; 4. LIS Web.

Denmark

	Income-Net; Per Household	Income-Gross; Per Person	Income-Gross; Per Household	Income-Net; Household/ cap	Disposable Income; Per Person
1963		37.00 (1)			
1976	31.00 (2)				
	37.00 (3)				
1979			40.65 (4)		
1980			41.27 (4)		
1981			30.99 (4)		
1982				22.00 (5)	
1983				21.60 (5)	
1984		41.00 (6)		20.50 (6)	
1985				20.10 (6)	
1986		40.00 (6)		20.00 (5)	
1987				20.90 (5)	25.40 (7)
1988		40.00 (6)			
1990		39.00 (6)			
1991		39.00 (6)			
1992		39.30 (6)			23.60 (7)
1993		38.00 (6)			
1994		38.11 (6)			
1995		36.00 (6)			26.30 (7)
1997					25.70 (7)

Sources: 1. Paukert 1973; 2. DHSS; 3. Van Ginneken and Park 1984; 4. Statistical Yearbook; 5. Atkinson et al. 1995; 6. Danmark Statistik Ten Year Review 1998; 7. LIS Web.

Finland

	Income-Net; Per Household	Income-Net; Household eq.	Disposable Income; Per Person
1966		31.80 (1)	
1971		27.00 (2)	
1976		21.60 (2)	
1977	30.45 (3)		
1979	31.06 (4)		
1981	32.04 (4)	20.60 (1)	
1983	30.98 (4)		
1985		20.00 (1)	

(Continued)

Finland (Continued)

	Income-Net; Per Household	Income-Net; Household eq.	Disposable Income; Per Person
1986		20.50 (1)	
1987		19.90 (1)	20.90 (6)
1988		20.40 (1)	
1989		20.50 (1)	
1990		20.40 (1)	
1991		20.20 (1)	21.00 (6)
1992		19.90 (1)	
1993		21.00 (5)	
1994		21.00 (5)	
1995		21.70 (5)	21.70 (6)
1996		22.70 (5)	
2000			24.70 (6)

Sources: 1. Atkinson et al 1995; 2. Atkinson, Rainwater and Smeeding 1995; 3. UN 1981; 4. Statistical Yearbook; 5. Uusitalo 1998; 6. LIS Web.

France

	Income-Gross; Per Household	Income-Gross; Household/cap	Income-Net; Per Household	Disposable Income; Per Person
1956	49.00 (1)			
1962	49.00 (1)			
1965	47.00 (1)			
1970	44.00 (1)	39.80 (2)		
1975	43.00 (1)	38.40 (2)		
1979	34.85 (3)		31.74 (3)	29.30 (5)
	40.30 (4)			
1981			27.88 (3)	28.80 (5)
1984	34.91 (3)		31.94 (3)	29.20 (5)
1989				28.70 (5)
1994				28.80 (5)

Sources: 1. UN 1985; 2. Atkinson et al 1995; 3. LIS Database; 4. Sollogeub 1988; 5. LIS Web.

Italy

	Income Net; Per Household	Income Net; Household/cap	Income Gross; Per Person	Disposable Income; Per Person
1948	42.00 (1)		40.00 (2)	
1967	40.00 (1)			
1968	40.00 (1)			
1969	40.90 (1)			
1970	38.00 (1)			
1971	40.00 (1)			
1972	38.00 (1)			
1973	42.00 (1)			
1974	41.00 (1)			
1975	39.00 (1)			
1976	35.00 (1)			
1977	36.00 (1)	33.40 (3)		
1978	36.00 (1)	33.80 (3)		
1979	37.90 (1)	31.20 (3)		
1980	37.00 (1)	30.60 (3)		
1981	32.00 (1)	28.70 (3)		
1982	31.00 (1)	28.70 (3)		
1984		30.10 (3)		
1986	33.00 (1)	30.20 (3)		30.60 (4)
1987	34.40 (1)	31.90 (3)		33.20 (4)
1989	33.90 (1)	29.70 (3)		30.30 (4)
1991	32.50 (1)	29.20 (3)		29.00 (4)
1993	36.30 (1)			33.90 (4)
1995	36.20 (1)			33.80 (4)
2000				33.30 (4)

Sources: 1. Brandolini 1998; 2. Paukert 1973; 3. Atkinson et al 1995; 4. LIS Web.

Japan

	Income Gross; Per Household	Disposable Income; Per Person
1962	37.20 (1)	
1963	35.70 (1)	
1964	35.80 (1)	
1965	34.80 (1)	
1967	35.10 (1)	

(Continued)

Japan ((Continued)

	Income Gross; Per Household	Disposable Income; Per Person
1968	34.90 (1)	
1969	35.70 (1)	
1970	35.50 (1)	
1971	36.90 (1)	
1972	33.40 (1)	
1973	32.50 (1)	
1974	33.60 (1)	
1975	34.40 (1)	
1976	33.90 (1)	
1977	33.30 (1)	
1978	32.90 (1)	
1979	33.90 (1)	
1980	33.40 (1)	
1981	34.30 (1)	
1982	34.80 (1)	
1985	35.90 (2)	
1986		29.30 (3)
1989	37.60 (2)	31.20 (3)
1990	35.00 (2)	
1992		31.10 (3)
1995		31.60 (3)
1998		31.90 (3)

Sources: 1. Mizoguchi and Takayama 1984; 2. Oshima 1994; 3. Shirahase 2001.

The Netherlands

	Income Gross; Per Person	Income Net; Household/cap	Income Gross; Per Household	Income Net; Per Household	Disposable Income; Per Person
1962	42.00 (1)				
1975		28.60 (2)			
1977		28.39 (2)			
1979		28.14 (2)			
1981		26.66 (2)			
1982		27.62 (2)			
1983			33.39 (3)	29.66 (3)	26.00 (4)

(Continued)

The Netherlands ((Continued))

	Income Gross; Per Person	Income Net; Household/cap	Income Gross; Per Household	Income Net; Per Household	Disposable Income; Per Person
1985		29.10 (2)			
1986		29.68 (2)			
1987			32.48 (3)	27.03 (3)	25.60 (4)
1989		29.60 (3)			
1991		27.58 (3)	30.59 (3)		26.60 (4)
1994					25.30 (4)
1995			31.60 (5)		
1996			32.00 (5)		
1997			32.20 (5)		

Sources: 1. Paukert 1973; 2. Statistical Yearbook; 3. LIS Database; 4. LIS Web 2000; 5. CSO.

New Zealand

	Income Gross; Per Household
1973	30.05 (1)
1975	30.04 (1)
1977	32.95 (1)
1978	31.90 (1)
1980	34.79 (1)
1982	33.93 (1)
1983	34.10 (1)
1985	35.82 (1)
1986	35.53 (1)
1987	36.45 (1)
1989	36.58 (1)
1990	40.21 (1)
1997	37.02 (2)

Sources: 1. New Zealand OYN; 2. CSO HES Web 1999.

Norway

	Income Net; Per Household	Income Gross; Per Person	Income Net; Household eq.	Income Gross; Per Household	Disposable Income; Per Person
1962	37.52 (1)				
1963		35.00 (2)			
1967	36.04 (1)				
1970			30.50 (3)		
1973	37.48 (1)		34.80 (3)		
1976	37.30 (1)		31.90 (3)		
1979	26.24 (4)			30.18 (4)	22.30 (6)
1982	32.43 (5)				
1984	32.17 (5)				
	30.57 (1)				
1985	31.39 (1)				
1986	28.35 (4)			30.36 (4)	23.30 (6)
1988	30.89 (5)				
1989	34.21 (5)				
1990	33.31 (5)				
1991	33.31 (1)			31.81 (4)	23.10 (6)
	28.80 (4)				
1996	32.35 (1)				
2000					25.10 (6)

Sources: 1. Statistical Yearbook (different years); 2. Paukert 1973; 3. Brandolini 1998; 4. LIS Database; 5. Statistical Control Office of Norway 1990; 6. LIS Web.

Spain

	Income Gross; Per Household	Income Net; Per Household	Income Net; Family eq.
1965	31.99 (1)		
1973	37.11 (1)		
1974	36.20 (2)		
1975		34.50 (3)	
1980			32.10 (4)
1981	34.23 (2)		
1990			30.60 (4)
1991	32.99 (2)		
1994		35.00 (1)	

Sources: 1. Statistical Yearbook (different years); 2. Goerlich and Mas 2000; 3. UN 1981; 4. LIS Web 2000.

Sweden

	Income Gross; Per Household (Source 1)	Income Gross; Per Household (Source 3)	Income Net; Family Eq. (Source 2)	Income Net; Per Household (Source 3)	Disposable Income; Per Person
1967	37.42		29.50		
1975	31.44		21.30		21.50 (4)
1976		28.14		23.72	
1978			20.00		
1980			19.40	32.44	
1981	29.35	34.69	19.10	29.22	19.70 (4)
1982		35.17	19.40	30.66	
1983			19.40	30.06	
1984		35.38	20.40	30.51	
1985		35.08	20.50	31.24	
1986		35.06	21.40	31.72	
1987	30.77	29.07		31.65	21.80 (4)
1988		28.43	20.40	26.17	
1989			21.00		
1990			21.90	27.15	
1991			24.30		
1992	31.11			32.44	22.90 (4)
1993			24.00		
1994			27.00		
1995					22.10 (4)
2000					25.20 (4)

Sources: 1. LIS Database; 2. Brandolini 1998; 3. Sweden SAS; 4. LIS Web.

United Kingdom

	Income Net; Household eq. (Source 1)	Income Net; Per Household (Source 2)	Income Net; Household eq. (Source 3)	Disposable Income; Per Person (Source 4)
1961	25.30			
1962	24.20			
1963	26.50			
1964	25.50			
1965	24.30			
1966	25.30			
1967	24.50			
1968	24.10			
1969	24.90	26.30		26.70
1970	25.10		25.50	
1971	25.70		26.20	
1972	26.00		26.50	
1973	25.10		25.50	
1974	24.20	28.56	24.70	26.80
1975	23.30		23.80	
1976	23.20		23.70	
1977	22.90		23.40	
1978	23.10		23.40	
1979	24.40		24.80	27.00
1980	24.90		25.30	
1981	25.40		25.90	
1982	25.20		25.80	
1983	25.70		26.40	
1984	25.80		26.60	
1985	27.10		27.90	
1986	27.80	33.29	28.80	30.30
1987	29.30		30.20	
1988	30.80		32.00	
1989	31.20		32.40	
1990	32.30		33.70	
1991	32.40		33.70	33.60
1994				33.90
1995		34.60*		34.40
1996	35.00*			
1999				34.50

*Income Net for Family equivalent; ** Income net per person (from Statistical Yearbook)
Sources: 1. Goodman and Webb; 2. LIS Database; 3. Atkinson, Rainwater and Smeeding 1995; 4. LIS Web.

United States

	Income Gross; Family*; (Source 1)	Disposable Income; Per Person (Source 2)
1947	34.28	
1948	35.16	
1950	36.02	
1952	35.10	
1954	35.66	
1956	34.20	
1958	33.92	
1960	34.88	
1962	34.80	
1964	34.70	
1966	34.68	
1968	33.50	
1970	34.06	
1972	34.46	
1974	34.16	31.80
1976	34.42	
1978	35.02	
1979		30.10
1980	35.20	
1982	36.48	
1984	36.90	
1986	37.56	33.50
1988	37.76	
1990	37.80	
1991	37.94	33.60
1994		35.50
1997		37.20
2000		36.80

*Families with more than one person.
From 1948 to 1990 the data for even years only are shown here.
Sources: 1. United States Bureau of the Census (different years); 2. LIS Web.

2. LATIN AMERICA

Brazil

	Income-Gross; Per Household	Income-Gross; Per Person	Income-Gross; Household/capita
1960	53.00 (1)		
1970	57.61 (2)		
1972		61.00 (1)	
1976	60.00 (1,2)		
1978		56.00 (1)	
1979		59.44 (3)	
1980	57.78 (2)		
1981	55.42 (2)		
1982	54.19 (4)		
1983		57.00 (1)	
1985		61.76 (2)	
1986	54.52 (2)		
1987	56.18 (2)		
1989		59.60 (2)	
		63.42 (5)	
1990			60.60
1996	58.13 (6)*		

Note: * The income receiving unit is "Family."
Sources: 1. Fields 1989; 2. Annuario Estadio do Brasil; 3. Psacharopoulos et al 1992; 4. UN 1985; 5. World Bank 1996; 6. WIDER database.

Chile

	Income-Gross; Per Household	Income-Gross; Per Person
1968	45.64 (1)	44.00 (2)
1971	46.00 (3)	
1980		53.21 (4)
1981		53.46 (4)
1982		59.98 (4)
1983		54.49 (4)
1984		55.85 (4)
1985		54.91 (4)
1986		55.69 (4)
1988		56.72 (4)

(Continued)

Chile ((Continued)

	Income-Gross; Per Household	Income-Gross; Per Person
1989		54.50 (4)
1990		51.88 (4)
1991		53.18 (4)
1992		55.38 (4)
		52.00 (5)
1993		50.00 (5)
1996	56.37 (6)	

Sources: 1. UN 1981; 2. Paukert 1973; 3. Fields 1989; 4. MIDEPLAN/WIDER; 5. IADB/ WIDER; 6. Szekely and Hilgert 1999.

Colombia

	Income-Gross; Per Household	Income-Gross; Per Person
1964		62.00 (1)
1970	52.02 (2)	
1971	51.00 (3)	
1972	51.00 (3)	
1974		47.82 (3)
1978	54.50 (4)	
1988	51.20 (4)	
1991	49.51 (5)	51.32 (6)
1992	49.24 (5)	
1993		61.00 (6)
1994		58.00 (6)

Sources: 1. Paukert 1973; 2. DANE 1970; 3. CEPAL 1984 and 1986; 4. World Bank Colombia; 5. Fiszbein 1995; 6. Chen et al 1995; 7.

El Salvador

	Income-Gross; Per Person	Income-Gross; Per Household
1965	53.00 (1)	
1977		48.40 (2)
1994	53.00 (3)	
1995	50.00 (3)	

Sources: 1. Paukert 1973; 2. Park 1980; 3. IADB Web 1997.

Mexico

	Income Gross; Per Household	Income Net; Per Household	Income Gross; Per Person	Income Gross; Household/cap	Disposable Income; Per Person
1950	52.60 (1)				
1957	55.10 (1)				
1958		53.00 (2)			
1963	55.50 (1)	55.00 (2)			
1968	57.70 (1)				
	52.60 (3)				
1969		58.00 (2)			
1975	57.10 (1)				
1977	50.00 (4)	50.00 (2)			
	49.60 (5)	47.28 (6)			
1984	42.90 (7)		50.58 (8)		44.80 (13)
1989	46.90 (7)		54.98 (8)		46.70 (13)
	46.90 (9)				
	53.09 (10)				
1992	53.41 (10)		57.00 (12)	53.10 (11)	48.50 (13)
1994	47.70 (7)		57.00 (12)		49.60 (13)
	53.61 (10)				
1996	52.76 (10)				47.70 (13)
1998					49.40 (13)

Sources: 1. Felix 1982; 2. Fields 1989; 3. Van Ginneken 1982; 4. Aspe and Beristein 1986; 5. Bergsman 1980; 6. UN 1985; 7. Gonzalez and Mckinley 1997; 8. Psacharopoulos et al 1992; 9. Farne 1994; 10. Szekely and Hilgert 1999; 11. Panuco-Lagetto and Szekely 1996; 12. IADB Web 1997; 13. LIS Web.

Panama

	Income Gross; Per Person	Income Gross; Per Households	Expenditure; Per Household
1969	48.00 (1)		
1970		57.00 (2)	
1979	49.00 (3)		
	48.76 (4)		
1980	47.47 (5)		
1989	57.00 (3)		
	56.47 (4)		
1997			48.50 (6)

Sources: 1. Paukert 1973; 2. van Ginneken and Park 1984; 3. IADB Web; 4. Psacharopolous et al. 1992; 5. Panama DEC; 6. World Bank 2000.

Peru

	Income Gross; Per Person	Income Gross; Per Household	Expenditure; Per Household	Expenditure; Per Person
1961	61.00 (1)			
1971		55.00 (2)		
1981	49.33 (3)			
1986			31.00 (4)	42.76 (5)*
1991		46.43 (6)		43.00 (7)
				39.00 (8)
1994		48.32 (6)		44.87 (9)*
1995		50.55 (6)		

* Expenditure net, per person.
Sources: 1. Paukert 1973; 2. Leon and Leon 1979; 3. Peru 1991; 4. Fields 1989; 5. Psacharopoulos et al 1992; 6. Szekely and Hilgert 1999; 7. IADB Web 1997; 8. Favaro and McIssac; 9. Chen et al 1995.

Venezuela

	Income Gross; Per Person	Income Gross; Per Household	Expenditure Net; Household/cap	Expenditure; Household/cap
1962	42.00 (1)			
1971	47.65 (2)			
1976		43.63 (2)		
1977		42.41 (2)		
1978		40.70 (2)		
1979		39.42 (2)		
1981	43.00 (3)			
	42.82 (4)			
1987	45.17 (5)			
1989	44.00 (3)			
	44.08 (5)			
1990	44.40 (6)			
1992			35.70 (7)	
1998				36.10 (8)

Sources: 1. Paukert 1973; 2. UN 1981; 3. IADB Web 1997; 4. Psacharopoulos et al 1992; 5. Chen et al. 1995; 6. Hausman and Rigobon 1993; 7. World Bank 1999; 8. World Development Indicators 2000.

3. ASIA

Bangladesh

	Income-Gross; Per Household	Expenditure; Per Person
1963	36.44 (1)	
	37.31 (2)	
1966	34.34 (1)	
1967	34.20 (2)	
1969	29.00 (3)	
1973	36.78 (4)	
1978	35.17 (4)	
1981	39.00 (4)	
1983	36.00 (4)	
1986	37.00 (4)	
1989		28.85 (5)
1992		28.30 (6)
1996		33.60 (7)

Sources: 1. Dowling and Soo 1983; 2. Jain 1975; 3. Fields 1989; 4. Bangladesh Statistical Yearbook; 5. Chen et al 1995; 6. World Development Indicators 1999; 7. World Development Indicators 2000

China

	Income-Gross; Per Household	Income-Gross; Per Person	URBAN Income-net; Household/cap	RURAL Income-net; Household/cap
1953	55.80 (1)			
1964	30.50 (1)			
1970	27.90 (1)			
1975	26.60 (1)			
1977			18.60	
1978			16.00	21.24
1979				23.66
1980		32.00 (2)	16.00	28.59
1981			15.00	23.88
1982		28.80 (2)	15.00	23.18
1983		27.20 (2)	15.00	24.59
1984		25.70 (2)	16.00	25.77
1985		31.40 (2)	19.00	26.35

(Continued)

China (Continued)

	Income-Gross; Per Household	Income-Gross; Per Person	URBAN Income-net; Household/cap	RURAL Income-net; Household/cap
1986		33.30 (2)	19.00	28.84
1987		34.30 (2)	20.00	29.16
1988		34.90 (2)	22.30	30.14
1989		36.00 (2)	23.00	30.00
1990		34.60 (2)	23.00	30.99
1991		36.20 (2)	24.00	30.72
1992		37.80 (2)	25.00	31.35
1993			27.00	32.00
1994			30.00	33.00
1995			28.00	33.20
1997				32.66

Sources: 1. Dowling and Soo 1983; 2. Ying 1995; the rest from WIDER 2000.

India

	National; Expenditure per person	URBAN; Expenditure per person	RURAL; Expenditure per person
1951	35.56	40.00	33.72
1952	35.12	37.30	34.37
1953	35.39	40.98	33.53
1954	34.41	37.53	33.27
1955	34.83	37.66	33.75
1956	35.03	37.46	34.13
1957	34.17	40.78	32.21
1958	34.46	36.40	33.74
1959	34.64	35.57	34.29
1960	32.59	36.39	31.65
1961	33.08	35.57	32.48
1962	32.60	36.28	31.61
1963	30.73	36.54	28.94
1965	31.05	35.57	29.71
1966	31.14	34.51	30.13
1967	31.06	34.69	29.69

(Continued)

India (Continued)

	National; Expenditure per person	URBAN; Expenditure per person	RURAL; Expenditure per person
1968	30.55	34.50	29.08
1969	31.86	34.25	30.97
1970	31.47	35.86	29.82
1971	30.38	34.69	28.76
1973	31.85	34.70	30.67
1974	29.17	30.79	28.54
1978	32.14	34.71	30.92
1983	31.49	34.08	30.10
1987	32.22	36.75	30.22
1988	31.82	35.57	30.14
1989	31.15	34.80	29.51
1990	30.46	35.59	28.23
1991	32.53	37.98	29.91
1992	32.02	35.51	29.88
1994	29.70 (1)	34.50 (3)	28.50 (3)
1997	37.80 (2)	36.12 (3)	30.11 (3)

Source: Datt (1995) for all except 1. World Bank 1999; 2. World Bank 2000; 3. Jha 1999.

Indonesia

	Expenditure; Per Person	Expenditure Net; Per Person	Expenditure; Household/cap	Income Gross; Per Household	URBAN Expenditure; Household	RURAL Expenditure; Household
1964	33.30 (1)					
1967	32.70 (1)					
1970	30.70 (1)					
	34.60 (2)					
1976	31.80 (1)	34.60 (3)		42.69 (4)	35.00 (3)	31.00 (3)
1978	34.80 (1)	38.59 (3)			38.00 (3)	34.00 (3)
1980	31.80 (1)	35.61 (3)			36.00 (3)	31.00 (3)
1981	30.90 (1)	33.73 (3)			33.00 (3)	29.00 (3)
1984	30.80 (1)	32.40 (3)			32.00 (3)	28.00 (3)
	33.00 (3)					
1987	32.00 (3)	32.01 (3)			32.00 (3)	26.00 (3)
1990	32.00 (3)	33.09 (3)			34.00 (3)	25.00 (3)
	31.18 (5)					

(Continued)

Indonesia (Continued)

	Expenditure; Per Person	Expenditure Net; Per Person	Expenditure; Household/cap	Income Gross; Per Household	URBAN Expenditure; Household	RURAL Expenditure; Household
1993	31.69 (6)					
1995			34.20 (7)			
1996			36.48 (3)		37.04 (3)*	28.60 (3)*

* The enumeration unit is Household per capita.
Sources: 1. Fields 1989; 2. Mizoguchi 1985; 3. Statistical Yearbook (different years); 4. Dowling & Soo 1980; 5. Chen et al 1995; 6. World Development Report 1996; 7. World Development Report 1998/99.

Malaysia

	Income Gross; Per Household	Income Gross; Per Person	Expenditure; Household/cap
1967	48.30 (1)		
1970	49.90 (1)		
	50.00 (2)		
1973	51.80 (3)		
1976	53.00 (2)		
1979	51.00 (2)		
1984	48.00 (2)		
1989		48.35 (4)	
		46.10 (6)	
1994			50.50 (5)
1997		49.90 (6)	

Sources: 1. Dowling and Soo 1983; 2. Bruton et al 1992; 3. Perumal 1989; 4. Chen et al. 1995; 5. World Development Indicators 1999; 6. Fields and Soares 2002.

Pakistan

	Income Gross; Per Household	Income Gross; Per Person	Expenditure Net; Per	Expenditure; Household/cap
1963	34.30 (1)			
	38.65 (2)			
1964		37.00 (3)		
1966	35.51 (2)			
1967	34.20 (1)			
1969	32.60 (1)		30.56 (4)	

(Continued)

Pakistan (Continued)

	Income Gross; Per Household	Income Gross; Per Person	Expenditure Net; Per	Expenditure; Household/cap
1970	32.99 (1)		29.21 (4)	
1971	34.50 (1)		31.45 (4)	
1979	35.67 (5)		32.32 (5)	
1985	35.16 (5)		32.44 (5)	
1986			32.15 (4)	
1987	32.78 (5)		32.13 (5)	
1988	32.38 (5)		31.43 (5)	
1991				31.15 (6)*
				31.20 (7)
1996				31.20 (8)

* Expenditure net per person.
Sources: 1. Burki 1989; 2. Dowling and Soo 1983; 3. Paukert 1973; 4. Pakistan Economic Survey 1990-91; 5. PHIES; 6. Chen et al 1995; 7. World Development Report 1998/99; 8. World Development Indicators 1999.

The Philippines

	Income Gross; Per Family	Income Gross; Per Household	Income Gross; Per Person	Expenditure; Per Person	Expenditure; Household/cap
1956	49.21 (1)				
1957		46.14 (2)			
1961	51.28 (1)	49.71 (2)	48.00 (4)		
		50.30 (3)			
1965	51.39 (1)	51.32 (2)			
		50.50 (3)			
1971	49.41 (1)	49.00 (3)	49.39 (4)		
1975	45.18 (1)				
1985	44.66 (6)	46.08 (2)		41.04 (5)	
		45.20 (3)			
1988	44.46 (6)	44.70 (3)	45.73 (2)	40.68 (5)	
1991	46.80 (6)	47.70 (3)			
1994	45.07 (6)				42.90 (7)
1997	49.60 (6)				46.20 (8)

Source: 1. Dowling and Soo 1983; 2. Statistical Yearbook (different years); 3. Estudillo 1997; 4. Paulkert 1973; 5. Chen et al 1995; 6. NSO-FIES Web 1999; 7. World Development Indicators 1999; 8. World Development Indicators 2000.

Singapore

	Income Gross; Per Household	Expenditure Net; Per Household
1973	41.00 (1)	
1978	37.00 (1)	
	38.20 (2)	
1980	40.69 (3)	
1983	42.00 (4)	
	43.29 (2)	
1988	41.00 (1)	
	41.97 (2)	
1989	39.00 (5)	
1993	37.84 (2)	41.01 (2)

Sources: 1. Rao 1990; 2. Singapore CSO; 3. UN 1985; 4. Fields 1989; 5. Oshima 1994.

South Korea

	Income Gross; Per Household	Income Gross; Per Person	Expenditure; Household/cap	URBAN Income Gross; per Household	RURAL Income Gross; Per Household
1965	34.34 (1)			41.67 (1)	28.52 (1)
1966	34.16 (2)	26.00 (2)			
1970	33.30 (1)			34.55 (1)	29.45 (1)
1971	36.01 (3)				
1976	39.10 (1)			41.18 (1)	32.73 (1)
	37.00 (3)				
1980	38.63 (4)				
1982	35.70 (1)			37.05 (1)	30.61 (1)
1985	34.54 (4)			36.94 (4)	29.69 (4)
1988	33.64 (4)			34.96 (4)	28.95 (4)
1993			31.60 (5)		

Sources: 1. Choo 1985; 2. Paukert 1973; Dowling and Soo 1980; 4. Korea NBS.

Sri Lanka

	Income Gross; Per Household	Expenditure; Per Person	Expenditure; Household/cap
1953	47.80 (1)		
	48.70 (2)		
1963	47.00 (1)		
	47.16 (2)		
1969	37.78 (2)		
1970	37.71 (3)		
1973	35.30 (1)		
	35.30 (2)		
1979	43.50 (1)		
	44.00 (4)		
1980	42.00 (5)		
1981	45.30 (1)		
	45.00 (4)		
1987	46.70 (1)	38.80 (1)	
1990			30.10 (6)
1995			34.40 (7)

Sources: 1. Datt 1994; 2. Dowling and Soo 1983; 3. Central Bank of Ceylon; 4. Fields 1989; 5. UN 1981; 6. World Development Indicators 1999; 7. World Development Indicators 2000.

Taiwan

	Income Net; Per Person	Income Net; Per Household
1964	32.24 (1)	
1966	32.43 (1)	32.30 (2)
1968	28.90 (1)	
1970	29.42 (1)	
1972	29.02 (1)	
1973	33.60 (1)	
1974	28.09 (1)	
1976	28.40 (1)	
1977	28.00 (1)	
1978	28.43 (1)	
1979	27.70 (1)	
1980	27.96 (1)	
1981	28.15 (1)	
1982	28.51 (1)	
1983	28.45 (1)	

(Continued)

Taiwan (Continued)

	Income Net; Per Person	Income Net; Per Household
1984	28.81 (1)	
1985	29.20 (1)	
1986	29.29 (1)	
1987	29.65 (1)	
1988	30.02 (1)	
1989	30.41 (1)	
1990	30.11 (1)	
1991	30.49 (1)	
1992	30.78 (1)	
1993	31.60 (1)	
1994		31.84 (3)
1995		31.70 (3)
1996		31.67 (3)
1997		31.88 (3)

Note: From the mid 1960s to the mid 1970s the data in Taiwan CSO and Fei, Ranis, and Kuo (1979) are roughly the same. Similarly, the Gini indexes in the LIS Databases are roughly similar to the data shown here from the mid 1970s onwards.
Sources: 1. Taiwan SPIDT; 2. Taiwan CSO; 3. Statistical Yearbook (different years).

Thailand

	Income Gross; Per Household	Income Gross; Per Person	Expenditure; Per Person	Expenditure; Household/cap
1962	41.40 (1)			
	41.28 (2)			
1968	42.90 (1)			
1969	42.63 (2)			
1971	49.90 (1)			
1975	41.74 (2)			
1981	43.10 (3)	47.50 (3)		
1986	47.40 (3)	50.40 (3)		
1988	47.40 (3)	48.80 (3)		
1989			43.81 (4)	
1990	48.80 (4)	50.80 (4)		
1992	51.20 (3)	54.00 (3)		46.20 (5)
1996	45.28 (6)			40.45 (6)*
1998				41.40 (7)

*Expenditure gross per household.
Sources: 1. Dowling and Soo 1983; 2. Ikemoto and Limskul 1987; 3. Ikemoto 1993; 4. Chen et al. 1995; 6. Statistical Yearbook 1997; 7. World Development Indicators 2000.

Turkey

	Income Gross; Per Person	Income Net; Per Person
1968	56.00 (1)	
1973	51.00 (1)	
1987	44.25 (2)	
1994		49.00 (3)

Sources: 1. UN 1981; 2. Statistical Yearbook 1994; 3. Household Income Distribution Survey.

4. AFRICA

Egypt

	Expenditure-Net; Per Household	Expenditure; Per Household	Expenditure; Household/cap
1959	42.00 (1)		
1965	40.00 (1)		
1975	38.00 (1)	38.00 (2)	
1991			32.00 (3)
1995			28.50 (4)

Sources: 1. Hansen and Radwan 1982; 2. Fields 1989; 3. World Development Indicators 1999; 4. World Development Indicators 2000.

Nigeria

	Income Gross; Per Person	Income Gross; Per Household	Expenditure Net; Per Person	Expenditure; Household/cap
1959	51.00 (1)			
1981		35.18 (2)		
1982		36.14 (2)		
1986			37.02 (3)	
1991				45.00 (4)
1992			41.15 (3)	
1993				45.00 (5)
1997				50.60 (6)

Sources: 1. Paukert 1973; 2. NFOS; 3. Ngwafon 1995; 4. World Development Report 1998/99; 5. World Development Indicators 1999; 6. World Development Indicators 2000.

Tanzania

	Income Gross; Per Person	Expenditure Net; Per Person	Expenditure; Per Person	Expenditure; Household/cap
1964	54.00 (1)			
1969		39.00 (2)		
1977		44.00 (2)		
1991			57.00 (2)	
1993				38.20 (3)

Sources: 1. Paukert 1973; 2. Fereira 1994; 3. World Development Indicators 1999.

Tunisia

	Expenditure Net; Per Person	Income Gross; Per Person	Expenditure; Per Person
1965	42.30 (1)		
1971		53.00 (2)	
1975	44.00 (3)		40.40 (4)
1980	43.00 (3)		
1985	43.00 (3)		43.43 (5)
1990	41.00 (3)		40.24 (5)

Sources: 1. van Ginneken and Park 1984; 2. Paukert 1973; 3. TINS; 4. Fields 1989; 5. Chen et al. 1995.

Zambia

	Income Gross; Per Person	Income Net; Per Household	Expenditure Net; Per Person	Expenditure; Household/cap
1959	48.00 (1)			
1976		51.00 (2)		
1991			43.51 (3)	
1993			51.40 (4)	46.20 (5)
1996			52.40 (4)	49.80 (6)

Sources: 1. Paukert 1973; 2. van Ginneken and Park 1984; 3. Chen et al 1995; 4. World Bank, Africa Department; 5. World Development Report 1998/99; 6. World Development Indicators 1999.

5. TRANSITION ECONOMIES

Slovak Republic

	Income Net; Household/cap	Income Net; Per Household
1958	30.60 (1)	
1988	19.40 (1)	
1989	18.06 (3)	18.30 (2)
1990	17.80 (3)	18.00 (2)
1991	17.96 (3)	18.00 (2)
1992	18.62 (3)	18.90 (2)
1993	19.68 (3)	
1994	20.81 (3)	
1995	20.00 (3)	
1996	24.83 (3)	
1997	23.36 (3)	

Sources: 1. Atkinson and Micklewright 1992; 2. Cornia 1994; 3. Transmonee Project.

Poland

	Income Net; Per Household	Income Gross; Per Person	Income Net; Per Person	Income Gross; Per Household	Income Net; Household/cap
1976	25.81 (1)				
1978		24.44 (2)			
1979		24.54 (2)			
1980		24.87 (2)			
1981		23.27 (2)			
1982		20.88 (2)			
1983		24.53 (2)	24.52 (3)		
1984		24.87 (2)	25.80 (3)		
1985		25.57 (2)	25.21 (3)		
1986		25.45 (2)	25.14 (3)	30.25 (4)	
1987		25.83 (2)	24.99 (3)		
1988		25.36 (2)	24.48 (3)		
1989			26.71 (3)		25.05 (5)
1990		26.24 (2)			18.81 (5)
1991		25.49 (2)			23.26 (5)

(Continued)

Poland (Continued)

	Income Net; Per Household	Income Gross; Per Person	Income Net; Per Person	Income Gross; Per Household	Income Net; Household/cap
1992		26.29 (2)			24.03 (5)
1993		33.06 (2)			31.71 (5)
1994					32.75 (5)
1995					32.40 (5)
1996					33.12 (5)
1997					34.20 (5)

Sources: 1. United Nations 1981; 2. Milanovic and Ying 1996; 3. Atkinson and Micklewright 1992; 4. LIS Database; 5. Transmonee Project.

3

ECONOMIC THEORY AND INCOME DISTRIBUTION

Inequality is a very large subject. Income distribution, which is the framework used in economics to study inequality, is itself a very large subject. David Ricardo, one of the pioneers of the discipline, wrote to Thomas Malthus: "Political economy you think is an inquiry into the nature and causes of wealth. I think it should rather be called an inquiry into the laws which determine the division of the produce of industry among the classes who concur in its formation" (quoted in Ferguson and Nell 1972, 437). Despite ups and downs in interest in income distribution, the subject is so large that small subsections of it can fill entire bookshelves. For instance, the Luxembourg Income Study (LIS) referred to in Chapter 2, which focuses almost entirely on OECD countries, has, by itself, produced more than 350 substantial working papers. There are hundreds of papers on the measurement of inequality in income distributions. Scores of papers and books focus on a single idea in distribution, the Kuznets hypothesis (more on which later in this chapter). All this is in the literature in economics alone. Inequality is also studied by sociologists. They focus on social inequality, social classes, and stratification, which together form perhaps the single largest subject area in the discipline, which has a literature that may be as voluminous as in economics.

Trying to summarize this vast literature while doing justice to all its important strands is an enterprise beyond my ability and well beyond the objectives of this chapter. Had there been some consensus, or even convergence, in the literature, the task might have been manageable. Part of the reason this literature is so vast is that there is no generally accepted theory of income distribution. One fundamental schism divides scholars. This schism is not disciplinary. It is not economics vs. sociology. Rather, within every social science discipline there is funda-mental divide, which I will call a metatheory divide.[1] This concerns basic beliefs about human nature, social institutions, and units of analysis. Chapter 1 outlined this divide in terms of a tripartite division of interests —self interest, group interest, and territorial interest—which is another way of saying that theories are either individualistic or they are not. (Another detailed treatment of the metatheory divide is presented in Chapter 4.) This chapter summarizes the individualistic approaches used in economic theory. It begins with a brief review of abstract theo-ries of distribution and show why they are less than useful in moving toward an understanding of the distributional patterns and trends identified earlier. Next, a more useful approach that focuses on under-standing the process of personal distribution of income is reviewed. The final, longest section focuses on theories of inequality change.

ABSTRACT THEORIES

The superstructure of distribution theory is concerned not with the distribution of income to individuals or households (which is what is reported in the previous chapter), but to the factors of production. These factors are land, labor, and capital, and, if we follow Jan Pen's (1971) argument, what he calls "entrepreneurial activity." The objective of factor theory (also called functional theory) is to examine how these factors of production are rewarded—per unit of land (with rent), per unit of labor (with wages), and per unit of capital (with interest). According to Atkinson (1997, 298) "... much of what can be found today in textbooks under the heading of the Theory of Distribution is concerned with the determinants of payments to factors.... In mainstream economic theory, the competitive theory of factor pricing determines the division of national income between wages, profit and rent." The reward for each factor is determined by its scarcity and the demand for it. That is, the basic principles of supply and demand govern factor prices. Wages are determined by the demand for and supply of labor. Interest rates are set by demand for and supply of capital. This textbook approach to distribution theory has been built upon the work of giants in the field, starting from the classical pioneers like Adam Smith and David Ricardo, but primarily through the work of the marginal utility theorists Walras, Menger, and Jevons. Marginal price theory is as fundamental to modern economics as differential calculus is to physics.

The initial trouble with the functional theory of distribution is that it is difficult to move from demand and supply forces in a small part of the economy to the national labor market. In other words, microeconomic principles have to be applied to the macro-economies of national markets. This creates analytical problems that are often intractable. According to Pen (1971, 17–18):

> A higher wage not only means higher costs, thus reducing the profit; it also means more purchasing power and more sales, thus increasing the profit. The wage–profit–wage spiral influences distribution, and that cannot be grasped by the pure theory of supply and demand. Micro-wage theory may even be misleading because particular wage rates move together: there is a "wage structure." Interest determination is really in all cases a macroeconomic problem, because the capital market is a "large" market. Capital is mobile, as a result of which the "submarkets" for various kinds of loans are interconnected.... And so we cannot say that we have brought functional distribution within the grasp of the theory by constantly murmuring the magic formula "supply and demand."

The bigger problem with functional theory is the inherent assumption that wage, rent, and interest rates are the outcome purely and solely of market forces, without the influence of institutions such as central banks and collective bargaining units, and without the exercise of power. This is the central divide in the economic metatheories of income distribution, described by economist David Starrett (1976, 261):

> When it comes to the theory of income distribution, economists have tended to gravitate toward one of two (heavily armed) camps. On the one hand, there are the so-called neoclassical economists who espouse the marginal productivity theory. While admitting that this theory is not powerful enough to give answers to all the important questions, they argue that competition leads to inequality of incomes based on genetic or environmental rent, that these inequalities are necessary if efficient outcomes are to result, and that feasible redistribution schemes are almost certain to distort incentives. On the other hand, there are the "radical" economists who argue that marginal productivity theory is either irrelevant or wrong and that the critical factors in determining

income distributions are the social institutions ... [which] are
pernicious in making the rich richer and the poor poorer.

The "radical" tradition in economics is the legacy of Karl Marx and his
critique of the institutions and processes of capitalism. What is radical
in economics, however, is perhaps the mainstream tradition in sociology (and the other non-economic social sciences such as anthropology
and geography), where the principles of mainstream (neoclassical)
economics are considered radical. Marx is a very important intellectual
figure in the study of inequality. His analysis of capitalism and capitalist institutions has provided much of the foundation on which other
key figures such as Max Weber, Emile Durkheim, and Ralf Dahrendorf
have erected many of the enduring theories and arguments in sociology.
It is necessary, therefore, to review the Marxian position on property
and returns to it.

Marx did not differ with the other functional theorists in the view
that human beings are essentially self-interested creatures, but rather
than see social order arising out of the harmonious operation of markets, he argued that order resulted from coercion. State power is used
to uphold unjust and exploitative systems of property ownership
(slavery, feudalism, capitalism) and is—or must be—resisted by the
social classes who do not own the means of production (land and
capital). These arguments are well known, and do not begin to capture
the magnitude of Marx's analytical achievement. Weber added several
critical elements to this analysis, namely the importance of human
emotions and their manipulation, and the existence of more complex
property relationships. Eventually this approach, emphasizing the role
of coercive and symbolic power, has become a dominant tradition
called conflict sociology.

The intellectual polar position from conflict sociology is held by
followers of functionalist sociology, which, in its assumptions, parallels
neoclassical economics and, to a lesser extent, structural-functional
anthropology. This position is perhaps best enunciated in the work of
Davis and Moore (1945) summarized thus by Grandjean (1975, 543):

> [They] have attempted to identify the universal causes accounting for
> inequality in the distribution of positional rewards in societies
> —stratification in their terminology. They contend that "the duties
> associated with the various positions" in a society are not equally
> important for "societal survival." Hence, higher rewards are attached
> to the more essential positions because it is more important that
> individuals be induced to fill these positions. Furthermore, qualified

persons are scarce and are more scarce the more talent or training required for the performance of a position's duties.

It is possible to argue that these two modes of thinking on the subject of inequality—the competition-based or functional mode, and the conflict mode—are not complete in themselves, but in fact are complementary. I will take up this theme later in Chapter 4. For now, it is not difficult to see that these abstract theories do not really aid our analysis of the questions raised in Chapter 1: why do patterns and trends in inequality vary so widely over time and space? If competition leads to a condition of, say, "natural" inequality, why would that level change over time (unless one presumes that the distribution of "natural" abilities also changes over time)? Also, if the distribution of natural ability is similar in all societies (as they must be) why is there such great variance in inequality levels? Similarly, if distributional outcomes truly depend only on state coercion then state transition should always lead to inequality change; later I will show that this is not the case. Moreover, it would stand to reason that more inequality would lead to more conflict. The empirical evidence, despite some serious methodological problems, indicates that there is no such robust relationship (see Lichbach 1989 for a summary). Therefore, these abstract theories are not immediately useful for answering our questions. Nevertheless, they remain important intellectual organizing principles, as we shall see in the remainder of this chapter and many other places in the rest of the book.

THEORIES OF PERSONAL INCOME DISTRIBUTION

One reason that abstract theories are unable to provide adequate explanation is that income data, which, as reported in Chapter 2, are quite difficult to collect, are not reported or cannot usually be reported in the frameworks used in the functional or conflict theories of distribution. It is typically not possible, therefore, to actually calculate inequality using functional or conflict theories. This implies a general implicit understanding in the inequality-research community: that a theory is only as good as its empirical confirmation. This section turns to theories that are empirically verifiable and have been empirically tested. These are the theories of personal income distribution, where the income is divided not between factors of production (as presumed in functional theories), nor between income classes (though, as we shall see later, it is possible to move toward class-based explanations, if not conflict-based explanations, using personal income data); the income is divided between persons or individuals.

There are a fairly large number of such personal theories, and to simplify the exposition, I shall collapse many strands into some overarching categories. There are distinct schools, schools within schools, overlapping approaches, and, sometimes, distinct ideological orientations. The first division, in fact, is an ideological one between what may be called "fatalistic" and "institutional" theories (see Sahota 1978 for this distinction and for an excellent overview of personal theories). Fatalistic theories argue that income inequalities are basically preordained or unalterable; they reflect random luck, or the distribution of abilities, or individual choice, and nothing much can be done (in terms of policy) to make a difference. The institutional theories argue that societies can and do create the norms and laws that determine how individuals are rewarded. This is the set to which I will pay special attention, focusing on two widely discussed approaches: human capital theories and inheritance theories.

Fatalistic Theories

The fatalistic theories are so called because, in these views, inequality is presumed to be immutable. The oldest and best known of these theories (in the sense that some version of them percolates in the public discourse) argues that inequality of income is a reflection of the inequality in ability in the population. Just as height and weight vary among individuals, it is suggested that mental and physical ability also vary, which gives rise to variation in productivity, and income inequality is simply a manifestation of that variation. This belief, which was commonplace in the nineteenth century, would require incomes to be distributed normally (in the shape of a bell curve); but Vilfredo Pareto's finding (1897) that incomes are distributed log-normally with a pronounced skew to the right, helped quash the normal-distribution theory. There have been many modifications of the basic approach. For instance, Pigou (1920) suggested that discrepancy between the distribution of abilities and incomes may arise from inherited wealth (more on that soon). Others have argued that there is not a single definition of ability, and multiple abilities interact multiplicatively rather than additively to create greater dispersion of talent. There is little doubt that ability, however defined, is distributed unequally. The key questions are: What determines ability and does ability alone have much income-generating capability without the addition of education and skills?[2] The two questions are obviously interconnected, and we can begin to disentangle the issues after I discuss the contributions of human capital and inheritance. Unless we can separate "pure" ability (congenital talent) from human capital (education and training)—and it is not clear that the numerous empirical studies on ability and human capital have been able to do so—it is rather pointless to argue the nature vs. nurture debate in sophomoric terms.

A second branch of fatalistic theories comes from the argument that the shape of the income-distribution curve is derived from chance or random occurrences. Called stochastic theory, this suggests that a given income distribution is not based on systematic forces, but on nonsystematic events such as windfalls and wipeouts, pure luck or disaster, etc. Stochastic theorists suggest that some initial distribution may be derived from returns to skill or ability (and may even be equal), but as time goes on and random events keep occurring (rewarding some and punishing others), the distribution soon begins to approach the log-normal right-skewed curve we are familiar with. The theory originated with the work of Robert Gibrat (1931) and has been in disrepute for some time, largely as a result of the methodological critique launched by Shorrocks (1975) and the empirical critique by Taubman (1975). Because this, at the core, is a technical argument, the reader can refer to several technical critiques summarized in Sahota (1978), which will not be detailed here. It is necessary to point out that though, on the surface, the stochastic argument appears to be absurd, it is not difficult to find real-world instances of rewards and punishments way out of proportion to talents and abilities. Nonetheless, these are probably outliers; to understand how the vast body between the outliers is rewarded, we have to turn to other, nonfatalistic theories of income distribution.

Human Capital Theory

Land, labor, and capital are the three basic factors of production and sources of income. Here capital, in its simplest sense, means money; hence financial capital is a basic ingredient of production. Now, if labor were an undifferentiated mass, not required to think or specialize in any way, we could leave the basic factors unchanged. But in reality, one of the hallmarks of every technological change—from the agricultural through the industrial and into the communication revolution—has been the increasing specialization or division of labor. Complex production systems and societies are divided into a number of smaller tasks and units; there is a hierarchy of complexity; higher-order tasks are more difficult to do because they require more knowledge or training; wages, to some extent (and this is where some of the debate has focused), are commensurate with the complexity of the tasks and the skills required to undertake them; hence, education/training/skill (or human capital) is an essential element of production. This fact has been well known for some time. Adam Smith wrote: "wages vary with the cost of learning the business" (Smith 1776, 100). Its modern conceptualization in the works of Theodore Schultz (1960, 1971) and Gary Becker (1962) and others is the idea that rational individuals make optimizing decisions on acquiring human capital to maximize lifetime or permanent earnings.[3] According to Sahota (1978, 12):

> Education [has] emerged as a key to several other forms of human investment. Educated as against less-educated individuals have been found: to work longer hours per year and to spend more time on in-service training, as well as to invest more on migration, job search, and retrieving and evaluating information. Educated parents, especially educated mothers, have been found to be an important determinant of the ability and educability of their children. It has been suggested that education interacts with entrepreneurship and drive. Consequently, the hard core of the "hard core" of human capital theory has turned out to be education.

Human capital theory has become a colossus in the social science discourse on education, welfare, growth, and distribution. Empirical analyses of wages/earnings in developed nations have shown that around half the earnings inequality is explainable by investment in schooling and post-school training (Mincer 1974). Investment in education has been used to explain earning variances between genders, age categories, labor groupings, and across occupations and regions.

There are some interesting models of economic growth and income inequality in developing nations showing both: (a) that the primary source of income inequality is the distribution of human capital (Galor and Tsiddon 1997, Eicher and García-Peñalosa 2001), and (b) that human capital accumulation is restricted and inequitable when there are credit market constraints (Chiu 1998, Mookherjee and Ray 2003). Some analysts have argued that educational attainment has a nonlinear effect on income inequality; in the early stages, the expansion of education creates educational and income inequality; later educational inequality declines, there is wage compression for individuals with higher levels of education, and income inequality also declines (Knight and Sabot 1983). This process is very similar to the Kuznets process discussed in a separate section below. There is evidence that in most countries there has been a decline in the inequality of human capital distribution (Castelló and Doménech 2002), and that "educational factors—higher educational attainment and more equal distribution of education—play a significant role in making income distribution more equal" (Gregorio and Lee 2002, 395). Birdsall, Ross, and Sabot (1995) have argued for a similar understanding based on their analysis of East

Asian economies. There is a convergence of ideas among development economists that educational attainment, economic growth, and progressive income distribution are interlinked outcomes, connected in virtuous cycles in specific countries, or, vice versa, connected in vicious cycles of low educational attainment, low economic growth, and regressive income distributions.

Despite the ability of human capital theory to explain a large proportion of the variation in earnings, there are several critiques of the approach, notably the one raised by labor economists on segmented labor markets. In these approaches, education is seen to be largely a screening device used to reinforce the existing class structure and income inequalities in developed nations (Bowles and Gintis 1973), or is limitedly applicable to only the formal sector of the labor market in developing societies where a large majority of jobs are in the informal sector; in these latter situations, workers compete for jobs rather than for wages, which are fixed by employers. Equally significant is the critique that links inequality in human capital acquisition to technological change (see Acemoglu 2002 and Brown and Campbell 2002 for good reviews), whereby there are increasingly higher returns to skills; as a result, there is greater wage dispersion without significant differences in human capital distribution. This link, according to many analysts, is the key to understanding the recent rise in inequality in many countries. This material is reviewed in the forthcoming section on globalization and trade liberalization.

Inheritance Theories

Wealth is substantially more concentrated than income. According to Edward Wolff (2000), the Gini coefficient of net worth in America increased from 79.9 to 82.2 between 1983 and 1998; in 1998, the share of the richest one percent of households was 38.1 percent (averaging USD 10.2 million per household), the share of the top quintile was 83.4 percent (average USD 1.12 million), and the share of the bottom 40 percent was 0.4 percent (average USD 1,100; also see Keister 2000). For the middle three quintiles, about 60 percent of net worth comes from equity in the principal residence; for the top one percent, almost 80 percent of the net worth comes from stocks, securities, business equities and non-home real estate. The American experience may be extreme, but very substantial inequalities in wealth exist in every society. These are deepest in polarized societies such as South Africa and Brazil, but are also significant almost everywhere in the world. In countries where the majority of the population still works in the agricultural sector, land is the most important asset; inequalities in the distribution of land often approach and exceed the wealth concentration levels discussed above (Chapter 5 details these land inequalities). What effects do these wealth inequalities have on the distribution of income?

The ability theory of inequality corresponds to the maxim: "the smart get richer"; human capital theory can be summarized as: "the educated get richer"; inheritance theories correspond to the hoariest of maxims: "the rich get richer." Inheritance theories do not, for the most part, dispute the claims of the ability and human-capital approaches, but raise questions on how and why some have "ability" and get educated while others do not. There are three bases of inheritance: material inheritance, genetic inheritance, and cultural or social inheritance. The first refers to property and capital (or wealth), the second to biological features such as health and physical characteristics, and cognitive and creative characteristics, the third to values and norms that are transmitted through families, social networks, and cultures. The latter two are generally considered to be directly immutable, and, at the extreme, to also be a function of the first variable. Biological inheritance is superior for the materially well endowed through a process of "assortative mating" or "homogamy"—the process by which wealth marries wealth and brings into its circle beauty and intelligence. Social inheritance has been studied most closely by sociologists and anthropologists, many of whom argue that the values that lead to financial success or failure are transmitted at the neighborhood scale, where neighborhoods themselves are clusters of the well-to-do or the poor. For a quick introduction to these ideas see the "contagion" and "collective socialization" models in Jonathan Crane (1991) and similarly organized economic models in Bénabou (1996). This is a key conceptual area that will be developed further in Chapter 4.

Inheritance theories therefore have focused on the first variable: material inheritance. According to James Meade (1976) inheritance can be made up of fortunes: inherited property, parental nurture and training, and social contacts; and "positive feedbacks" in terms of favorable demographic factors and higher returns on bigger fortunes. The latter argument follows one of the better-known analytical approaches to inheritance theories; it is from the Cambridge school led by Luigi Pasinetti (1962) and Nicholas Kaldor (1956, 1957). In Kaldor's model, the rich (capitalists) continually reinforce their economic position following a cycle of savings and investment. They save more, which they are able to invest, which provides higher returns than wage labor does; so the capitalists accumulate even more, invest at even higher levels, and accumulate yet more. Because new investment is the basis of economic growth, in this approach inequality goes hand in hand with growth. Investigations of this thesis have focused on the question: Do the rich really save more? There is no consensus in the empirical findings, where the propensity of different classes to save is seen to vary over space and time and under different macroeconomic employment conditions. Critics argue that Kaldor's denial of human capital and interclass mobility makes his argument less compelling than it could have been.

But how much interclass mobility is likely? Writing about the U.S., where income mobility is reputed to be very high (according to political conservatives, income mobility is supposed to make up for income inequality), Paul Krugman (1992) notes:

> Census data show that 81.6 percent of those families who were in the bottom quintile [the poorest 20 percent] of the income distribution in 1985 were still in that bottom quintile the next year; for the top quintile the fraction was 76.3 percent. Over longer time periods, there is more mixing, but still not that much. Studies by the Urban Institute and the U.S. Treasury have both found that about half of the families who start in either the top or the bottom quintile of the income distribution are still there after a decade, and that only 3 to 6 percent rise from bottom to top or fall from top to bottom …. Even this overstates income mobility, since (i) those who slip out of the top quintile (say) are typically at the bottom of that category, and (ii) much of the movement up and down represents fluctuations around a fairly fixed long-term distribution.

Fields (2001) summarizes a handful of studies of income mobility in Peru, Malaysia, Chile, China, Ivory Coast, and India. In most cases, a mobility matrix is presented. These show that generally about 60 percent of income earners in the top quintile remained there during the next study period; about 75 percent stayed in the top two quintiles. Similar data are reported for the bottom quintiles, with perhaps a little more mobility; but not to the top quintile—generally only around three percent of the bottom quintile population could be seen in the top quintile in the next time period. There is little data from developing nations on mobility at the very top, the one percent that owns a quarter to a third of all land and property. With fewer windfalls and wipeouts than in developed nations, it is difficult to imagine that there would be much mobility into this stratospheric group.

Demography

The demographic transition is one of the most widely accepted stylized facts of modernization. All societies are seen to transition from virtual steady state populations in high flux (high birth and death rates), through exploding populations during one to two generations of transition (high birth rates eventually converging with falling death rates), into a virtual steady state population in low flux (low birth and death rates). This reality, in combination with the fact that individual earnings over a lifetime follow a fairly regular cycle, have given rise to at least two distinct approaches that link demographic change to changes in the size distribution of income. The simpler of these "life cycle" models posits that income inequality within an age cohort (a group of similarly aged persons) increases over time, as either random luck or endowed ability brings greater returns. Therefore, the aging of a population should increase inequality in the full population. Summarizing a study of two developed and two developing countries, Deaton and Paxson (1997, 97) conclude that: "There is evidence in favor of the life cycle model's prediction that within-cohort inequality of consumption and of total income—though not necessarily inequality of earnings —should increase with the age of the cohort." The second theory is also intriguing. According to Higgins and Williamson (2002, 269):

> The cohort-size hypothesis is simple enough: fat cohorts tend to get low rewards. When those fat cohorts lie in the middle of the age-earnings curve, where life-cycle income is highest, this labor market glut lowers their income. ... Earnings inequality is moderated. When instead the fat cohorts are young or old adults, this kind of labor market glut lowers earnings at the two tails of the age-earning curve.... Earnings inequality is augmented.

Higgins and Williamson estimate the variation in inequality across countries using age-cohort data, controlling for education, the "so called natural resource curse" (discussed later), and other variables, and find strong empirical support for the life-cycle hypothesis (which also happens to mirror the Kuznets curve). Similar support is found for case studies of Taiwan in Greenhalgh (1985) and Chu and Jiang (1997); on the other hand, Brandolini and D'Alessio (2003) do not find strong support for this thesis in their analysis of inequality in Italy.

How do we account for the contradictory findings? First, "fat cohorts" are also likely to have political heft. If wages and benefits are set institutionally, then fat cohorts can influence institutions to get high returns despite the labor market glut. Second, secular changes include not only the demographic transition but increasing women's participation in the labor force, changes in the relative earning power of men and women, shifting definitions of "children" and values on what constitutes child labor, etc. In other words, the size of an age cohort is a single variable that may have explanatory power at a relatively simple level of analysis, but when it is deconstructed the simple explanations may not hold up under examination.

Summary

Most sensible readers would agree that all of the four main propositions above have some merit. Ability matters, education and skills matter, inheritance matters, and age matters in determining an individual's earnings. It is very difficult to empirically disentangle these different threads: What is ability? How much does ability matter? How much of ability is inherited? How much of ability comes from education? To what extent does inheritance matter in acquiring education? How much does education matter? Can "pure" ability be separated from education? If so, which matters more? What is luck, and how much does it matter? Aside from the problems of empiricism on these issues, economic theory seems ill equipped to handle such charged and often hard-to-define issues in a simultaneous framework. Further complicating this already complex scenario is the fact that these questions go to the heart of some of the most important political questions of modern times: on justice, fairness, and deservingness, and on taxes and welfare. Therefore, politicians are tempted to take the partial answers as complete and turn them into slogans. I will try to unravel some of these complications in the following chapters.

THEORIES OF INEQUALITY CHANGE

Inequality has long been a subject of considerable interest in the high-income nations, as the foregoing discussion on personal theories of inequality shows. However, because inequality in these nations was generally thought to be unchanging (in Henry Aaron's words: "It's like watching grass grow"), or even better, changing to more equal conditions, there was little analytical attention to long-term distributional change in these nations. Till the recent rise in inequality in many (most Anglophone) countries, questions on inequality change were considered relevant only to developing nations. The explanations considered can therefore be considered distributional theories in development (even if, as we shall shortly see, increasingly there are overarching explanations that cover both high- and low-income nations). I argue that these explanations are of two types: *deterministic approaches* and *particularistic approaches*.

The deterministic paradigm comes from development economists who have tended to study distribution by focusing on the relationship between growth and inequality. Whatever the causal direction in these analyses (i.e., from growth to inequality or vice versa), these are deterministic approaches because change is continual, universal, and linear, and therefore, they are necessarily ahistorical. Long-term inequality data suggests different evolutionary models—as discussed in Chapter 2, these are gradualism and punctuated equilibrium—in which any society or nation has the potential for rapid or slow distributional change, but is generally marked by distributional stability. The second approach is the antithesis of the deterministic paradigm in that it includes a variety of particularistic methods and angles focused on policy and governance. In the most important of these approaches, globalization and the technological changes and policies associated with it (such as structural adjustment, trade liberalization, and privatization), are seen as the key to understanding recent distributional changes. Perhaps the most widely discussed element in this policy paradigm (as it encompasses the developed as well as the developing world, more the former than the latter), is the issue of "free trade" or trade liberalization, which is identified as the cause of both globalization and increasing inequality within nations. This section is therefore also devoted to a detailed examination of the most important of these ideas on growth and globalization, and their links to income distribution change.

Deterministic Approaches

The development economics literature tends to use deterministic models of growth as the focus of explanation for distributional change. These approaches have led to many critical and revealing insights; paraphrasing Czeslaw Milosz (who was writing about deconstructionist poetry), many of these models are dazzlingly intelligent constructions, which, however, have led to a dead end as far as explanation is concerned. I suggest that the lack of explanation in these models comes from the underlying evolutionary assumption about history in general, and development history in particular. I will explain what I mean after a detailed exposition of the two main theories on the growth-inequality relationship.

Does Growth Increase Inequality? One of the most widely researched and oft-quoted ideas in development is the Kuznets hypothesis (Kuznets 1955), which argues that income inequality increases during the early phases of economic development and declines during the later phases;

that is, the curve for inequality traces an inverted-U or bell shape over the level of development as measured by GNP per capita. This has been considered one of the "stylized facts of development." Professor Kuznets observed that the distribution of income was substantially more unequal in developing than developed nations (he had just five cases), and that the now developed countries with low levels of inequality had had higher levels of inequality earlier in their industrial histories. He argued that these facts could be explained by an inverted-U shaped curve. He proceeded to illustrate this intuition using a simple simulation.

The implications of the Kuznets hypothesis were not seriously scrutinized for several years. Following Kaldor, analysts expected a trade-off between growth and inequality, and growth issues so dominated the development discourse that distributional issues were generally given much less attention. Moreover, reliable income-distribution data for developing nations were scarce and empirical investigations were difficult to undertake. Two early studies, by Kravis (1960) and Oshima (1962), generally confirmed the Kuznets hypothesis. By the early 1970s, however, dissatisfaction with the growth process had led to questions on distribution, even among many mainstream economists. The emerging feeling then was that growth was not automatically achieved by following the prescriptions laid down earlier, that many countries had failed to grow at expected rates, and most important, that among both slow growing and rapidly growing countries the benefits of growth were not reaching the poor. The Kuznets hypothesis was discovered and became the focal point of research. The early studies were all saddled with the same problems—that not enough time had passed after the beginning of development for the effects of structural change to become apparent, and that longitudinal income- distribution data were generally not available; the few studies that existed used a variety of definitions for income and income-receiving unit, were of poor quality, and rarely were derived from income surveys (but cobbled together from other surveys and national accounts statistics). Despite these drawbacks, the perceived urgency of the situation demanded some investigation, and a number of scholars decided to use the available single data points to undertake cross-sectional studies.

Among the early writers, Adelman and Morris (1973), Paukert (1973), Ahluwalia (1976), and Lydall (1977) largely confirmed the Kuznets hypothesis but with caveats. For instance, Ahluwalia warned: "It appears that if there is a 'trickle down' process, that it takes substantially longer to reach the bottom." Numerous other studies confirmed the Kuznets hypothesis (to some degree) from the 1970s through the 1990s (see Chenery and Syrquin 1975, Adelman and Robinson 1989,

Milanovic 1994, and Jha 1996). There are substantial variations among these studies in terms of the data used for analysis, the number of countries in the study, the additional variables used in the models, etc. Even for these confirmatory studies, the extent of inequality variation explained by income alone remains very low, rarely higher than 0.1 in the regression models.

However, there have always been dissenters. Cline (1975), Papanek (1978), and Fields (1980) were among the early critics. Some authors have criticized the methodology by which the inverted-U finding has been made on the basis of cross-sectional studies. Saith (1983), Campano and Salvatore (1988), and Ram (1988) have shown that the curve is sensitive to the data set being used, especially to the inclusion/exclusion of specific countries. Several critics have pointed out that the inclusion of Latin American countries—most at moderate levels of development with high levels of inequality—tends to show more support for the Kuznets curve in cross-sectional studies. Anand and Kanbur (1993) innovatively estimated the turning point of the inequality curve using several different inequality indices: the theoretical values estimated ranged from a high of $1003 (using the log-variance measure) to –$1727 (using a decomposable transform of the Atkinson index). More recently, Gustav Ranis criticized the longevity of the thesis and argued that, "It is time to give a decent burial to that famous 'law'" (Ranis 1996, 50).

It is not difficult to see why the Kuznets hypothesis has been so influential. First, its implications for development policy are far reaching: if it is correct, then developing nation governments are best advised to "grow now and redistribute later." In other words, the Kuznets hypothesis warns of a substantial trade-off between growth equity during the early years (decades?) of development, a consequence of which is the distinct possibility of hampering growth (and therefore, welfare) by paying too much attention to distributional issues at an early stage. Second, the divergence–convergence thesis is a deeply satisfying one for mainstream economists, who firmly believe in the equilibrating and harmonizing nature of market forces. That this thesis was suggested in a simple and elegant model with minimal assumptions no doubt was helpful in establishing its importance and longevity.

The early students of the growth–inequality relationship had to rely on cross-sectional data because long-term data on income distribution were not available for developing nations. This is no longer true. The long-term data reported in WIDER (2000) incontrovertibly show that the Kuznets hypothesis cannot be supported by the data. Nor is there any relationship between growth and distributional change. According to Stiglitz and Squire (2000, 140): "In 88 decade-long spells of growth drawn from across the world ... inequality worsened in about half the cases and improved in the other half, but in most cases the changes were small." Similarly, Fields (2001) shows that in low-income countries the Gini coefficient increased with growth in ten cases and decreased with growth in eleven cases; among high-income developing nations, in nine the Gini increased with growth, in ten the Gini decreased. Therefore, there is no evidence of the inverted-U curve of inequality through the development process, and more important, there is no relationship between the level of development and the level of income inequality (see Bourguignon 1998). Finally, the recent significant inequality increase in several high-income nations raises serious questions about the second part of the Kuznets curve, where inequality is supposed to fall to some equilibrium position. I have to agree with Professor Ranis: it is time we went beyond the Kuznets hypothesis.

Does Inequality Hinder Growth? Among scholars who have gone beyond the Kuznets hypothesis, attention has shifted to the idea proposed by endogenous growth theorists (Perotti 1993, Persson and Tabellini 1994, and others) that the causal connection between growth and inequality runs the other way—that high initial inequality is a barrier to growth, which means that unequal countries grow more slowly. This argument flies in the face of several long-standing positions. First, there is the basic understanding of the growth process itself, which is supposedly driven by savings. In Kaldor's well-known class-based Neo-Keynesian models of distribution (discussed earlier in this chapter), capitalists save more than workers; therefore, the higher the share of capital income, the higher the level of national savings and the higher the rate of growth.[4] As a result, higher inequality can be expected to lead to faster economic growth. Second, growth may rely on certain kinds of investments that are indivisible (i.e., they cannot be provided at smaller scales), which may require the existence of very wealthy individuals (Aghion, Caroli, and Garcia-Penalosa 1999). Third, as discussed in the section on the personal distribution of income, redistribution is considered fundamentally inefficient; a well-known illustration comes from Arthur Okun's (1975) warning that redistribution is like carrying water from the rich to the poor in a "leaky bucket."

On the other hand, here is a summary of Gary Fields' arguments on why high initial inequality may lead to low subsequent growth (Fields 2001, 201–202):

- High inequality gives more economic and political power to high-income people, thereby increasing their leverage and ability for "rent seeking," leading to suboptimal allocation of resources.
- High inequality causes the median voter to support populist (and wasteful) programs, and the poor to engage in "rent seeking" from the middle and upper classes.
- High inequality leads to political and macroeconomic instability.[5] High inequality (in the distribution of land) leads to less efficient agricultural performance because small holdings are more efficient than large ones. At the same time, because access to credit and other productive assets for small holders is poor in high inequality situations, small holdings are less productive than they can be.
- Under conditions of high inequality, the education system favors the upper and middle classes by spending more on higher than primary education, and the health care system spends more on advanced rather than primary care. As a result, resources are inefficiently invested in these areas that are critical for generating human capital.
- High inequality, when combined with poverty, creates large numbers of people who are too unhealthy, malnourished, and weak to work effectively, and who cannot afford to educate their children (because their labor is needed for productive purposes).

These appear to be reasonable arguments in support of the contention that initial high inequality is a growth retardant in the long run. On the other hand, as Putterman, Roemer, and Silverstre (1998, 897) point out: "the political-economic models proposed for explaining it [the equality-to-growth hypothesis] must be taken with a grain of salt because … it is an oversimplified description of politics in a democracy; it is stretching credibility excessively to apply it to non-democracies." Not surprisingly, the empirical evidence from cross-sectional growth regressions is inconclusive. Some studies support the thesis (Clarke 1995, Birdsall, Ross and Sabot, 1995, Bénabou 1996b), and some do not (Brandolini and Rossi 1998, Forbes 2000). In a major critique of the thesis, Forbes (2000, 871) writes:

> Results suggest that in the short and medium term, an increase in a country's level of income inequality has a strong positive correlation with subsequent economic growth … [I] find that data quality, period length, and estimation technique all influence the sign and significance of the coefficient on inequality … [these

results] are highly robust to many permutations of the original sample and model. The one caveat is that these results may not apply to very poor countries, since inequality data for these nations are still limited.

Perspectives on Growth and Inequality It may be fruitful to ask why there is such contradictory evidence on the two major theories discussed above. We saw that the relationship between inequality and growth or development that Kuznets hypothesized does not exist in reality. The long-term data presented in Chapter 2 prepared us for this outcome; the mixed results from the cross-sectional studies simply confirm it. We also see that the relationship between initial equality (or relatively progressive distributions) and higher growth rates is also merely hypothetical; there are equally good reasons to believe and disbelieve it, and the cross-sectional evidence is inconclusive at best.

Is the method of investigation then at fault? Certainly, cross-sectional regressions, in these situations, have very serious problems. In Chapter 2 I pointed out that in a given country, for a single year there may be multiple estimates of inequality with varying definitions of income, income-receiving unit, time of survey, equivalence scales, etc. A researcher can often cherry-pick the estimate that best supports his case. Let us discount that possibility and presume that researchers do not "massage" the data to get the desired results. However, in the earlier studies (in the 1970s and 1980s) these variations were never accounted for; therefore, these studies should simply be ignored. The more recent studies, on the other hand, largely do try to take account of these variations, usually by using the Deininger and Squire (1996) data set. However, to create perfectly comparable estimates of inequality, these newer studies also usually make some arbitrary or tautological assumptions.[6] It is not at all clear that even in these latest studies the inequality data are comparable.

Temple's (1999) critique of cross-country growth regressions can be applied to these models.[7] The measurement error problem identified above is just one of several potential pitfalls. "Parameter heterogeneity," whereby vastly different countries with very different social and political systems are brought into the same equation, is the one that bothers most economic historians and scholars from outside economics. In some equations, given the number of observations or cases, "outliers" (or cases that are far from the mean) become "leverage points" that drive the models. There is a high degree of "model uncertainty" (this is particularly true of the inequality models); which means there are many significant variables (especially when the work of all researchers is combined), many of which are "fragile" in the sense that their significance depends on what other explanatory variables are in the model.

Perhaps most important is the problem of "endogeneity." Is it possible that both the dependent and independent variables are determined in a larger system, where they are not so much related in causal terms as much as they are the outcomes of other, more significant forces? Even more than in growth regressions, this is a problem in inequality regressions which, for instance, typically use some measures of education or literacy as explanatory variables. Is it reasonable to argue that growth causes inequality to change (the Kuznets argument) or inequality causes growth levels to change (the new political economy argument) mediated by some factors such as education? Or is it more reasonable to argue that both growth and inequality levels are determined by larger political and social forces and their manifestation in laws and norms?[8] Of course, it is very difficult to agree on, instrumentalize, and measure a concept like "norm." And if the objective of measuring these amorphous concepts is to insert them into cross-country regressions then the purpose of measurement or understanding is lost. We will run into the same problems of measurement confusion and error, outliers, and fragile models. The best one can say about the current line of equality-to-growth research is that now it is difficult to argue that inequality is good for growth. That, in itself, is a considerable achievement, and should be kept in mind when evaluating the varieties of neoconservative "trickle down" theories that often overwhelm the public discourse.

Fundamentally, the methodology of cross-sectional regressions (applied to the inequality question) is deeply flawed because it presumes a gradualist evolutionary model of inequality change. It is clear from the evidence presented in Chapter 2 that most inequality change is episodic, and if evolutionary metaphors are to be used, one of the appropriate models is punctuated equilibrium, which simply cannot be captured by cross-sectional regressions. Note, that if the linear evolutionary model was correct, the following discussion of globalization or trade liberalization and inequality would have been unnecessary.

Particularistic Approaches

We can see that the evolutionary approach discussed above tends to be over-inclusive and is generally less mindful of the specifics of particular social settings and histories. The approaches discussed below take a different tack (but often use the same methodology) by arguing that particular institutional and policy conditions in specific countries are the primary determinants of inequality. We begin with the most important of the particularistic approaches, which is the very large discourse around trade liberalization or globalization.

Globalization and Inequality Globalization is the word of the new century. It evokes strong passions in academia and among a large section of informed lay persons. We must begin with the recognition of a clear distinction between two contrasting overarching views of globalization. One school of thought sees globalization as a homogenizing process, an economic and cultural assault led by the American juggernauts of Coca colonization and McDonaldization. Some academics (such as Behrman and Rondinelli 1992) have gone so far as to suggest that, to succeed in the global economy, there are certain universal "cultural imperatives" that must be followed. The opposite view is that globalization promotes, more than anything else, difference and plurality—of culture and values, of taste, of political formations, of identity—and at the same time generates resistance that is empowering and liberating (see Robertson 1992, Hall and Hubbard 1998).[9] This dichotomous view of globalization is reflected in popular accounts such as *Jihad vs. McWorld* (Barber 1995) and *The Lexus and the Olive Tree* (Friedmann 1999), and in academic discourse in terms of the global and the local, and the ungainly term of choice among some social scientists: glocalization (Grant and Short 2002).

Globalization has two overlapping elements. The more commonly recognized is its international dimension: increased international trade, improved communication and reduced transport costs, and general technological change (not only in communication but also in production). The second, less recognized, but just as significant element, is the convergence of ideas about governance, usually encapsulated under the umbrella of the Washington consensus (Williamson 1990, 2000).[10] In developing economies this convergence or consensus on governance has led to structural adjustment programs that include fiscal austerity measures, budget cuts, exchange rate adjustments, dismantled import barriers, privatization of state-owned industry, and, of course, trade liberalization. In developed countries, this has led to the formation of regional trading blocks (such as the North American Free Trade Agreement [NAFTA] and the European Union) and a general lowering of trade tariffs; for instance, in developed nations, tariff barriers declined from 40 percent in the late 1940s to less than seven percent by the late 1970s (Wood 1994). Also, according to many scholars, globalization has led to increased inequality.

The inequality question is the one that concerns us here, but before we can get to that a number of issues need to be disentangled. I will consider them in the following order:

1. Why should there be a relationship between trade and inequality?
2. How do the developed and developing worlds differ in the degree of globalization as measured by international trade or foreign capital penetration?
3. What does the evidence on trade liberalization and inequality show in the developed and the developing worlds?
4. What summary conclusions can be drawn on this relationship and the debate?

In economics, the theory used most commonly to explain the relationship between trade and wages is the Heckscher-Ohlin model of international trade, in which countries specialize in the production of goods that most intensively use the factors of production the countries are best endowed with. Hence, developed countries specialize in the production of those goods that are skill intensive, while developing countries specialize in the production of goods that intensively use unskilled labor. Now, in Burtless (1995, 803–4):

> The factor price equalization [Stolper-Samuelson] theorem ... asserts that under the assumptions of the Heckscher-Ohlin model and a regime of unrestricted free trade, prices of the factors of production will be equalized among trading partners.... That is ... free trade between the United States and Mexico will equalize U.S. and Mexican wages for equivalent labor and will equalize rents for a standardized unit of land, even if the factors of production cannot move across the Rio Grande.

If one follows this argument through, it stands to reason that workers with low skills in high-income countries will see their wages decline to the levels obtained among similarly skilled workers in low-income countries that are also strong trading partners. Hence, U.S. workers with skill levels equivalent to Mexican workers are going to face wage reductions. This should lead to an increase in inequality in the U.S. Similarly, high-wage workers (say, in information technology) in developing countries should see their wages rise to the level of similarly high-skill workers in developed countries. As a result, inequality in developing countries should also increase. There is considerable disagreement among trade and labor economists about the assumptions and hence the applicability of the Heckscher-Ohlin model and the

Stolper-Samuelson theorem (see Bhagwati and Dehejia 1994). I will not detail these issues here, but prefer to deal with the evidence after looking at some data on how developed and developing countries differ on the extent of globalization.

Consider some recent data on summary indicators of global integration.[11] Two points are highlighted in data from the World Development Indicators (World Bank 2001, Table 6.1) on two crucial indicators —trade in goods and gross foreign direct investment (FDI)—measured at two points in time (1989 and 1999) covering the decade of economic globalization's full flowering. First, economic globalization, whether measured by trade or capital flow, is primarily a First World phenomenon; and just as significant, this is increasingly true. In 1989, trade in goods accounted for more than 28 percent of purchasing power parity (PPP) gross domestic product (GDP) in the high-income economies; by 1999 it accounted for more than 37 percent. The corresponding numbers for the low-income economies was 7.2 and 7.8 percent. In 1999, trade in goods and services was worth $10,589 billion in the high-income countries, $1,231 billion in East Asia and the Pacific, $772 billion in Latin America, and only $187 billion in sub-Saharan Africa and $173 billion in South Asia (World Bank 2001). Similarly, FDI as a percentage of GDP is far more important in high-income economies than in low-income ones. As with trade in goods, this difference is increasing—from 15 fold to 25 fold in the ten-year period. "Fifteen emerging market economies, mainly in East Asia, Latin America, and Europe, accounted for 83 percent of all net long-term private capital flows to developing countries in 1997" (World Bank 2001, 317).

There is great variation in the significance of trade among developing nations. In several countries, notably in Africa, trade in goods has actually declined, whereas the greatest gains have generally been seen in the Latin American economies. In China, India, and Brazil, vast countries with large economies, trade in goods accounts for small proportions of their economies (8 percent in China, 3.6 percent in India). In general, trade is seen to be most significant in the relatively small, open economies (South Korea, Malaysia, Thailand, and, perhaps as a result of NAFTA, Mexico). Remember that these trade figures include exports *and* imports, which, of course, include oil. The FDI data are similar to the trade data: general decline in Africa (where in every country other than Nigeria and Zambia, gross FDI accounts for less than one percent of PPP GDP), some increase in Asia (also where the vast majority of countries have FDI at less than one percent of PPP GDP), and significant increases in Latin America. Except in Latin America, FDI generally accounts for a minuscule proportion of the GDP. As a result, in almost all developing nations, the domestic economy continues to be over-whelmingly important.

We can see that trade liberalization has had rather different impacts in the developing and developed worlds, and the latter is significantly more involved in global trade. Therefore, one would expect that the income distribution effects, if any, would be felt more deeply in the developed world. Indeed, popular discourses (and some academic ones) are replete with accounts of job and wage losses arising from deindustrialization in the West and the concomitant rapid industrial-ization of the global South; onetime U.S. presidential candidate and maverick entrepreneur Ross Perot called this a "giant sucking sound" of jobs leaving the U.S. for Mexico. No one can doubt that the manu-facturing sector in developed countries has suffered tremendous job losses; this sector provided well-paying jobs to relatively unskilled labor who must now either retrain or find work in the far less remunerative parts of a fragmented service sector. Therefore, when well-paying jobs in manufacturing are replaced by lower-paying jobs in consumer services, there should be an increase in inequality. Is free trade, then, the source of rising inequality in developed nations?

Remember from Chapter 2 that not all developed nations have seen increasing inequality over the last two decades. Rather, the new distri-bution patterns are seen in some developed countries, most acutely so in the U.K., the U.S., and Australia, but not so clearly in several other cases such as France, Sweden, and Canada (see Gottschalk, Gustafsson, and Palmer 1997). Therefore, without detailed analyses, it is possible to presume that even if there is a direct link between trade liberalization and increasing inequality, the link may not be straightforward. Indeed, the evidence is rather mixed. Burtless' (1995, 801) review suggests that: "Analysts approach this question from a variety of starting points, so it is hardly surprising if their research yields conflicting results." The default approach, outlined above, has been taken by Borjas and Ramey (1994), Wood (1995, 1997), and Leamer (1998), who find that trade liberalization leading to international competition has led to increasing inequality in the developed world. The alternative approach argues that, rather than trade liberalization per se, the worldwide skill-biased technological change (whereby there is a growing gap between the wages of skilled and unskilled workers because of the increasing skill-premium) accounts for the increasing inequality (see Lawrence and Slaughter 1993, Sachs and Shatz 1994, Bhagwati and Dehejia 1994). A rapid rise in productivity created by intense technological change in the leading sectors of the economy creates larger wage gaps between workers, along with a shift of labor to these leading sectors and a shift of low-technology production to low-wage economies. In this perspective, free trade explains very little of the increased inequality, especially when compared with technological change as an explanatory variable.[12]

This argument between the two perspectives—whether increased trade or technological change is the primary cause of inequality increase in some developed nations—has been carried over to the developing world. Paraphrasing the argument of Hanson and Harrison (1999), Esquivel and Rodriguez-Lopez (2003, 544) write:

> If trade was behind the relative wage movements in developed countries, we should observe a movement in the opposite direction in the relative wages of developing countries. That is, if trade with developing countries was increasing the wage gap between skilled and unskilled workers in developed workers, we should observe a corresponding reduction in the wage gap in the former countries. However, if skill-biased technological change was the main force behind the relative wage movements in developed countries, a similar pattern should be present in developing countries too.

Similarly, if, as suggested earlier, the production that moves from high-income to low-income countries is low skill in the former but high skill in the latter, then inequality in developing nations can also be expected to increase (Feenstra and Hanson 1996). In short, there are good reasons from economic theory to expect that wage (and therefore income) inequality in developing nations can increase or decrease as a result of trade liberalization. Some of the most cogent theoretical arguments on this subject have been made by Marjit and Acharyya (2003). They show how the existence of dissimilar factor endowments and trade in inputs could lead to increasing wage inequality in both developed and developing nations.

Some empirical studies have now looked at this question: Does trade liberalization cause increased inequality in developing nations? The detailed studies to date have focused on Latin American nations. On Mexico, Esquivel and Rodriguez-Lopez (2003, 543) write: "During the period 1994–2000 the effect of trade liberalization on the wage gap was nil, thus suggesting that the slight increase in wage inequality that occurred during this period was also driven by technological progress." Writing on Argentina, Galiani and Sanguinetti (2003, 497) conclude that "trade deepening can only explain a relatively small proportion of the observed rise in wage inequality." On Colombia, Attanasio, Goldberg, and Pavcnik (2002, 1) find that the "overall effects of the trade reforms on the wage distribution may have been small" despite the facts that there are higher returns to education, the low-skill intensive industries have been wage squeezed, and the informal sector with low wages and benefits has grown. On Chile, Beyer, Rojas, and Vergara (1999) find that trade openness contributes to widening the wage gap between skilled and unskilled labor. The Chinese case of rapidly rising inequality during the period of trade openness (post-1984) is well documented in many sources, though it is unclear how much of the increase is directly due to openness. Finally, a meta-analysis of micro-studies in several developing nations by Goldberg and Pavcnik (2004) suggests that the overall wage impacts of trade liberalization are small or indeterminate. At this point there are, to my knowledge, no other detailed analyses of trade liberalization and wage or income inequality in specific developing nations.

What have we learned about the link between trade liberalization and inequality?

- The major participants in international trade are developed nations. Barring a handful of exceptions, developing nations are not major participants in global trade.
- Economic theory suggests that inequality can increase as a result of international trade or as a result of technological change (and its impacts in the labor market).
- There is a heated debate in developed nations on the "real" cause of increasing inequality (though many developed nations have not seen any such increase). On balance, free trade may have some inegalitarian wage impacts, which probably are lower than the wage impacts of technological change.[13]
- There is less direct evidence from developing nations on the link. The Latin American data suggest that the wage divergence effects of trade liberalization may be quite small.

So far, I have looked exclusively at the role of markets in influencing the patterns of income or wage distribution when trade liberalization policies are enacted. However, remember two points. First, trade liberalization is only one—and not even always the most significant one —of several new polices that many developing nations have adopted in the preceding two decades; this set of policies pertaining to weakening the role of the public sector by privatization of production units and the elimination of subsidies of many kinds (to agricultural producers, urban consumers, etc.), fiscal austerity, exchange rate adjustments, etc., are subsumed under the banner of structural reforms. These reforms have coincided with rising inequality in many developing nations, and, as a result, many critics of globalization and capitalism think that the reforms have directly caused these inequality increases. There is little analytical work in this area. Much of the attention has focused on Latin America (where the inequality increases were supposedly greatest); but according to several scholars of recent Latin American inequality, given the severe macroeconomic conditions under which the structural reforms took place, the distributional consequences without reform would likely have been worse (Psacharopoulos et al. 1995). In fact, some of this discourse has reverted back to the growth–inequality nexus; after reforms, it is argued, economies in recession have seen increasing inequality, growing economies have seen their inequality levels decline.

Second, the approach discussed thus far is devoid of political content. We assume that disinterested policy makers, with the best interests of their citizens in mind, have enacted policy reforms that are applied to populations without political beliefs or interests and without the ability to influence the policies that they have been placed under. This may be a caricature, but is not too much of a distortion of the reality that economic theories on trade liberalization do not allow for the insertion of political interests or institutions that may have an interest in or ability to influence wages. As soon as we recognize the political element, the discussion becomes murkier. What do policy makers really want? Whose interests do they really serve? What institutions can and do influence wages? Are there generalizable outcomes on who wins and who loses from structural reforms? Do the poor lose more or the middle class or the rich? Do the winners compensate the losers? What role does the state play in refereeing (a virtuous view) or manipulating (a cynical view) the distribution process? How do reforms enable or encumber the state's redistributive capacity?

Consider two typically contrasting views. According to Lustig (1998, 293):

> ... the short run effects of opening the economy are likely to exacerbate the problems of poverty and inequality. The rich can insulate themselves from the costs of the adjustment, using the same economic and political tools that in many countries helped them resist adjustment in the first place. The rich are educated, have financial and physical assets, and have access to capital markets; thus they are able to exploit the new opportunities that liberalization of trade and investment bring. The poor ... benefit little, at least in the short run, from the opening of economies.

Others see the new situation in a more positive light. Writing in the same volume as Lustig above, Alesina (1998, 299–300) writes:

> ... since the very poor have relatively little political voice, the redistributive process is captured by various vocal interest groups, such as urban trade unions, civic servants, and university students.... So-called redistributive policies, including social spending on health, education, social security, and public employment, favor parts of the upper and middle classes, and several powerful interest groups, but almost never the very poor ... (who) often suffer not because of stabilization policies but because of the so-called social policies that created the macroeconomic imbalances.... Cuts in benefits for vocal interest groups and reallocation of government spending can improve the welfare of the neediest.

Note the ambivalence in the positions taken by both Lustig and Alesina. Lustig is at pains to point out that her arguments are true "in the short run," whereas Alesina theorizes the pro-poor potential of liberalization without actually spelling out the mechanisms by which the "very poor" can get political voice under the new dispensation. This ambivalence is taken a step further by Stewart and Berry (2000, 50) who argue that "in developing countries, the expected effects of liberalization on income distribution vary with the type of the economy, making any general prediction implausible." They suggest that developing nation economies are of four types: the manufacturing-goods export producers such as Thailand, and the primary-goods export producers such as Ghana and Uganda are "likely to experience an improvement in income distribution from liberalization;" Mineral exporters such as Zambia and Nigeria and import-substitution industrializing countries such as many Latin American countries are likely to see their inequality levels increase.

In other words, the experience on the movement of wages within individual countries is diverse, partly because there is great diversity in the level of global integration in individual countries, and partly because there are significant policy variations within these countries. In addition, the inherited economic structures and resource endowments of these economies are quite diverse. As a result, this paradigm ends up being particularistic on the prospects of income distribution change under globalization in developing countries.

Other Particularistic Explanations

The explanations discussed above are the main ones in the literature, but they are by no means the only ones. Other explanations exist and many of these can be classified under a general category called "destiny" because they imply that income distribution is not amenable to specific policies. Examples of such explanations include: dependency or foreign capital penetration (both of which are expected to raise inequality),[14] democracy (which is expected to diffuse political and economic power and lower inequality), natural resource endowment (whereby reliance on commodity exports raises inequality),[15] and absence of desired resources (which leads to more competition and greater inequality). There are clear theoretical problems with these approaches, besides the methodological problem of using cross-sectional regression analysis, which, as discussed earlier, is a flawed tool for this particular purpose. Let us very briefly examine the most important of these explanations.

Democracy Do democratic nations have lower levels of inequality than non-democratic ones? Are nations that do become democratic able to lower the levels of income inequality over time? Several political scientists have argued that the answer to both questions is yes. The argument goes like this: The concentration of political power also permits and leads to a concentration of economic power and thereby high levels of inequality; in democratic societies political power is decentralized, which leads to the decentralization of economic power, resulting in lower levels of inequality. As with the growth–inequality debate, the democracy–inequality question (it is too much of a fringe argument to be termed a debate) also hinges on the direction of the causal arrow. Does democratic politics make a country more equal, or do relatively equal distributions permit the rise of a middle class or bourgeoisie that then attempts to solidify its economic power into political power by demanding democracy?

However the question is asked (and it is very much more the former than the latter), the methodology for answering is always the same: cross-sectional regressions with control variables representing level of socioeconomic development, regional dummies, etc. Some researchers have found empirical support for the hypothesis (Weede 1982, Muller 1988, Crenshaw 1992, Burkhart 1997); others have found none (Bollen and Grandjean 1981, Bollen and Jackman 1985). These studies seem largely unaware of problems with the inequality data—of measurement, comparability, income definitions, etc. This alone is sufficient to discount the findings. Moreover, there is no attempt to analyze long-term changes in single nations. As we have seen, inequality can increase in some democracies during some periods and decline in those same democracies at other periods (the U.S. and U.K., for instance); inequality can decline in non-democracies and rapidly increase in new democracies (like the transition economies). Therefore, regardless of the reasonableness of the "decentralization of power" argument, being a democracy is not a sufficient or even necessary condition for inequality to be low or to decline. This kind of simple-minded argumentation does little to advance our understanding of inequality change.

THE STATE OF INCOME DISTRIBUTION THEORY

How much do we know about economic explanations for income distribution patterns and trends? I would submit the following two summary judgments: the terrain of theory is contested, and because it is dominated by economic theorists, the social terrain is not well covered.

Perhaps the most striking feature of income distribution theory is the degree of contestation and, often, polarity in positions. The contestation starts at the meta-theory level, where we seek to understand how people behave in social settings. They either compete rationally and individually, or they form classes or groups and seek domination over other groups, which, of course, leads to conflict. The possibility of cooperation or having moral or ethical consciousness is almost never discussed. At the individual level, society rewards those with "ability" or those with "luck"; ability is either entirely individually acquired through character or genetic "luck," or it is socially acquired through a process of gaining education and skills that are imparted through social institutions such as schools and communities, or it is inherited, not merely through genes, but through intergenerational transfers of wealth. For a nation as a whole, inequality may be good for growth, or it may be bad for growth. Globalization, especially free trade, has led to increased inequality in developed nations alone, or in both developed and developing nations; or trade has little to do with inequality change, which is really the result of technological change. The positions in opposition are not marginal in the discipline; rather they are central, and reflect, perhaps, the centrality of inequality as social, political, and economic issue.

Despite the centrality of income inequality in social life, economics is the discipline that dominates the theoretical discourse by far. This is not entirely surprising, as economics is the discipline that is best suited to examine issues of income and wealth. Moreover, the analytical tools in the discipline are useful for undertaking the empirical assessments necessary for hypothesis testing and falsification. I suggest that, despite the apparent advantages of using the lens of economics to study all issues related to income, its distribution is a different issue. The distribution of income is influenced by history (ideological shifts and path dependence), politics (the power of the state in relation to groups), sociology (the existence of groups and the power relations between them), and geography (the fragmentation of economic space). The following three chapters use approaches from economic sociology and economic geography to delve deeper into the structure of income distribution. Economic sociology stresses the idea of the "embeddedness" of human thought and action. Economic geography builds upon the fundamental insight of Alfred Marshall (1919) that physically dense interactions provide "increasing returns." These two ideas are used to show how societies and spaces are fragmented and how distributional patterns and changes can be explained in terms of these fragmentations.

4

SOCIAL THEORY AND INCOME DISTRIBUTION

We have seen that the major economic theories of income distribution —informative, intriguing, and even brilliant on occasion—are not able to explain the diverse patterns and trends in income inequality seen worldwide. The primary reason for the failure of mainstream economic theory, I suggested, was its inability to take into account those variables that do not conform to the fundamental assumptions of economic theory. These social variables, on the other hand, have been studied intensively in the other social sciences, and their economic implications have been explored in the disciplines of economic sociology and economic geography. However, because many of their principles, including the critical ones relating to embeddedness and increasing returns, are not amenable to the simplifying sparseness of economic theorizing, they have not been incorporated into any general theory of income distribution.

In this chapter I will attempt to reconcile the relevant principles from economic sociology and economic geography with theories on supply and demand to create a analytical framework that, it seems, is not as elegant or parsimonious as economic theory, but is more realistic and therefore better able to explain what we know about income distribution patterns and trends. The material is presented in two sections. The first presents a social theory of income distribution beginning from a deconstruction of the rational, self-interested individual of standard economic theory. The second section derives a analytical framework from the social theory developed in the first section, and presents a simplified numerical illustration incorporating the fundamental assumptions of the social theory.

TOWARD A SOCIAL THEORY OF INCOME DISTRIBUTION

Knowledge and action are the two basic elements of human existence, and how individuals earn incomes has to be understood from the firmament of our understanding of how knowledge is acquired and informs action. The strength and weakness of neoclassical economic theory come from its simple principles on knowledge and action: everyone has perfect information (or knowledge) and is perfectly rational in evaluating that information; everyone acts solely to further his or her self-interest, which is to maximize utility over the long run. These assumptions give strength because they allow the analyst to study a large range of social and economic situations. Unfortunately, these assumptions are not only simple but are incorrect in that they fundamentally misunderstand the bases of knowledge and action. These assumptions presume a biology of human behavior that is unsupported by evidence, and in assuming such a restrictive biology, mainstream economic theory wishes away the reality of a more complex biology and the very notion of culture (or institutions) and power. In this section I will first critique the key assumptions underlying economic theory, specifically those pertaining to rationality and self-interest. Next I will propose new principles of analysis by assuming that knowledge and action are embedded in time and space. Four ideas will be presented:

1. Individual knowledge and action rules are informed and constrained by cultural and institutional contexts.
2. Self-interest is often subsumed by group-interest, whereby societies are characterized by in-group cooperation and out-group competition.
3. The concentration of power, in the market or in non-market institutions, influences the distribution of resources and income.
4. The appropriate geographical scale for understanding income generation and distribution processes is the local scale.

Individuals

Let us begin the construction of the framework for understanding income distribution realities by examining the fundamentals of neoclassical economic theory. At the core of the mainstream economic approach are unproven assumptions and axioms about human nature and the social world. *Homo economicus* or "economic man" is rational, self-interested, has perfect information, operates in perfectly competitive markets, and makes decisions only to maximize individual utility. These assumptions have been thoroughly critiqued in many places. Many scholars have shown that these assumptions are somewhere between unrealistic and absurd, so that, for many of the more complex social issues, such as inequality and crime, mainstream economic theory is simply unable to provide adequate understanding or policy guidance. My objective is not to list yet more "straw man" arguments, but to deconstruct and reform *homo economicus* with new knowledge gained from sociology, behavioral economics, sociobiology, evolutionary economics, and social psychology. The review in this section relies substantially on the arguments of Amartya Sen (1977, 1987), Andrew Kamark (1983, 2002), Samuel Bowles (1998, 2004), and Geoffrey Hodgson (1998), economists all, who are able to offer professional as opposed to armchair critiques. Bowles (2004) has gone so far as to suggest that neoclassical (or what he calls Walrasian) economics is no longer the appropriate framework for analyzing micro-level human behavior. Some of the distinctive features of evolutionary social science, the more appropriate framework in his view and mine, are: relationships are usually noncontractual and take place in noncompetitive settings; there are increasing returns in technology and social interactions; equilibria are multiple and nonstationary; preferences and institutions co-evolve in embedded social systems; and preferences are self- and other-regarding. We will see that these features are important in the theoretical framework used here.

How rational are human beings? The rationality axiom in economics suggests that: "(1) People have full knowledge of what is in their best interest; (2) They should act rationally if they wish to optimize their well-being; (3) They really do act rationally to optimize their well-being" (Kamark 2002, 45). However, a reading of the specialized literature in psychology and the classics of fiction leads one to the conclusion that there are two possible answers to the question: Humans, in making the most important decisions in their lives, are not rational at all, but are driven by irrational passion (think of characters from Shakespeare's Macbeth, Othello, and Hamlet, through suicide bombers from Sri Lanka to Palestine); or, everyday human decisions are based on limited knowledge, perception rather than reality, and seek to minimize the cost of decision-making and the outcome of the decision itself—in Herbert Simon's terms (1955), humans (and firms) "satisfice" rather than "optimize," and their actions show "bounded rationality" rather than "pure rationality." In his Nobel Prize acceptance lecture Daniel Kahneman (2003, 1449–50) writes:

> Economists often criticize … psychological theories of intuitive thinking [because] they cannot match the elegance and precision of formal normative models of belief and choice, but this is just another way of saying that rational models are psychologically unrealistic. Furthermore, the alternative to simple and precise models is not chaos.… The guiding ideas [from psychology] are (i) that most judgments and most choices are made intuitively; (ii) that the rules that govern intuition are generally similar to the rules of perception.

A large literature in behavioral psychology and now a fairly substantial one in behavioral economics (see Slovic et al. 2002, Epstein 1994) show how intuitions are formed from "vibes" from past experiences, concrete images, metaphors, and narratives. They also differ from rational judgments; the former are oriented toward immediate action and pleasure-pain rather than the distant future and logical orientation of perfect rationality. In other words, human decisions and actions are based not on sound objective reality and perfectly informed logical analysis, but on experiential, personal, and image-based perceptions. Human beings panic, stampede, and riot, and also experience ecstasy, rapture, and blood lust. None of this is purely "rational" even if it is possible to recast these emotions and experiences in terms of utility maximization. Even something as information-rich as the stock market can induce "irrational exuberance" or panic. "One would have to be extremely committed to rationality not to agree that in the area of financial economics, the heart of traditional economics, a number of important market phenomena are well explained by assuming that not all behavior is fully rational" (Russell 1997, 90).

The dominant neoclassical assumptions of perfect information and rationality have been challenged within the discipline itself, from "old" institutional theorists such as Thorstein Veblen and John Commons through John Galbraith and Gunnar Myrdal, followers of the post-Keynesian school out of Cambridge University, evolutionary economists and game theorists, and sundry heterodox and "non-autistic" economists worldwide. Hodgson (1998, 171 & 178) summarizes the position of institutionalists, which, to varying degrees, is also adopted by other non-mainstream economists:

> In general, institutional economists approach the analysis of macroeconomic systems by examining patterns and regularities of

human behavior, expecting to find a great deal of imitation, inertia, lock-in and "cumulative causation."... [Thus] Habit can be defined as a largely non-deliberative and self-actuating propensity to engage in a previously adopted pattern of behavior. A habit is a form of self-sustaining, nonreflective behavior that arises in repetitive situations ... [Among philosophers and psychologists] instead of habits being explained in terms of rational choice, rational choice was explained in terms of habits. All ideas, including beliefs, preferences, and rational modes of calculation, were regarded as evolutionary adaptations to circumstances, established through the acquisition of habitual propensities.

The "institutional" conception of habit is not very different from the idea of *habitus* suggested by the eminent social theorist Pierre Bourdieu. In his theory of embodied practice, "the world imposes its presence, with its urgencies, its things to be done and said, things made to be said, which directly govern words and deeds...." (Bourdieu 2002, 276). Great literature takes the *habitus* for granted. Here, for example, is Saul Bellow (1984, 177): "The emotional struggles of mankind were never resolved. The same things were done over and over, with passion, with passionate stupidity, insectlike, the same emotional struggles repeated in daily reality—urge, drive, desire, self-preservation, aggrandizement, the search for happiness, the search for justification, the experience of coming to be and passing away, from nothingness to nothingness. Very boring."

Let us now consider the second major assumption in neoclassical economics: that self-interest is the primary drive for human action. Had the axiom been milder—incorporating a generous definition of self (including family and community or group) and a weaker version of maximized utility (sub-optimal or satisficing returns)—the intellectual and theoretical problems might not have been insurmountable. As the assumption stands now, it dwarfs every other possible human motivation or reward, including family, community, love, honor, altruism, and spirituality. So much so that it leaves individuals without free will: if every action must have as its goal the maximization of utility for the self, then it does not allow one to choose some other alternative that does not further the maximization of self-interest (Kamark 2002). Therefore, the primacy of self-interest overturns much of our most basic understanding of human nature.

Game theory offers a good window into the structure of self-interest. Consider the "Ultimatum" game in which a sum of money is divided by one person, and the division has to be accepted by a second person for both persons to get the money thus divided. Following neoclassical economic theory, in the equilibrium condition the divider leaves a minimum, say one percent, for the decider, who should accept any nonzero amount. Repeated experiments have shown that actual divisions do not follow these theoretical expectations; rather, in society after society, the split tends to be around 60:40 or 50:50, and substantial positive offers that are viewed as unfair are frequently rejected.[1] Fehr and Fischbacher (2002) provide a good account of why social preferences and non-selfish motives matter in real-world decision-making. The counter-argument by neoclassical economists is that non-selfish or other-regarding behavior is more an outcome of the absence of ideal markets rather than being intrinsic to human nature. They show that when game conditions more closely approach market conditions, the Ultimatum game tends toward self-regarding neoclassical solutions. According to Bowles (1998, 88), "market-like anonymity generates behaviors differing from those induced by more personal settings." I agree that morality is not fixed or absolute; as argued in the previous and following sections, it is conditioned by institutions, where the market is itself a major institution. If (state) institutions can generate mass violence or genocide—certainly the institutions would have to shape individual and group morality to achieve those ends—an institution like the market will surely affect morality and behavior. However, it does not follow that in perfect markets all human interactions are perfectly morals-free. Even if we do not accept the judgment of philosophers that humans are essentially moral beings, we are far from understanding the biology of ethics, and accepting unproven assumptions cannot further our understanding of human action.

The rationality and self-interest axioms inhabit the core of individuality —rationality is the fundament of knowledge, thereby belief, which in turn is one basis of action; self-interest is the motivation, the other basis of action. I suggest that there is more than adequate evidence that the rationality axiom must be modified. People make decisions and act on the basis of images and perceptions; these images and perceptions are shaped by habit, or the ability to transform a large variety of conditions to relatively few known or experienced situations with reasonably predictable responses; habits, in turn, are shaped by institutions (the state, culture, community, market, etc.) whereby they have a large overlap with norms (more on this soon).

Perhaps the most disturbing implication of the self-interest thesis is the implicit assumption that it is true at all times and in all places. Culture has no influence, social norms do not matter, personal ethics do not exist. The assumed and unproven biological instinct of self-interest is supposed to be strong enough to dominate all forms of learned and social behavior. Actually, a good case can be made for the opposite position: that giving primacy to self-interest itself is culturally conditioned. It has reached epic proportions in modern America, where the discourse has created a belief system that appears to be much more willing to entertain the possibility of unbridled self-interest than are other nations, including other western industrial democracies.[2] Peoples' actions are shaped by what they believe; ultimately, individual and group belief systems are conditioned by the societies within which they are embedded. Therefore, the self-interest thesis too must be qualified, not because it is unimportant, but because it has to be modified by other interests, the most important of which is group interest.

Groups

The self-interest assumption is supposedly derived from evolutionary principles. Nature, so goes the conventional wisdom, is unforgiving of the weak. In the struggle for survival only the strong can make it, and that strength comes from relentlessly pursuing one's individual interest at the cost, if necessary, of the interests of others.[3] These are the lessons some have taken from Darwin's theory of evolution and, more recently, from Richard Dawkins' *The Selfish Gene* (1976) and Steven Pinker's *The Blank Slate* (2002). Yet in Darwin's own words (Darwin 1952, 322):

> It must not be forgotten that although a high standard of morality gives but a slight or no advantage to each individual man and his children over the other men of his tribe, yet then an increase in the number of well-endowed men and an advancement of morality will certainly give an immense advantage of one tribe over another.

In other words, cooperation is necessary for a group to survive (and one must remember that it is the species or group that survives, not just an individual member). Group solidarity and sacrifice for the group are seen commonly in the animal world (weak animals team up to kill a stronger animal even at the cost of losing some members of the team), not to mention in the human world, where self-sacrifice is considered one of the noblest of qualities. There is empathy and altruism too in the animal world (primates who refuse to hurt other primates for food, even at the cost of starving themselves); our world is full of examples of empathy and altruism and sacrifice.[4]

So far, we have proceeded on the assumption that the relevant unit of social analysis is the individual. In economic analysis, the individual (person, household, or firm) is indeed the only relevant analytical unit. However, in the other social sciences, especially sociology and anthropology, the most important unit of analysis is not the individual, but the group. I suggest that it is necessary to incorporate groups —specifically the concepts of in-group cooperation and out-group derogation or conflict—to move toward a social theory of income distribution.

To incorporate socialized or group behavior it may not be *necessary* to make radical adjustments to the self-interest element of the *homo economicus* proposition. If we follow strictly functionalist assumptions—that is, human actions and institutions are all functionally oriented for individual survival—it is possible to argue that competition and cooperation are both efficient responses to different types of situations. That is, we do not have to answer the question whether human nature is only self-interested. Lenski's (1966) synthesis of the conservative and radical traditions of sociology shows how this is possible.

> The potential for rivalry arises because humans are naturally inclined to their selfish or partisan group interests above the needs of others, the demand for the objects of human desire generally exceeds the supply, and individuals have unequal genetic endowments. The potential for cooperation emerges because humans are naturally gregarious, and individual needs and desires can be fulfilled more efficiently through joint undertakings and mutually beneficial exchanges. In the distribution of amenities, humans are capable of both hoarding and sharing. (Haas 1993, 296).

This understanding of human behavior—being both competitive and cooperative—is fundamental to many disciplines including social psychology, and has a strong tradition in philosophy (among twentieth century philosophers, Isaiah Berlin's theory of the coexistence of selfish and altruistic impulses is well known). This may come about naturally (because humans are social, gregarious, somewhat altruistic, etc.), or as a result of understanding one's own group and society as an extension of oneself, whereby pursuing group interests is at the same time self-serving. As a result, individuals are embedded in social norms that, in the interest of serving group interests, circumscribe individual self-interest.

Though in-group cooperation is usually the norm, cooperation between groups (or with out-groups) is much less so. According to Charles Tilly (1998, 7–8):

Large, significant inequalities in advantages among human beings correspond mainly to categorical differences such as black/white, male/female, citizen/foreigner, or Muslim/Jew rather than to individual differences in attributes, propensities, or performances. In actual operation, more complex categorical systems involving multiple religions or various races typically resolve into bonded pairs relating just two categories at a time.... Durable inequality among categories arises because people who control access to value producing resources solve pressing organizational problems by means of categorical distinctions ... these people set up systems of social closure, exclusion, and control.

There is little doubt that ethnocentric behavior is not only common, but may even be a defining feature of social life. By ethnocentric behavior I mean the phenomenon of favoring in-groups (or we-groups) and derogating out-groups (or other-groups). Let us examine first the possible evolutionary basis of such behavior, and then the social psychological explanations.

Doyne Dawson's (1999) review of genetic and cultural theories of group evolution suggests three possible approaches to the evolutionary question: Why do groups exist? There is the possibility of "strong biological evolution," which comes from sociobiological theories in which group formation is a direct outcome of genetic signals; "biocultural coevolution" theories argue for the joint influence of genetic and cultural tracks; "autonomous cultural evolution" suggests that ideas and institutions (that is, culture) supporting group survival derive directly from Darwinian rules, independent of genes and biology. In other words, either our genes carry the codes for group formation, or our genes combine with our institutions to do so, or, most interestingly, our institutions alone do so, but following Darwinian rules. In any of these approaches it is possible to understand how altruism and sacrifice for the group come about.[5] Following the behavior of social insects and primates we can see that "natural selection promotes the survival and reproduction not only of individuals but also of their close relatives, who share much of the same genetic heritage" (Dawson 1999, 85; also see Sober and Wilson 1998).[6] Dawson (p. 96) goes on to argue:

Groupishness, or ethnocentricity, is the product of long ages of cultural selection, quite possibly abetted by genetic selection. The trait is clearly self-perpetuating. It has survival value because a culture that achieves cognitive consistency will function better at everything. Primitive groups seem quite conscious of the value of homogeneity ... they seem to know that their survival depends upon meticulous loyalty to the group norms, and that if they fail to uphold these they will be replaced by other groups.

The last sentence indicates that group solidarity is good for the group primarily because other individuals are also organized into groups. In other words, there is competition between groups that results in intergroup bias or conflict. This bias can escalate from competition to warfare to genocide; we are all too well aware of examples of each of these outcomes. Let us now consider theories from social psychology that address the causes of intergroup bias. Hewstone, Rubin, and Willis (2002) identify five such general theories, of which three seem to be more plausible:

1. *Social identity theory* derives from the instinctual human need for self esteem. In-groups provide social identity for its members and thereby bolster individual levels of self esteem.
2. *Subjective uncertainty reduction theory* proposes that people seek to reduce uncertainty and risk and identify with groups that provide clear normative guidelines on behavior.
3. *Social dominance theory* derives from the dominating drive of individuals who seek positions atop hierarchies and promote ideologies that create rivalrous in- and out-groups.

Perhaps more to the point are the empirical findings based on group size, status, and power (Hewstone, Rubin, and Willis 2002, 585):

- Groups in a numerical minority tend to show more bias than those in a numerical majority.
- Members of high-status groups express more bias than low-status groups, especially when the status gap appears to be closing.
- Members of low-status groups show more bias when the status differential is perceived to be illegitimate or unstable "and group boundaries are seen as impermeable."
- When the status gap is large and considered legitimate, that is, when the low-status group members view themselves as inferior, they actually show out-group favoritism.
- Members of high- and equal-power groups show more bias than members of low-power groups.
- Bias and discrimination by high-power numerical minorities is particularly high.

Though these findings come primarily from developed nations, often from laboratory settings,[7] they are likely to be replicated in all societies, albeit to different degrees. The degree or intensity of out-group bias is culturally and temporally specific. The groups that proliferate in a given area differ from region to region, and an intergroup relationship in a specific region is formed through specific historical interactions. In short, intergroup relationships are dynamic and embedded. Bias in some settings may turn into discrimination in others and outright physical conflict in yet other settings.

Groups are relatively easy to define, at least in binary terms. Many group identities are ascribed, that is, individuals are born into virtually unchangeable identities of race, gender, ethnicity, caste, and religion. Other group identities are acquired, primarily in relation to work and income generation. Income class is a big tent that can incorporate many such work-related group identities—such as landed or landless in peasant societies, formal-sector or informal-sector worker in developing nation cities, mental or manual labor in industrial and post-industrial nations. The intersections of ascribed and acquired group identities create variegated or plural societies with narrow, shifting, and often amorphous groups at large geographical scales. When ascribed and acquired identities overlap significantly—that is, ethnic and class identities overlap—the likelihood of intergroup bias is higher. Later I will show how it is possible to simplify plural groups to binary terms by reducing the geographical scale of analysis. For now, let us declare that *individual self-interest is often subsumed by group-interest, whereby societies are characterized by in-group cooperation and out-group competition.* This formulation does not deny the existence of in-group competition, but suggests that there are significant and systematic income differences between groups. This intergroup inequality is the primary component of *social inequality.*

Embeddedness

Consider how knowledge and action are influenced in real social settings where humans behave not like economic robots but as biological beings. According to sociologist Mark Granovetter (1985), individuals in neoclassical and classical economic theory are "atomized" and "undersocialized." On the other hand, modern sociology is often burdened by the assumption of "oversocialized" individuals who are completely bound by social customs and norms, are overly eager to fit in, and therefore are completely complaisant and obedient. Granovetter (1985, 482) goes on to argue for a middle ground of "embeddedness" in which "the [individual] behavior and institutions to be analyzed are so constrained by ongoing social relations that to construe them as independent is a grievous misunderstanding."[8] According to Anderson

(1996, 732–4), in social analysis "it is necessary to assume embeddedness. That is, to locate individuals, groups, and structures in social and *spatial contexts*.... The social relations that emerge have been constituted through processes that are gendered, racially defined, and class differentiated" (emphasis mine).

The idea of embeddedness has a distinguished past, originating with the works of Karl Polanyi and Clifford Geertz.[9] After Granovetter's seminal article, embeddedness has "become a central concept in the new economic sociology" (Dequech 2003, 462). This concept has a very large degree of overlap with what is called the "old" institutionalism approach in economic theory.[10] Both institutionalism and embeddedness suggest that individual knowledge and action are circumscribed by context. Zukin and DiMaggio (1990) suggest that embeddedness works in four ways:

1. Cognitive embeddedness refers to the limits of the mind and their impact on rational thought and decision-making.
2. Cultural embeddedness refers to the idea that specific cultures have narratives and scripts that signify and symbolize the values and norms that constrain social and economic behavior.
3. Structural embeddedness refers to "the contextualization of economic exchange in patterns of ongoing interpersonal relations" (Granovetter 1985, 18).
4. Political embeddedness refers to the shaping of institutions and exchange rules by the relations of power between economic and institutional actors.

Now, consider how institutions influence economic behavior. According to Dequech (2003), institutions play:

- A restrictive function, whereby there are constraints on economic behavior arising from cultural regulations
- A cognitive function, which refers first "to the information that institutions provide to the individual, including the indication of the likely action of other people" (also termed the informational-cognitive function by Dequech), and second to the idea that institutions shape individuals' sense of reality and information organization and interpretation (a deeper cognitive function)
- A motivational function, in which a culture provides a set of values and ideal norms of attainment, achievement, service, community, etc.

- An emotional function, "through which institutions influence the emotions guiding economic behavior ... [this] is related to the expressive or affective aspects of culture" (Dequech 2003, 464).

Note that, in this perspective, institutions are virtually indistinguishable from cultures. It is possible to shed much semantic blood distinguishing between these two entities (certainly the anthropological understanding of culture is broader than economic versions of institutions), but for the purpose of my argument no such distinction is necessary. As we can see below from Hodgson's (1998, 179) characterization of institutions, what an economist calls institutions can just as easily pass for culture to an anthropologist.

All institutions involve the interaction of agents, with crucial information feedbacks.

All institutions have a number of characteristic and common conceptions and routines.

Institutions sustain, and are sustained by, shared conceptions and expectations.

Although they are neither immutable nor immortal, institutions have relatively durable, self-reinforcing, and persistent qualities.

Institutions incorporate values, and processes of normative evaluation. In particular, institutions reinforce their own moral legitimation; that which endures is often—rightly or wrongly—seen as morally just.

It matters little whether we conceive of the social system in terms of embeddedness (as sociologists do), culture (as anthropologists do), or institutions (as economists do). In any case, the system produces "norms" that regulate behavior and desire. Norms regulate social and economic behavior, reining in or exaggerating the worst instincts of aggressive and powerful groups and individuals through the use of symbols, myths, and images of past social orders and outright sanctions. But norms do more than merely constrain action. They also enable action by reducing the cost of decision-making, by providing information on individual agents and groups, and by relieving the decision-makers of the burden of constant intense calculation. Most important, norms are inscribed with the relations of power in a society —between genders, classes, social groups, and between the state and its subjects/citizens. They are the most direct expressions of group interests, and the interesting aspect is that this happens without constant collective action. Therefore, in moving toward a social theory of income distribution, it is possible to declare that *individual knowledge and action rules are informed and constrained by cultural and institutional contexts.*

Power

In previous sections, the unit of analysis was changed to include groups along with individuals. Now, consider the idea that perfect markets are impossible because all markets are mediated by power. The term "power" captures a fundamental dynamic of social and economic relations between individuals, groups, territories, and institutions. Some individuals have power over other individuals, some groups have power over other groups, some territories (nations, kingdoms) have power over other territories, and the state has power over its citizens. Power is minimally the ability to act, and more usually it is the ability to make others (individuals, groups, territories) follow one's wishes; in extreme but common situations, the powerful are able to enforce their wishes despite resistance from the less powerful. Power comes from having something that others want; in the sociological worldview, the struggle for control over such scarce resources is the defining element of social life at all analytical scales.

The concept of power is virtually absent in economic theorizing (except the special case of monopoly or oligopoly power to set market prices); it is central in social theory, so much so that preeminent social theorists—from Marx and Weber to Gramsci and Foucault—have made the study of power central to their analyses.[11] Marxian ideas of power are class-based where classes are constituted in terms of the relationship to the mode of production, whereby the owners of these means dominate those with only labor power. Weber enlarged on the idea of economic class with the idea of social status and the drive for status domination (this is a more individualistic position). Gramsci explored the role of hegemony, specifically cultural hegemony, in maintaining state-domination in the interest of the owners of capital. Foucault analyzed the link between knowledge (or language) and power and showed how discourses of normal authority (experts, specialists) legitimize the use of power. In between these grand theories of power are fascinating ideas such as Peter Blau's (1964) argument that, in market exchange, people with less capital subordinate themselves to those with more because "the power to command compliance is equivalent to credit."

It is easy to see that power asymmetries exist in every social relationship. Parents have power over children, men have power over women (especially in patriarchal or traditional societies), employers and corporations have power over employees, landlords have power over the landless, lenders have power over borrowers, etc. A defining element of modern democracies is the attenuation of traditional power using legal and other institutional means—by providing children, women, employees, the landless, borrowers and others in weaker power positions with more rights and therefore more power through the institutions of the state and changing social norms. It would be wrong to presume, however, that the state is necessarily an honest broker or referee arbitrating power struggles between unequal classes and groups, or that it always acts in favor of the weaker class or group. The state usually acts in its own interest: in evolutionary terms, for survival. In Marxian class theory, the state is a handmaiden in the interest of capital, creating conditions to subjugate labor in the domestic and international arenas. In liberal individualistic theory, the power of the state can be curbed only by creating inviolate social and legal institutions that protect individual property rights.

The subject of state power is too vast to cover in any detail here. As discussed above, Marx, Weber, Gramsci, and Foucault have argued the idea extensively and creatively from radical critical perspectives. They are well known among students of social theory. Also well known are the more mainstream liberal accounts offered in political science (see Robert Dahl 1989). Such concepts as democracy, civil society, process, authority, autonomy, etc., which are important in political theories of state power, will not be discussed here. Some of these issues will inevitably arise in discussions that are forthcoming in other chapters. In fact, later I will argue that state ideology, or what the state believes is right, which becomes the basis for state action, is a very significant variable for analyzing income distribution change. For now, I will focus on a single idea that is critical for understanding power from the micro to the macro scales. This is the concept of monopoly or concentration.

In a monopoly a single entity or institution is able to dictate the terms of transaction or exchange. The state derives its power from having a monopoly on violence. It has the ability to tax, to take land and other property, and to take life, using its monopoly on violence and its ability to coerce. Where the state has a monopoly on violence, there is order, where it does not, there is anarchy. We are not so concerned here with a state's ability to monopolize violence, but are interested in seeing, first, how this monopoly leads to the rules that govern market and non-market exchanges, and second, how state institutions shape the production and distribution of information and education, and thereby shape cognition and human capital acquisition. The more powerful the state or the greater the concentration of power in state institutions, the more hegemonic is the state's ability to create and enforce laws and shape social norms. ·

It is useful to also consider the more common conceptualization of monopoly, which is the ability of a single agent or a limited number of agents (an oligopoly) to set the terms of market exchange by having disproportionate control of scarce resources (capital, land). A monopolist has the ability to set the price of goods, the quantity of goods in the market, and labor's wages. Economists from Adam Smith on have been concerned about the market distortions that arise from the existence of concentrated power (see Elliott 2000). A monopoly is a special case of concentration, and all concentrations of power, be it in wealth or market share or land or politics, lead to inefficient and inegalitarian outcomes. Therefore, *the concentration of power, in the market or in non-market institutions, influences the distribution of resources and income.* Power asymmetries exist at multiple levels and scales. In a simple hierarchy, the state is the most powerful institution, followed by groups, followed by individuals (which implies that there are power hierarchies within groups).

Scale

So far, my three arguments have been (1) that knowledge and action are socially and institutionally embedded, (2) that intragroup cooperation and intergroup conflict is characteristic of all societies; and (3) that market and non-market power is concentrated to some degree. The question now before us is this: are these relations of embeddedness, group dynamics, and power homogenous over entire societies and populations? In general, the answer is presumed to be yes, because the scale of analysis is assumed to be national. That is, the same social norms and strictures, and group and power relations are assumed to apply to all citizens of modern nations. This, I believe, is a serious mistake. Anthropologists (see Berreman 1978) and geographers have long argued that the appropriate scale of social analysis is something much smaller than a nation. Geographers' distrust of large scales is best expressed in the "ecological fallacy" principle, whereby associations and causal connections that are observed at one scale cannot be presumed to be true at larger or smaller scales. What is true for nations cannot be assumed to be true for its constituent regions; what is true for regions may not be true for the groups that make up the regions; what is true of groups cannot be assumed to apply to individuals in the group. There is disagreement over what "appropriate" scale is, mainly because different scales are appropriate for different social processes or interactions. The organization of the modern state implicitly recognizes that different social processes and institutions are most effectively managed at different geographical scales—defense and communication at the national scale, education and health at a regional or local scale. Similarly, all social processes have some elements that operate society-wide, but there are other social processes that are most clearly manifested and understood at the sub-national or local scale. I suggest that we need to disaggregate social and economic processes to smaller units than whole nations or societies. Consider the reasons for this claim:

1. Embeddedness is inherently a spatial concept. Some institutional or cultural features, such as federal and religious laws, are manifested society-wide. Other features, such as customs and rituals, tend to be local. Individuals and groups are embedded in space just as they are embedded in time (remember that laws, customs, and norms change over time).
2. At a society-wide scale it is often quite difficult to identify binary oppositional groups because each individual is a member of several groups, some by ascription, some acquired through labor. At a local scale, however, the plurality of group identities is significantly more simplified. Hence intergroup dynamics is best understood and analyzed at local rather than national scales.
3. Power relations between and within groups are most clearly manifested locally. Nationwide monopolies are rare, but local monopolies or oligopolies are quite common. It is not at all unusual to find oligopolies that control land, labor, and credit markets at local scales, especially in rural settings, and thereby control rents and wages. A large landholder can impose his will on the local population much more easily than in places where he does not own land.
4. The most significant power relations may exist at the interregional scale, where one area or territory dominates another in terms of average income and all the benefits and superior life chances that income brings. This is the most important reason for incorporating geographical scale because this is the source of *spatial inequality.*

How does spatial variability affect income distribution? To answer this question it is necessary to disentangle two key concepts—social norms and social contract—that have unfortunately been jumbled in much of the literature. The latter applies to the relationship between ruler and ruled, which is to say that the social contract is one that legitimates or creates consensus for a given system of governance. It does not cover all social norms, nor does it apply to distributional norms, which are primarily local (see John Rawls 1971 for the most widely discussed recent statement on the social contract). I find James Coleman's understanding to be persuasive. Coleman writes (1974, 759–62):

> They [social contractarians such as Rousseau, Locke] conceived of society as a single fabric of institutions which one made a single contract to join, while I conceive of society as consisting of distinct corporate actors, only one of which is the encompassing state.... All these "single contract" theories ... are more appropriate to something like (though more voluntaristic than) states characterized by "state socialism" than to the pluralistic societies of Western democratic states....

I suggest that not only are there multiple social contracts (the principal one of which is with the state), but that there are multiple scales at which the different contracts operate. On income distribution, we can make the following assumptions:

1. Inequality levels at a small scale have to be sustainable inequalities at that scale. That is, the local inequality level cannot be so high that poverty will physically destroy marginal labor, nor can it be so high that it leads to local social unrest or revolution.[12] The destruction of marginal labor is not in the interest of capital, as that can only serve to raise the cost of labor or lead to challenges to the social order. This can be understood as a self-preservational, rational actor argument.
2. Distributional judgments on fairness and justice are made at a small scale. Most people are indifferent to incomes earned by people far away; their reference groups and individuals are local.[13] This argument is closely allied to the arguments on limited information and image/history-based perception that have been outlined earlier. The cognitive universe of individuals cannot hold information about incomes worldwide or even nationwide. Even if some individuals more than others are able to carry more information on distant places, they recognize that they have virtually no ability to influence the incomes of people far away. Social and distributive change, it is well recognized, must take place locally.
3. Social reproduction, social inheritance, and social capital generation take place at a small scale. This is an example of increasing

returns arising from localization economies or externalities, whereby the interaction of dense local networks creates institutional and economic features that could not have arisen without the density. (This is a key idea about "increasing returns," which will be covered further in Chapter 6.) According to Ronald Bénabou (1996, 237) certain essential inputs in the process of accumulation of human capital

... are determined neither at the level of individual families nor that of the whole economy, but at the intermediate level of communities, neighborhoods, firms or social networks. Not only is this the case with school resources when funding is decentralized, but also with many forms of "social capital": peer effects, role models, job contacts, norms of behavior, crime, and so on. Through these fiscal and sociological spillovers, the next generation's distribution of skills and incomes is shaped by the manner in which the current one sorts itself into differentiated clusters.

It follows that the distributional contract is also local/regional. The idea that social relations are local rather than national is not new. The most far-reaching consequence of local conditions may lie in the long-term implications of the influence of local environments on technological and social change; this idea is most eloquently detailed in Jared Diamond's (1997) popular account in *Guns, Germs, and Steel.* In economics, this idea has entered the analytic literature through models of chaotic and cybernetic systems. Rosser (1999) summarizes a large literature showing, among other things, that regional agglomeration and/or economic/racial segregation can take place assuming only minor variations in preference, and that most such "complex economics" models assume local relationships among individual actors rather than general relationships that are meant to apply society-wide. Therefore, it is possible to declare that *the appropriate geographical scale for understanding income generation and distribution and values and judgments on income inequality is the local scale.*

Summary The self-interested rational actor of mainstream economic theory must be replaced by an agent with the following characteristics:

- He has bounded rationality and limited knowledge. His actions are informed by perceptions, images, and norms derived from his specific social context. This is usually more efficient than going through endless calculation on every decision.

- His self-interest is limited by group-interest. Since group survival is evolutionarily important, this too is an efficient response.

Under these circumstances, it follows that:

- The units of social analysis must include both individuals and groups.
- Self-interest is expressed in the drive to acquire power—within groups, between groups, and in institutions.
- Markets are mediated by power: the power of the state, followed by the power of groups, followed by the power of individuals within groups.
- Market and social relations thus defined vary over space. It is necessary to disaggregate a society geographically to understand the dynamics of these relations.

THE ANALYTICAL FRAMEWORK

These arguments can now be incorporated into a simple analytical framework based on individual choice within a social system (see Figure 4.1). This framework is based on one fundamental assumption: that every person is, at the same time, an individual agent and a social agent. As an individual agent, each is endowed with some inheritance and human capital and is governed by and responsive to market forces and market rules. That is, following the principles of basic economics, each individual operates within a market system. However, in the social system (which includes market and non-market elements), that individual is also a social agent; he or she acts as a member of some collective and community and is influenced by institutional laws and group norms. Our objective is to understand how this dual existence as an individual and social agent within a market and a social system affects an individual's income and the income of others in the same society.

The Market System

First, consider an individual agent. Let us say that every individual has some income-earning potential. In the first instance, this income-earning potential is a function of inheritance. If property (land, real estate, stock, etc.) is inherited, it may be possible to earn an income without any other input. Individuals also inherit genes, some of which affect their health, temperament, etc., and which also contribute to that nebulous entity called ability. However, following the discussion in Chapter 3, inherited ability is useless without the acquisition of human

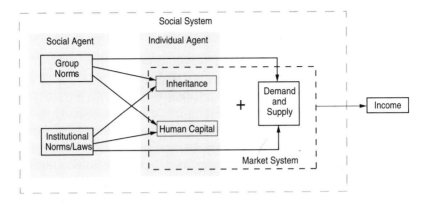

Fig. 4.1 Analytical framework for income determination in a social system.

capital in the form of education and training; this may be formal schooling or informal/traditional apprenticeship or learning by doing. The level and quality of human capital acquired may, in turn, be a function of property or wealth inheritance; this is a big debate that was outlined in Chapter 3; it is not necessary to settle that issue at this point. Nor is it necessary to assume that the acquisition of human capital is an individual decision based on time-discounted estimates of all future earnings. On the contrary, we will assume that the most important human capital acquisition decisions are taken not by the individual concerned, but by his or her family. The decision to attend first grade is surely not an individual's to make, though future decisions on human capital acquisition, after having attended several grades, may have some input from the individual. Similarly, the decision not to attend first grade determines, to a very large extent, future possible acquisitions of human capital; if a family does not or is unable to send its child to first grade, the possibility that the child will acquire human capital through schooling is virtually eliminated at that point. Therefore, we leave this first proposition at a simple level: every individual has some income-earning potential, which is a function of inheritance and human capital.

However, inheritance and human capital do not by themselves determine what income an agent will receive in the market. The interplay of supply and demand for an agent's inheritance and human capital will determine what wage, rent, or interest one receives. Random shocks such as technological change or a shift in taste or preference may quickly alter the earning potential of specific kinds of inheritance or human capital. Today, mastery of a dead language such as Sanskrit is likely to provide far lower returns than elementary knowledge of a technical language such as Visual Basic. Ownership of hundreds of hectares of land in Utah may provide returns that are a mere fraction of the returns provided by the ownership of a single hectare of land in Los Angeles. In short, temporal and geographical market forces determine how a specific inheritance or human capital is rewarded. It may be very much more difficult to master Sanskrit than to learn Visual Basic at an elementary level; it may require more time and more money. However, the salaries of the Sanskrit expert and the Visual Basic novice will be nominally set by the supply of Sanskrit experts and Visual Basic novices and the demand for them. "Ability" may have very little to do with it, as may the quantity or quality of human capital embodied in these agents. In a well functioning market, these wages are signals to others considering the acquisition of human capital: acquiring knowledge of Sanskrit is difficult, expensive, and relatively unrewarding; acquiring knowledge of Visual Basic is simpler, less expensive, and pays higher wages. More individuals will then train in Visual Basic and fewer will train in Sanskrit. In theory, the supply of people with knowledge of Visual Basic will match demand at some equilibrium quantity of Visual Basic graduates; similarly so for Sanskrit experts. Further supply and demand of Visual Basic and Sanskrit graduates will nudge but not seriously disrupt the quantities and wages set in equilibrium.

The Social System

It is necessary to reiterate here that the market system is a part of the social system, which, according to the framework suggested here, includes individuals and groups, and markets and non-market institutions. As a social agent, each individual's income potential is constrained and, at the same time, that person's income-related decisions made cognitively simpler by membership in groups and by the actions of institutions. Following the discussions in the preceding section, group membership influences individual inheritance and human capital endowments and labor market conditions. Similarly, institutions influence individual endowments and demand and supply or labor market conditions. We have already discussed the more subtle ways in which this happens. Consider the broad outlines again.

Institutions   The more obvious ways in which institutions affect income generation are through laws (created by institutions of the state) and norms (created through non-state institutions such as the market, religion, and social groups). Laws directly influence both inheritance and the acquisition of human capital. Norms do so less directly, and, in modern nations, perhaps less effectively. Briefly examine how laws may influence the potential income of agents. Laws cannot influence the inheritance of genetic traits. Therefore, it is possible to pass on some elements of raw ability, such as mathematical reasoning or musicality, through genetic inheritance. But the state certainly can affect property inheritance. It can tax incomes, estates, and intergenerational inheritances, redistribute land or limit the size of landholding; all these actions diminish power differentials in existing social arrangements. Alternatively, its policies can strengthen the power of large estates through consolidation and allow distress sales of small holdings; either of these latter actions will increase the magnitude of property inheritance within and between generations.

The state's role in enabling human capital acquisition is also quite clear. Human capital may be acquired through informal apprenticeship systems (as in the guilds of European city states). But, in modern states, human capital is acquired largely through formal pubic education systems. The reach and quality of the state education system determines who has access and at what level. The division of resources among the primary-, secondary-, and higher-education systems determines the reach and quality of education that individuals can potentially receive. Most developing nations, for instance, have invested more heavily in higher education than in primary education, a decision that has left significant proportions of their populations illiterate.

The role of norms in influencing inheritance and human capital acquisition is less obvious. Genetic and property inheritances are influenced by social norms that encourage, even dictate, assortative mating or homogamy (more on this in the next chapter). With an empirical, perhaps heuristic, knowledge of genetic inheritance, well before the advent of genetics, societies created customs that blessed unions where both partners were from the same group and social class and discouraged unions that broke group or class barriers.[14] The acquisition of human capital is affected by social norms through the same assortative channel: if education is correlated with property inheritance, and there is abundant evidence that it is (see Chapter 3), then norms can create social rigidities and hinder group and class mobility. Other ways in which norms can influence inheritance are through family size, primogeniture, and patrilineage.

Demand and supply conditions are also directly affected by institutions. State institutions have a strong influence on demand and supply conditions. The channels of influence include the state's roles as an industrial producer in most developing and all socialist nations (creating demand for labor), the buyer for many privately produced goods from food to aircrafts (affecting demand for labor), and the primary provider of public education (creating labor supply at different skill levels). Social norms can influence the demand for and supply of certain categories of workers, such as priests, language teachers, sex workers, soldiers, etc. Socially prescribed gender or race roles can limit both labor force participation rates and what kind of work an individual may be eligible to do. In fact, social norms may significantly define, at birth, what a person can be expected to do in life.

Groups How does group membership influence inheritance and human capital endowments? Earlier I argued that different groups—identifiable by ethnicity or class—occupy different positions in the social hierarchy. For instance, whites and blacks in South Africa and the U.S., whites and Indians in Brazil, Brahmins and Dalits (lower castes) in India, are identifiable social categories with very unequal average endowments and life chances. These identity-based group differences coexist with class-based group differences between landed and landless, formal sector and informal sector, mental and manual labor, etc. Again, the latter category in each pair faces inferior life chances and has lower endowments. Often the ascribed and acquired identities overlap, so that South African blacks are also the landless and the Dalits are also informal-sector workers.[15] Clearly, these social and market identities, or group memberships, influence property inheritance and human capital acquisition.

Groups influence supply-and-demand conditions by institutionalizing in-group favoritism and out-group derogation in hiring, lending, buying, and selling decisions. When white employers hire only white workers, or white-run banks lend primarily to white borrowers, the demand-and-supply conditions in the labor and credit markets are affected, usually to the detriment of the weaker groups. Powerful minorities, such as land-owning oligopolies in many countries, are able to control the supply of critical resources and thereby set prices and wages. Of course, weaker groups can organize, and when they form unions, or are settled densely in proximity, or form networks, they are able to generate social capital. Some forms of social capital can be converted to human capital. However, as useful as social capital can be, it is not a perfect or even reasonable substitute for financial capital or property. In addition, it is difficult to argue that the social capital of the poor and powerless can compete in effectiveness with the social capital of the rich and powerful, who also form clubs, associations, and networks.

A Numerical Illustration

Consider the distributional implications of the social theory framework using some numerical illustrations. I have made two substantial changes to conventional analysis: first, I have redefined self-interest to include group-interest; second, I have changed the basic unit of distributional analysis from the societal or national level to a local scale. It is possible, using just these two changes, to investigate different distributional outcomes based on a variety of assumptions on the nature of social and spatial relationships; including institutional arrangements and power hierarchies. In this section I discuss the results of a numerical illustration in the tradition of Kuznets (1955) to show how inequality at the societal level changes based on different assumptions about intragroup, intergroup and interregional relationships. The numerical illustration itself, with its technical details and basic findings, is an appendix to this chapter.

It may be useful to begin by visualizing the spatial setup of the illustrations—there are two regions populated by two groups each, where there is inequality within *and* between groups, and between regions. Therefore, there are four relevant forms of inequality in the numerical illustrations that are based on a two-group, two-region model.

- Within-group inequality reflects the reality of within-group competition and power hierarchies and variations in inheritance and human capital. Groups or classes are not homogeneous by any means, but as discussed earlier, within-group inequality levels can be expected to be low, at least lower in small localized regions than in entire populations. In other words, at small scales there is less within-group variation than at large scales.
- Between-group inequality, or what I have earlier called social inequality, captures the reality that group averages can be different, often very different. The illustrations are based on different assumptions about the extent of this difference—from none at all to situations where the average of the high-income group is three times that of the low-income group.
- Between-region inequality, represented by the ratio of average regional incomes, which is what we have earlier called spatial inequality. As with between-group inequality in the illustrations, this ratio is assumed to be between 1 and 3; i.e., from no interregional difference to a threefold difference.
- Societal inequality is the inequality in the entire two-group, two-region society. The objective of the illustrations is to calculate

societal inequality for different combinations of within-group, between-group, and between-region inequality.

The simulation results (detailed in the appendix) lead to the following conclusions:

- It is possible for low levels of local (or within-group and between-group) inequality to coexist with high levels of societal inequality. In such cases between-region inequality levels drive the level of societal or national inequality. These are situations of *spatial polarization.*
- It is possible for low levels of between-region inequality to coexist with high levels of societal inequality. In such cases between-group inequality levels drive the level of societal inequality. These are situations of *social polarization.*
- The level of societal inequality is not substantially influenced by the levels of within-group inequality *in the presence* of large between-group and between-region inequalities. All combinations of within-group inequalities tend to converge to similar levels of societal inequality with increasing levels of spatial and social polarization.

Putting the Numerical Illustrations in Perspective   The primary purpose of the illustrations is to examine some "what if" scenarios when all the economic, social, and spatial variables discussed earlier are considered together. It is possible as a result to ask questions about different combinations of within-group, between-group, and between-region inequality. For instance, we can ask what happens to societal inequality when within-group and between-group inequalities are low and between-region inequality is high. Alternatively, we can surmise the level of between-group inequality, for instance, when we know the levels of within-group, between-region, and societal inequality. This exercise is not meant to be explanatory. It is meant to be exploratory.

First, ask whether the assumptions of the illustrations are reasonable. I argue that localized within-group inequality levels are likely to be low because of redistribution within the group—to maintain group solidarity, to create public goods and social capital available exclusively for the group, and because redistribution is one of the identifying characteristics of a group. This assumption follows from the so-called first law of geography: everything is related to everything else, but proximate events are more closely related. It is also a standard assumption in spatial and nonspatial statistics: the smaller an area the less variance there is. There is empirical support for this idea in Snodgrass' (1980) work on the Bumiputeras, Chinese, and Indians in Malaysia. On the other hand, there is little data on between-group income inequality at the *local* level. Part of the problem, as discussed earlier, is that paired groups can be identified in many ways; some pairs are more significant in some places than in others. The landowner–landless or latifundia–minifundia relationship may be meaningful in some regions, the white–black or colonizer–colonized relationship may be more important in others, and the upper caste–lower caste or Christian–Muslim or native–immigrant relationship may be most important in yet other regions. The group income ratios may indeed go up to three and higher (especially in the earlier pairs among the examples above).

The between-region inequality numbers assumed here are quite conservative. Regional inequalities at the state or province level between the highest income and lowest income units range from around 1.5 in Japan, 2 in the U.S., 3 to 4 in Brazil and India, and higher in China and Russia. At smaller scales such as counties or districts it is not uncommon to see income ratios as high as 15–20 in China and India. Regional income data showing such differences are presented in more detail in Chapter 6. Urban–rural income differences too have a wide range, from around 1.5 in the advanced industrialized nations up to 5 and more in some African nations.

It is useful to remember that the simulation set up is an abstraction. Its purpose is to demonstrate that if we conceive society to be made up of competitive groups (with individual competition within groups) broken into relatively small spatial units (that are also in competition for investment and other limited resources), the level of societal inequality is driven by intergroup and interregional differentials. I do not mean to suggest that there are only two groups at any local scale, but that there are relations of power and domination at all scales that can be effectively captured in a two-group model, especially at small scales. Similarly, a two-region model captures the fact of regional differentials in all nations; it is not meant to suggest that all societies are composed of only two regions. Therefore, this two-group/two-region model becomes a fractal unit of large societies. It is possible to aggregate fractals and undertake similar analysis at larger and larger scales. Hence, we can move from societies composed of two villages to twenty villages and a town, from two rural districts to twenty rural districts and a metropolitan district that make up a state/province, to two states or provinces, to a nation made up of several states or provinces, to two nations or the international system made up of many nations. *At every higher level of spatial aggregation we need to generalize and aggregate groups* and thereby lose much of the richness of ethnographic or anthropological detail. I suggest that this loss of group-level detail at larger spatial aggregations has made it difficult for analysts to study income distribution in terms of social fragmentation. The strength of the approach used here is that the variety of group identities at large spatial scales could be simplified using such a micro-foundation approach; it recognizes that pluralism can be deconstructed to smaller spatial scales where the meaningful group identities are binary rather than plural.

The idea that inequalities can be decomposed into within-unit and between-unit components is not new. In fact, one of the desirable elements of a good measure of inequality is that it should be decomposable into within- and between-unit components. A large number of studies of decomposed inequality are available: these decompositions are usually spatial (using different administrative units of a country, for example), but they have also been occupational, educational, etc. For instance, studies of world inequality by Milanovic (2002) and others have repeatedly shown that the principal source of inequality at the global scale is the difference in national per capita incomes (which is equivalent to between-region inequality in our terms), rather than within-nation inequality, and till China's recent economic surge, the level of world inequality had been increasing as a result of increasing divergence in national per capita income levels (which is equivalent to increasing between-region inequality levels). The key intuition of the approach taken here is that, in its simplest sense, within-region inequality is further decomposed into within-group and between-group inequalities. As a result, we can begin to understand and analyze inequality at a national scale by looking at its principal components: inequalities within and between groups at a local scale, and inequalities between regions.

The Task Ahead   I have identified the two principal sources of variation in inequality levels at the national level—social inequality and spatial inequality—but we are not much closer to an understanding of why particular combinations of social and spatial inequality are seen in reality, and whether and how these conditions change. We can guess at what the important factors are that affect social and spatial inequality, namely history and institutions, but are far from developing a good theoretical understanding. Similarly, we are no closer at this point to an understanding of the evolutionary models of inequality change—punctuated equilibria and gradualism. The next two chapters will move toward creating the theoretical bases for understanding these variations: social inequality is covered in Chapter 5, where we will see how punctuated equilibria shape particular settings of social inequality; spatial inequality is covered in Chapter 6, where the focus will be on the gradualist model of inequality change.

APPENDIX 2

A Numerical Illustration

The objective in this appendix is to create a set of numerical illustrations where different levels of within-group, between-group, and between-region inequality combine to create societal inequality. The results of these illustrations are discussed in the final section of Chapter 4.

Assume a society made up of two spatial units R1 and R2 with populations p_{R1} and p_{R2} with average incomes y_{R1} and y_{R2} respectively, where $y_{R2} \geq y_{R1}$ (i.e., R2 is potentially the higher income spatial unit). Each of these spatial units—for simplicity, call these "regions" for now—is populated by two groups G1 and G2 with populations p_{G1} and p_{G2} with average incomes y_{G1} and y_{G2} respectively, which are the means of distributions d_{G1} and d_{G2} respectively, where $y_{G2} \geq y_{G1}$. Assume that the y_{R2}/y_{R1} ratio can take one of five possible values: 1.0, 1.5, 2.0, 2.5, and 3.0. That is, under the most spatially egalitarian conditions, the two spatial units (regions) have equal average incomes; under the most inegalitarian conditions the average income of R2 is three times that of R1. Similarly, between the groups, G2 is potentially the higher-income group, so that the y_{G2}/y_{G1} ratio can be 1.0, 1.5, 2.0, 2.5, and 3.0. Under the egalitarian setting $y_{G1} = y_{G2}$; in the most inegalitarian setting y_{G2} is threefold y_{G1}. Finally, the distributions d_{G1} and d_{G2} can take one of four variations, with the corresponding Gini Indexes equaling 16, 20, 24, and 28 as shown below. Each row represents a distribution; the numbers in the row are quintile shares, going from the poorest to the richest.

- Distribution 1: 12.5, 15, 20, 25, 27.5: Gini = 16
- Distribution 2: 10, 15, 20, 25, 30: Gini = 20
- Distribution 3: 7.5, 15, 20, 25, 32.5: Gini = 24
- Distribution 4: 5, 15, 20, 25, 35: Gini = 28

I wish to examine the impact on income distribution for the whole society (made up of R1 and R2) based on different values of p_{R1}, p_{R2}, p_{G1}, p_{G2}, y_{R1}, y_{R2}, y_{G1}, y_{G2}, d_{G1}, and d_{G2}. In other words, this is a society of two regions (which can, for the sake of convenience, be thought of as rural and urban), each composed of two income groups (a LIG or low-income

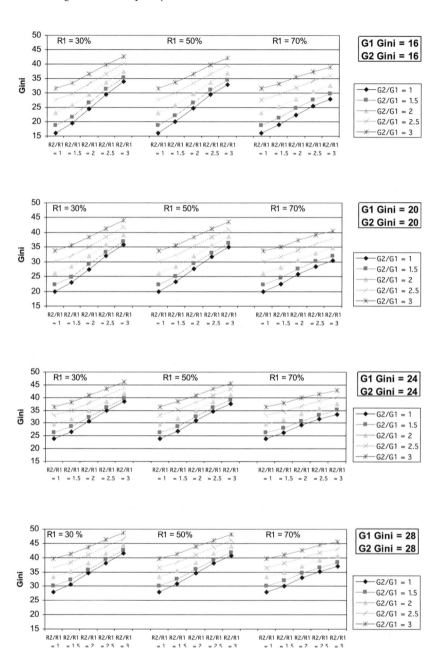

Fig. A2.1 Simulation results with equal intra-group inequality

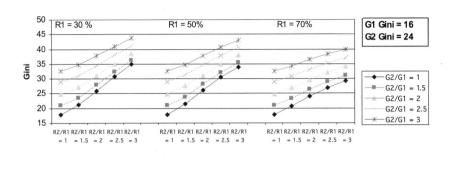

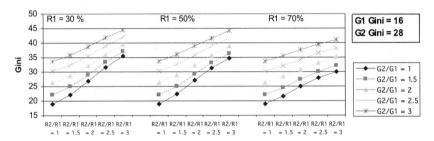

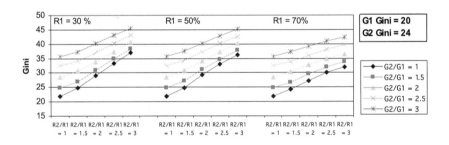

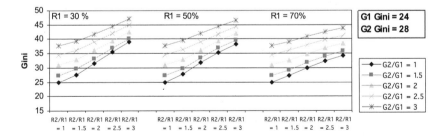

Fig. A2.1 (Continued)

group, and a HIG or high-income group) where the LIG represents 80 percent of the population.

In this setup, there are four relevant forms of inequality.

- Within-group inequality, represented by the Gini Index of the distribution of income within a group.
- Between-group inequality, represented by the ratio of average group incomes.
- Between-region inequality, represented by the ratio of average regional incomes.
- Societal inequality, represented by the Gini Index for the combined population of R1 and R2. The objective is to calculate societal inequality for different combinations of the above three forms of inequality.

Some results are shown in Figures A2.1 and A2.2. All possible results are not shown. Two variables have been held constant in the data presented. First, the proportion of people in the higher-income group (G2) has been kept constant at 20 percent. I have argued in the main text (Chapter 4) that the more powerful, higher-income group is likely to be a minority (of course, there are exceptions). This assumption can be easily changed, without substantially affecting the shapes of the curves. Second, the same conditions of within-group and between-group inequality levels in both regions are presumed here. That is, d_{G1} and d_{G2} in R1 are identical to d_{G1} and d_{G2} in R2. This assumption derives from the argument that institutional arrangements are likely to be similar nationwide.

Figure A2.1 shows the results when d_{G1} and d_{G2} (i.e., within-group inequality) are identical; that is, the LIG and HIG have the same internal distribution. Figure A2.2 shows the results when HIG inequality is higher than LIG inequality. Four sets of d_{G1} and d_{G2} combinations are shown in each figure, where each pair is represented by a panel of three sets of curves. These three sets show the results for different shares of R1 in the total population: 30, 50, and 70 percent from left to right. Each curve in each of these sets shows changes in societal inequality at different levels of between-region inequality for fixed levels of between-group inequality. The five curves in each graph set represent the five levels of between-group inequality. Note that each setting of G2/G1 = 1 in the graphs represents situations of no between-group inequality. In all such situations there are no discernible groups. When R2/R1 = 1 it implies that there is no between-region inequality. Therefore, in all such situations, the graphed inequality level represents within-region inequality for that particular level of between-group inequality.

Consider the first set of curves in Figure A2.1, to the left in the top panel. These curves represent situations of very low levels of within-group inequality (Gini = 16). The lowest curve in this set represents measures of societal inequality at different levels of between-region inequality with no between-group inequality (both groups have the same average income, therefore, effectively there are no groups). From a condition in which societal inequality is at Gini = 16 (there is no between-group inequality, and no between-region inequality), the curve moves to a societal inequality level of Gini = 34 simply as a result of the between-region inequality ratio increasing to 3.0. Conversely, when the between-group inequality ratio rises to 3.0 with the between-region inequality ratio at 1.0 (there is no between-region inequality), the societal Gini rises to about 32. When both between-group and between-region inequality levels rise to 3.0, the societal inequality level rises to Gini = 42. The set of curves in the middle of this top panel show results when R1 has half the overall population. The results are not very different from the R1 = 30 percent set. The set on the right, where R1 has 70 percent of the overall population, shows similar results, but the curves rise less steeply; therefore, at peak conditions, the Gini levels are three to four points lower in this set.

The four panels under Figure A2.2 show situations where within-group inequalities are different, with the G1 Gini less than the G2 Gini. In these cases, inequality within the HIG is presumed to be higher than within the LIG. The patterns identified in the previous set of graphs is repeated here. When there is no between-group or between-region inequality, societal inequality is driven purely by within-group inequalities. These levels are somewhere between the inequality levels of the two groups; for instance, in the second panel, with G1 Gini = 16 and G2 Gini = 28, societal Gini is around 19. As before, the level of societal Gini increases with increasing between-region inequality or with increasing between-group inequality, reaching a peak when both between-region and between-group inequalities also peak. This peak is between Gini levels of 44 and 47 in all of the R1 = 30 percent and R1 = 50 percent cases shown. At R1 = 70 percent, as in Figure A2.2, the peaks decline by about three Gini points.

5

PUNCTUATED EQUILIBRIA AND SOCIAL INEQUALITY

Let us now move toward an understanding of the processes by which changes in social inequality create punctuated equilibria in income inequality. Consider again some of the main arguments that have been detailed earlier. I have shown that inequality trends often follow patterns of punctuated equilibria, which is a term borrowed from evolutionary biology in which species change takes place not by gradual, minute adaptation, but by rapid, significant changes punctuating long periods of very little change. I have also argued that social inequality, defined primarily to be the inequality between groups at sub-national scales, is one of two key elements that determine the level of income inequality in a nation. This chapter considers these two arguments together; that is, examines the causes of and conditions under which social inequalities follow punctuated equilibrium patterns. I do not suggest that social inequalities change only in patterns of punctuated equilibrium, or that gradual change in social inequalities is not possible; toward the end of this chapter I argue that when there is a plurality of groups in market settings, gradualism may indeed become the only model of distributional change. The bulk of this chapter, however, is focused on showing when and why social inequalities tend to change rapidly and dramatically.

A punctuated equilibrium series goes: equilibrium–punctuation–equilibrium–punctuation–equilibrium.... We need to understand two phenomena: the equilibrium conditions and the punctuation conditions. To recast this in language that is more common in the social sciences:[1] Equilibria are steady state conditions, punctuations are transitions. After every transition a system goes into a steady state; this steady state serves as the initial condition upon which another transition takes place. Therefore, what we need is a theory of initial conditions and a theory of transitions in order to move to a theory of punctuated equilibria in income inequality.

This chapter presents the evidence and arguments in three parts. The first part discusses the elements of a theory of initial conditions and institutional transitions that can explain the observed trends. Continuing from Chapter 4, I situate or embed the basic elements of a social system: individuals, groups, and institutions. I show how initial conditions can be understood in terms of norms and laws: within-group and between-group norms, and laws instituted by the state. Using an evolutionary framework, I show how transitions to different norms and different laws take place. The second part of the chapter presents evidence on several types of institutional transitions in modern history using the elements of the theoretical framework identified in the first part. I discuss five specific transitions: colonization (in Latin America and South Asia), post-colonial nationalism (in India and Indonesia), socialism and post-socialism (in Russia, China, and Poland), non-socialist revolutions (in Bolivia and Iran), and postwar reconstruction (in Japan, Taiwan, and South Korea). Finally, in the third part of this chapter, I consider four key questions: Why do all institutional transitions (such as nationalism and reconstruction) not lead to distributional change? Why do similar transitions (such as post-socialism) lead to different distributional outcomes? How do markets affect distributional transitions? Why do between-transition inequality levels not change?

A THEORY OF INITIAL CONDITIONS
AND TRANSITIONS

Let us first work toward a model of initial or equilibrium conditions of income distribution using the key elements and variables we have identified in the preceding chapter. The key elements are individuals, groups, and institutions, and the key variables are inheritance and human capital. I have shown that individuals are important because inheritance and human capital, which are the sources of income generation, are endowments at the individual level. Groups are important because significant constraints and externalities that have income generation effects are created by group norms. Institutions are important because institutions create laws that, like group norms, generate constraints and externalities on individual levels of inheritance and human capital acquisition, and thereby on individual income generation. I have also argued that social inequality levels are determined by different combinations of within-group and between-group inequality levels. Under equilibrium conditions, these levels of within- and between-group inequality levels remain relatively unchanged.

The discussion below refers to the analytical framework shown in Figure 5.1. The purpose of the framework is to identify the general factors and the relationships among the factors that give rise to social inequality, where the latter is determined by the extent of within-group inequality (or solidarity) and between-group inequality (or mobility gap, to be discussed shortly). If either of these variables (within- or between-group inequality) is to change, there must be some change or transition agent. I will show later that there are basic differences in distributional impacts based on whether the transition agents are endogenous or exogenous. These transition agents affect change in two fundamental ways: Some agents (usually endogenous ones) change the norms that influence distribution at the group level (primarily between groups). Other agents change norms (or laws) at the institutional level, where the most significant institution is the state. Let us now see how these factors are determined. Note that the discussion below progresses somewhat differently from the summary outlined in this paragraph. For reasons that will be obvious, I discuss change agents last.

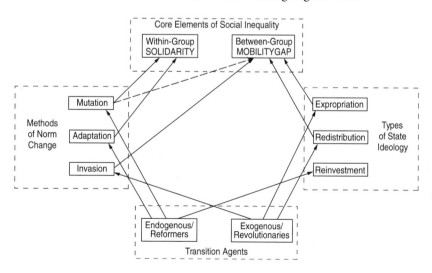

Fig. 5.1 Analytical framework of distributional change.

Finally, before we begin discussing the framework, it is useful to understand one key term: *norms*. A norm, as used in this chapter and book, is a collective belief or belief system whose primary function is to simplify decision-making. Norms exist to simplify both within-group and between-group interactions and transactions. Therefore, in many instances, norms solve the problem of collective action. Norms are enforced or institutionalized through collective sanctions, and usually (by definition) become so internalized that sanctions become unnecessary for enforcement. Norms must be distinguished from *laws*, which are rules of interaction and transaction designed by the state and enforced by the state's coercive power when necessary. Hence, norms are social by nature, whereas laws are institutional.

The Core Elements of Social Inequality

Consider how within- and between-group inequality levels are determined. A group, which is a class, race, ethnicity, religion, or caste, or a combination of these categories, is internally homogenous along at least one important identity variable. Which is to say that members of a well-defined group are usually selected at birth; they do not have much of a choice in the selection. This identity homogeneity does not, however, lead to homogeneity along all other important dimensions. Income, which is the variable of interest here, is not homogenously distributed within a group because the determinants of income (which are inheritance and human capital) are not homogenously distributed within a group. Now, these determinants of income are also the determinants of life chances. Inheritance and human capital determine, to a very large extent, an individual's income level, longevity, and what Amartya Sen generally calls "capabilities and functionings" (Sen 1985). Let us summarize all these possibilities—income, health, longevity, resources, capabilities, etc.—into a single concept "opportunity," and the realization of opportunity in the term "outcome" (analogous to Sen's "functionings").[2] The distribution of opportunities and outcomes within a group is not homogenous, but, as suggested in Chapter 4, the variance of opportunities and outcomes within a group must stay within a relatively narrow range if a group is to maintain its identity. The concept of within-group opportunity/outcome is an important one, and I will refer to this idea at several points in this chapter.

The question we need to begin with is this: Why do groups exist? In evolutionary terms, groups exist because they make some contribution to individual survival. Threats to individual survival may not only have external origins (from other groups, in our terms between-group rivalry) but may also have internal origins (which means again that groups are not homogenous, that there is within-group variance). Most internal group norms arise from the need to ensure group survival. Internal threats may arise from dissent within the group, and dissent is most likely to arise from a lack of consensus within the group. If individuals within a group perceive that opportunities for within-group mobility are limited, or that opportunities and outcomes are systematically biased toward or against some sub-group, the ability to create within-group consensus may become constrained. Hence, to maintain within-group consensus, it is necessary for groups to institute norms that reduce the variance in within-group opportunities and outcomes. This is done through redistribution and reciprocity within the group, and by making opportunities and positions of status open to all members of the group (see Coleman 1974). If this is not done, it becomes possible for groups to splinter into sub-groups.

The primary threat to group survival comes from other groups, which also have institutionalized norms on redistribution and reciprocity that generate group solidarity. Hence, the difference between groups lies not in their internal construction, but in the difference in average outcomes between groups. Let us say that our basic social unit is made up of two groups: a low-income group (or LIG) and a high-income group (or HIG) where the difference between the groups can be expressed in terms of the difference in average outcome. This difference in average outcome is the *mobility gap* between groups.[3] The mobility gap is analogous to the power gap between groups. The objective of HIGs is to maintain or increase the mobility gap; the objective of LIGs is to decrease or at least not increase the mobility gap. Between-groups norms are generated to deal with (maintain, increase, decrease) the mobility gap. HIGs create norms (such as proximity to divine authority, skin-color codes) that justify their superior average outcomes and other norms (such as assortative mating) that maintain the mobility gap.

A few words on assortative mating (and the identical concept of homogamy used in sociology) are necessary here. The idea is that in a stratified society marriages take place between economic and status equals. This is a very important concept. Homogamy is the key element in social reproduction—that is, the intergenerational transmission of status and economic position, and the transmission of group values and norms (Weber 1968, Schumpeter 1951; see Haller 1981 for a focused review). Think of the social changes possible if marriage partners are randomly chosen: family status simply cannot emerge as an important social variable, family values cannot be monolithic, many social norms as we know them cannot exist, as cannot, to the extent that it does now, the intergenerational transmission of income and wealth inequality (which is the main ingredient of inheritance-based inequalities, as understood in arguments I have made earlier).[4] In short, assortative mating or homogamy is one of the most important features of social life, with great significance for the emergence of within- and between-group norms.

In summary, we can identify two sets of social norms that arise from the existence of groups.

- One set of norms derives from the need to maintain within-group solidarity. These norms prescribe redistribution, reciprocity, and conformity within the group.
- The second set of norms derives from the desire to maintain between-group differences or mobility gaps. These norms, therefore, prescribe differences in status and power through institutionalized customs (on dress codes, for example), worker roles, property inheritance, and most important, marriage.

How Do Norms and Laws Change?

Human nature does not change in a matter of years or even centuries, but the institutional settings within which humans operate do. Similarly, social norms (which, I have shown in Chapter 4, may have evolutionary origins) also do not change radically in a short period, but laws, which are creations of the state, can and do. Let us begin from this broad understanding—that norms are slow to change, whereas laws can change quickly—to examine the general ways in which norms and laws change. Remember that the significance of changing norms and laws lies in the ways in which they influence behavior, which in turn depends on how individuals acquire and interpret information. People derive knowledge in the usual generic ways—from institutions such as the state and the market, and groups such as identity-based or occupational collectives. Their actions are also constrained and simplified in the usual generic ways—through institutional laws and collective or group norms. What distinguishes one institutional setting from another? How does the fact that norms are more robust than laws affect income distribution? Let us consider these questions in this section, paying particular attention to the significance of institutional ideology.

Let us refer to fundamental changes in legal regimes or systems as *institutional transitions*. Recall that the core argument made in this chapter identifies institutional transitions as the punctuation points in a model of punctuated equilibria in long-term inequality. However, rather than creating a model of institutional transitions alone, let us try to move toward an understanding of norm and law change in general terms. Continuing the biological terminology and metaphors used in this evolutionary approach, I suggest that there are three modes of norm/law change: mutation, adaptation, and invasion.

- Mutation refers to situations where individuals, within groups or institutions of the state, spontaneously choose to question the prevailing group norm or institutional law.[5] This is a form of endogenous change that is characteristic of all societies—from Martin Luther's challenge to the Christian orthodoxy, or the refusal of Chinese peasants to pay onerous taxes in dynasty after dynasty, to the rise of romantic love as the basis for marriage replacing the tradition of arranged marriages in Renaissance Europe. This form of dissent or resistance is unpredictable in its origins, hence the similarity with random variation in evolutionary biology. When this form of dissent or mutation is adapted or copied by many others, it becomes a dominant characteristic, a new norm that replaces an older norm. The existence of the possibility of spontaneous cultural mutation is exciting, and in a way, uniquely human. Herein lies the possibility of originality and innovation, which are necessary for material development and social change.
- Adaptation refers to situations in which individuals, groups, or institutions copy norms from other individuals, groups, or institutions. That is, the mutation originally takes place in some group or institution, and is perceived to be a superior solution for a proximate problem by other groups or institutions. Some of the dominant ideas of the modern period, especially its political ideas, have diffused by adaptation; these ideas include scientific rationality as the basis for decision-making, nationalism as the political organizing principle of modern territorial units, and democracy as the means of identifying the rulers. Again, in cases of successful adaptation, old norms are jettisoned in favor of new norms.
- Invasion refers to situations where a powerful group or institution is able to introduce new norms, usually by law, and by force over groups and institutions at varying levels of willingness, comprehension, and resistance. This form of institutional change is also common; colonialism, socialism, non-socialist revolutions, postwar reconstructions are all examples of institutional change where new norms/laws have been imposed by outsiders with the power to force compliance. The longevity or durability of new

norms/laws created by invasion may be less robust than that of new norms created by mutation or adaptation.

It is useful to understand that these forms of norm or law change are not mutually exclusive. For instance, it can be argued that mutations can be successfully introduced into whole populations (groups) only by adaptation; mutation or invasion alone is unlikely to be successful by itself. Similarly, invasion may introduce undesired laws that benefit the invader, but at the same time may introduce the possibility of other norms or ideas (such as nationalism) that, in the long run, work against the invader. I will refer to this idea again later in this chapter.

Ideology and Changing Norms

Let us now consider how norms that affect income distribution can change. I have already outlined the general ways in which norms can change. Now I consider the influence of the major institutions—markets and states—in terms of their influence on norms. Let us focus on the state. As before, I begin from the organic question: Why does the state exist? In evolutionary terms, it exists because it improves the survival chances of individuals and groups that are protected by it. However, we must look beyond this naïve and benevolent view of the state and recognize that the state has its own evolutionary goal: first it must survive. This singular purpose can be broken into two goals: it must be considered legitimate and thereby have the moral authority to maintain order; and it must be able to advance its own ideological interests. Legitimization can be sought in many ways: through divine authority, through the exercise of power, through popular support in the form of representative government, or through the creation of new identities, the most important of which is a national identity. Each of these processes of legitimization seeks to override individual and group interests and identities. The state must be able to override these interests and identities because it takes from every individual and group a proportion of its output; this is often called the surplus though it is unclear that there is always a surplus to be taken. How much the state takes and what it does with the take depends on the ideological orientation of the state. Three general forms of "surplus" taking can be identified, and each of these forms corresponds to a set of ideologies and norms that affect income distribution:

- Expropriation describes conditions in which the surplus is largely spent on the maintenance and aggrandizement of the state itself. This condition is characteristic of exploitative regimes, feudal orders, and colonial rulers. The political instruments of surplus expropriation are the HIGs; therefore, under conditions of expropriation we can expect between-group inequality levels to be high, made possible by laws created by the state.

- Redistribution describes conditions where the state reallocates output or income or resources from HIGs to LIGs. Redistributive state ideologies, which focus on reducing the mobility gap between groups, are often formed in reaction to the social inequalities maintained under surplus expropriation regimes and are characteristic of revolutionary states.

- Reinvestment describes conditions where the state is growth- and modernization-oriented, and therefore invests the surplus in infrastructure and productive enterprises. Reinvesting states are usually not directly concerned about between-group inequalities, being more interested in supplanting group identities with national or modern identities.

The pre-modern and colonial states were surplus-expropriation states that maintained large mobility gaps that created high levels of social inequality. Socialist states are defined by their redistributive approach and their declared goal of removing between-group inequality or the mobility gap. Nationalist and market regimes are surplus reinvestment states. Nationalist regimes often have moderately high mobility gaps; as a result, social inequality under nationalism may also be moderately high. Market regimes are distinct from all other types of states in that within-group inequalities may not be low; therefore, though the mobility gap is in the low to moderate range, the overall level of social inequality is variable. This is an important idea that will be elaborated further in the third and final part of this chapter. In summary, institutional or state laws tend to influence between-group norms more than within-group norms, and reflect the ideological orientation of the state.

Transition Agents

Finally, we come to the question at the heart of the analytical framework: Who are the change agents? As suggested earlier, the agents of change can come from anywhere—from the lower rungs of LIGs, or the upper rungs of HIGs, or vice versa—or from outside. The key distinction, I suggest, is the location of the transition agents. Let us then distinguish between two types of agents: endogenous and exogenous. *Endogenous agents* of institutional transition are members of the society in question; more specifically, they are members of known groups within a given society. Endogenous agents change norms by mutation and adaptation, and seek to address within- and between-group norms.[6] In other words, they are reformers who are also insiders. The Indian social activists who helped abolish the institution of *sati* (widow burning) and introduced the possibility of widow remarriage were reformers. The North African activists who have resisted and helped outlaw female circumcision are reformers. *Exogenous agents* of institutional transition are typically not members of the society in transition. They are colonizers, expatriates, victorious armies, technical advisors, missionaries, or bandits. In a general sense of the word, they are outsiders who have the potential to be revolutionaries. They are far more interested in capturing the state and changing state ideology (thereby changing between-group norms) than they are in reforming within-group norms.

If endogenous agents primarily seek to change within-group norms, usually with the goal of increasing group solidarity and reducing within-group disparities, and if the process of changing within-group norms is slow and time-consuming, then it follows that the actions of endogenous transition agents, if they do influence income distribution, do so gradually rather than dramatically. On the other hand, exogenous transition agents, who seek to capture the state and alter between-group norms, do so by changing the legal structure. As a result, exogenous agents' transformative actions on the pattern of income distribution have far more immediate effect. As mentioned at the beginning of this section, norms are difficult to change and the process takes time; laws are easier to change, especially under revolutionary conditions. As shown before, new laws that change the structure of the ownership of the means of production—land in agricultural societies, capital in industrial ones—can very quickly change the level of social inequality and the pattern of income distribution. According to Jessop (1971, 7):

> Reform and revolution are both types of social change. They have been variously distinguished. Some writers have argued that it is the content of their belief systems that distinguished reformist from revolutionary movements.... The more radical the beliefs ... the more revolutionary the movement. Others have argued that it is the means used to implement or promote the beliefs and proposals that is the distinguishing characteristic. Typically the criterion is the use or threatened use of violence.... Others again have emphasized the suddenness of the changes effected by the movement in question.

The conceptualization of ideological transition and reform/revolution used here is unconventional. I place primary emphasis on the location of the transition agent and secondary emphasis on his ideology. Many thoughtful, careful scholars have studied state transitions, especially the event of revolution, at great depth (see Tilly 1978; Parsa 2000). I take very seriously the works of Barrington Moore (1966, 1978) on revolutionary social change in feudal and peasant societies and on power and resistance, E.P. Thompson's (1963) writings on social change during proto-capitalism, and other, more recent work on "histories from below," which generally give greater emphasis to the role of the commoner, peasant, or subaltern (see the literature on subaltern histories by the South Asian group led by Ranajit Guha). I also take seriously the idea that dominant ideologies are meant to uphold the solidarity of the dominating and not the dominated class (Abercrombie and Turner 1978). Indeed, the idea of mutation and adaptation (or within-group reform) is posed in contradistinction to invasion to capture just such a dynamic: where the ideologies and norms of stronger and weaker groups are different, and where the legal structure is designed to further the intentions of the stronger group that controls the machinery and arms of the state. Revolutionaries, in this framework, are not necessarily the romantic heroes of egalitarian and justice movements, but are any group that seeks to capture the state and *thereby radically transform state ideology*. In this understanding, Boris Yeltsin, the Russian Federation's first real post-socialist President, and his "shock therapy" advisors are revolutionaries, no less than Castro and Mao.

The distinction I make between norms and laws, however, is a critical one. Movements and social changes from below do have the potential to change patterns of income distribution, but mainly within groups, and slowly, and not necessarily in more egalitarian directions. Certainly, without capturing the state and thereafter changing its distributional ideology, it is not possible to rapidly change between-group mobility gaps (which I have shown before are the primary determinants of social inequality) or to create punctuation points in distributional equilibria.

INSTITUTIONAL TRANSITIONS

Let us now turn to a discussion of specific types and cases of major institutional transitions and the inequality changes they have or have not engendered. I am going to look at five types of transitions here: to colonialism, to nationalism, to socialism and post-socialism, to non-socialist revolutions, and to postwar reconstructions. I will not be able to detail any of the cases I will consider. Nonetheless, the main outlines will be sufficient to make the points suggested in the theoretical framework presented in the preceding section. I will use the terms of the framework and focus on the key elements identified in it: between-group inequalities and transition agents (their locations and ideologies).

But before I begin the main discussion, it will be useful to consider some of the significant findings from the research on the origins of economic inequality. This too is a large subject area, replete with its own arguments and controversies. I will consider only some broad outlines of this research. The first important point to note is the idea that equality (or what may pass for equality because perfect equality of status and outcome seems not to have existed in agricultural societies)[7] is associated with simple societies, and inequality is associated with social complexity.

The origins of economic inequality can be linked to the practice of settled agriculture, which was a more complex enterprise than what preceded it: nomadic hunting and gathering. As long as humans were nomadic, as they were for between thirty and sixty thousand years, it was difficult for their societies to become hierarchical for two main reasons. From an evolutionary institutional perspective, hierarchies would have attenuated group solidarity, which was the key to survival in harsh conditions with many external threats. Also, in practical terms, it is difficult to acquire the material markers of status when one is always on the go. Acquisition and the desire to acquire became possible with the act of settling down in one place. There is some debate on exactly how social stratification or inequality came about.

According to one school of thought, the primary cause of emergent inequality was competition for land, which was of variable quality and increasingly limited because of population growth. This condition, combined with the reality of unequal ability, led to early forms of social inequality (Midlarsky 1999). A second school suggests that the generation of an agricultural surplus (possible only with settled agriculture) led to issues of distribution, settled by rulers and lawmakers, that is, the state. In this view, incipient inequality is linked to state formation, where the state finds it functionally necessary to create a division of labor and, associated with it, unequal rewards and status (Fried 1967). A third view takes the position that population growth fueled warfare between territorial units, which necessitated the creation of a defensive and redistributive state, which led to status differentiation and stratification (Carneiro 1970).

It may be impossible to ever know exactly how stratification and inequality started; whether the process began as a result of creating an agricultural surplus or in the process of creating it, or whether the surplus had little to do with it, being more related to warfare and defense. We can, however, conclude that, regardless of the original proximate causes of stratification, some features of social organization are its inevitable concomitants. We always observe a division of labor in stratified societies and we see a state that at a minimum is responsible for security and often goes beyond defensive security to engage in preemptive warfare. To maintain its security apparatus, the state is always involved in collecting taxes; to have the power to collect taxes, the state must also maintain an enforcement or taking authority. As a result, every agrarian society sooner or later becomes stratified, with the state at the top of the hierarchy followed by local tax collectors (who are usually the large landowners), followed by artisans, share-croppers, and landless peasants. When we arrive at the early modern period, i.e., the European expansion beginning in the sixteenth century, the world is already somewhat but not very uneven in terms of regional average outcomes (life expectancy, material welfare), and it is a world extensively populated by poor peasants living Hobbesian lives that are nasty, brutish, and short.

Colonialism

So we enter the colonial period, beginning in the sixteenth century in the Americas and the eighteenth century in Asia, with the soon-to-be colonized regions at reasonably stable levels of social inequality. Our information about this pre-colonial period is rather sketchy on inequality matters, and the sparseness of the record reflects not a lack of interest in the issue but a relative lack of documentary evidence. A wealth of material exists on status and hierarchy in both the Americas and Asia. In fact, many of the theories of the origins of inequality have been buttressed with Native American evidence (Paynter 1989), and South Asia has famously and with justification been dubbed the land of *homo hierarchicus* (Dumont 1972; Béteille 1983). A range of archaeological methods—including analysis of skeletal remains, burial details, ceramics, lithics, gourds, etc.—are used to estimate inequality indirectly. In addition, where written records exist, especially legal records on land and other property, it is possible to make judgments on economic inequality. Therefore, we have fairly good ideas about status hierarchies in both regions, but relatively less knowledge on how these status differences translated into income (a concept with little meaning for peasants 500 years ago) or material inequalities. Let us, in the absence of specific data, generalize about inequality in the Americas and South Asia from what we know about status and, in some cases, the distribution of land.

The Americas   When the Americas were colonized, North America was populated sparsely by a large number of tribes, none of whom had dominion over a large population or land mass (i.e., there were no empires). These tribes were either nomadic or they practiced subsistence agriculture, and as a result they were quasi-egalitarian. There were status differences within tribes and villages, to be sure, but the opportunities, such as they were, were generally meritocratic (the myths and symbols of most tribes celebrated bravery and sacrifice for the tribe/group), and there appear to have existed few distinct groups with demonstrably different average outcomes. In short, there were no between-group differences and minimal within-group differences.

Central America was largely a territory of the Aztec empire, and South America was largely under the dominion of the Inca. The two empires had substantial differences (particularly in terms of the extent of direct control on subject lands, which was more extensive under the Inca), but were similar in actions and policies that impacted on inequality and status. Both were centralized, surplus-expropriating, slave-owning regimes that collected taxes to keep the war machine growing and constructed public works for redistribution. The rulers and the ruled existed in what has been called a "core-periphery" relationship (more on this in the next chapter). At every spatial scale there were status, power, and material differences between the rulers and their representatives on the one hand and the vast majority of ordinary peasants on the other. In other words, there were some, possibly significant, between-group differences, though it is difficult to estimate the size of the HIG or the exact extent of the difference. The peasants, on the other hand, practiced within-group reciprocity and redistribution; there were few within-group differences in opportunity or outcome.

Colonialism was an invasion. A group of outsiders, external to the existing social system, captured the state and imposed its ideology of expropriation using tools that could best extract surplus.[8] The colonizers (British, Spanish, and Portuguese) initially came to plunder, stayed to govern, and eventually became a new people in the new world. The two critical acts that laid the foundation of the distributional system were the expropriation of land on a massive scale and the widespread use of slavery and indentured servants to work the land. The indigenous population was decimated by new diseases like smallpox (to which they had no immunity) and by warfare. Their land was taken by force and large quantities of land became the property of a small number of colonizing individuals. People were needed to work the land, but the remaining local population were too few and too resistant to doing degrading work, so slaves were imported from Africa to labor in the large sugar, cotton, coffee, and banana plantations, and, in the nineteenth century, to work in the coal, copper, and tin mines. These were the plantation colonies (Angeles 2004). We do not know what levels of land inequality existed in the colonial period, but land inequality data from the middle of the twentieth century indicate how deep those inequalities would have been. (We presume that land would not have been distributed substantially more unequally in the mid-twentieth century than it was in the eighteenth or nineteenth centuries). The Gini coefficient of land distribution in Peru (1961) was 94.7, in Venezuela (1961) it was 93.6, in Argentina (1970) it was 87.3, in Colombia (1960) it was 86.5, in Brazil (1960) it was 84.5, and in Uruguay (1966) it was 83.3 (see Sundrum 1987).[9]

For instance: Mexico became independent in 1821; in 1910, 80 percent of peasants had no land (Angeles 2004). In other words, there were deep between-group inequalities in South and Central America during colonial rule, and these differences were race-based. According to Reynolds (1996) and Glade (1996) these inequalities were much higher than existed in the pre-colonial period, they have persisted to the end of the twentieth century and have formed the basis of the inequalities that pervade the social system in Latin America at all geographical scales. Just as the invader's ideology became, over time, the established ideology (or set of social norms), the land-distribution patterns that resulted from the new ideology became, over time, the settled land-distribution patterns. This, in turn, became the most significant determinant of inequality in Latin America in the early twentieth century.

South Asia   On the eve of colonization South Asia had an empire in decline (the Mughals) and a large number of kingdoms that were either independent or semi-independent (paying few taxes to a central authority). Warfare was common, and the state everywhere had to maintain a large army with taxes. The ruling class was omnipresent in the form of large landlords (known as *zamindars* and *talukdars*) who were the tax collectors for a king who might or might not have needed to pay a share to the emperor. Therefore, as in Central and South America, the rulers and the ruled were differentiated by status and material markers. In addition, there was the caste system, a system of hereditary lineage for occupation, education, and status. The ruled, in the villages of South Asia, were therefore also differentiated into unequal subgroups. In short, there were significant between-group and within-group differences in status and income in pre-colonial South Asia.

Colonization in South Asia was also an invasion by outsiders, but unlike the version in the Americas, this invasion did not kill off the natives, and consequently the social structure was not reinvented. South Asia was colonized piece by piece by the British over more than half a century, largely by the traders of the East India Company, beginning in the late seventeenth and early eighteenth centuries. The Empire lasted for almost 200 years. During this time, fundamental changes to the legal and taxation systems were undertaken for the purpose of expropriating the surplus of Indian agriculture. The British, for the most part, did not use their direct representatives for tax-collection purposes, but used different types of intermediaries in different parts of the country (a method called "indirect rule"). Depending on when a region was colonized and what the man in charge then thought would be a good way to collect land revenue, three different methods were used: landlord-based systems (*zamindari*), individual cultivator-based systems (*raiyatwari*), or village-based systems (*mahalwari*). The *mahalwari* system often resembled the *zamindari* system, which, by giving local chiefs or large landlords the authority to collect taxes with broad enforcement capacities, often led to exploitation, usury, distress sales, and grinding poverty for the masses of peasants.[10] In addition to hardening the *zamindari* system (in much of North and almost all of East India) the British "divide and rule" strategy also hardened—by using censuses, categorical systems, and the revival of an ancient but defunct code of law (the *Manusmriti*)—caste differences and hierarchies.

Therefore, British colonization created new between-group inequalities (by adding themselves at the top of the group hierarchy) and exacerbating existing between-group inequalities (between landlord and peasant, and between castes). There is little reason to believe that within-group inequalities increased, especially inequality within the majority group of sharecroppers and small farmers. Social inequality in South Asia increased, but not to the extent of what happened in the Americas. The Gini coefficient of land distribution in India (1953–54) was about 69, in Pakistan (1972) it was about 52, and in Bangladesh (1977) it was about 45 (Sundrum 1987).[11] Why the big difference from Latin America? Were the British colonizers more humane than the Spanish or Portuguese? Did they demand less of the agricultural product? There are no indications that this is the case. There were, however, two significant differences: First, the British did not expropriate the land because they could not; there were too many people and they were not especially susceptible to European viruses. Second, the British did not create a system of slavery to work the land because they did not need to; there were already enough people to do the work. In short, the population density of South Asia contributed to a gentler form of colonization (that retained and even hardened most of the basic elements of the social structure) than in the Americas (see Sokoloff and Engerman 2000; Acemoglu, Johnson, and Robinson 2001).

We can conclude that colonization increased social inequality in the Americas and South Asia (the situation in Southeast Asia, which is not covered here, is very similar to South Asia), more so in the former than the latter, primarily by increasing between-group inequality levels. The colonizers' ideology, by definition, was one of surplus expropriation, which was morally justified by a series of assumptions and declarations about racial superiority and divine authority (captured in the aphorism "God, gold, and greed").[12] But the colonizers in Asia also brought something else with them: fresh ideas about identity and governance, which were absorbed in the colonized regions by mutation and adaptation. The most important of these new ideas, the transition we turn to now, was the idea of the nation and nationalism (see Chatterjee 1986).

Nationalism

The colonized regions of Asia and Africa became independent nations during the two decades after the end of World War II. The American nations had started becoming independent of Europe in the eighteenth century. Since less is known about post-independence social inequality in the American nations (whose independence movements were based on economic rather than identity nationalism), I will discuss only the Asian experience here (with very brief reference to some African experience) by focusing on two large nations: India and Indonesia. There is little doubt that the transition to independence was a major event in recent history. The question before us is this: Did the transition to nationalist independence change the level of social inequality in these nations? The answer, as we shall see, is "very little."

Indian nationalism began in the late 1800s and gathered steam after the partition of Bengal in 1905.[13] The Congress Party, led by Mohandas Gandhi and Jawaharlal Nehru, agitated for independence, which finally arrived in 1947. In the process was also formed Pakistan, a Muslim majority nation, because the Muslims (who had fallen behind the Hindus under colonial rule) feared for their group rights under Hindu hegemony. The partition of India led to a bloodbath between Hindus and Muslims in North and East India. The foremost task of independent India's leaders then was to restore communal peace and create a new national identity among its polyglot, multi-ethnic, multi-religious population of 350 million. The challenges facing the new leadership were daunting: overpopulation, illiteracy, linguistic chauvinism, religious bigotry, unemployment, chronic food shortages, the threat of a "red revolution," and inequality of course.

Nehru, a Fabian socialist, approached the inequality problem from two fronts. He focused on women's equality by raising the age of marriage to 15, legalizing widow remarriage and property inheritance, and outlawing the dowry system (which is very much alive even now). He addressed the land-distribution issue by banning absentee landlordism and by allowing actual, documented cultivators to take ownership of the land under their cultivation. However, because these laws ran smack against power structures and norms that were well established, they had virtually no impact initially and little impact in the long run in most regions. As I have shown earlier in this chapter, the distribution of land did become more equal and that should have reduced between-group inequality to some extent. The *zamindari* system was abolished (as were princely estates) and the heavy revenue burden on peasants was removed. However, the *zamindars* became urban landlords and continued to realize the benefits of intergenerational "increasing returns." Meanwhile, the peasants were now taxed indirectly through a series of policy initiatives on urban industrialization that probably created some urban and metropolitan bias.[14] As we have seen in Chapter 2, the level of income inequality in India has remained virtually unchanged over the last four decades. Nonetheless, it is likely that between-group inequality levels have declined to some extent, but not rapidly. Within-group inequalities have probably remained unchanged. Indian nationalists were reformers, not revolutionaries (in the sense I have adopted in this work), and their reforms did little to change social inequality quickly.

Indonesia was colonized by the Dutch at about the same time, using processes that were not dissimilar to those used by the British in India. The rise of anti-colonial nationalism under the leadership of Achmed Sukarno was also similar to the Indian situation, as were the daunting challenges facing the newly independent nation. Independence was effectively achieved in 1950 after bloodshed. The Dutch resisted decolonization with arms. Along with the Dutch, violence was visited upon the ethnic Chinese, the entrepreneurial middle class who were viewed with suspicion as collaborators. The new nation faced serious challenges to national unity. There was an "ethnic problem" with the presence of the Dutch, the Chinese, and native Malay, three groups whose economic positions were in inverse proportion to their numerical strength. There were linguistic differences, which at that point were only partially solved by the adoption of Bahasa Indonesia (a minority language of traders) as the official language, as well as significant regional differences in terms of average condition (I will take up this theme seriously in Chapter 6). There were religious differences due to the presence of sizable Hindu and Buddhist minorities in a Muslim-majority country.

Therefore, like socialist Nehru, socialist Sukarno could hardly think of inequality issues because the nation had to be constructed first. "The PNI [Sukarno's Party] had no constitutional proposals, economic policy, or social program; achieving independence was its central goal" write Bevan, Collier, and Gunning (1999, 199–200). After independence there was political uncertainty for several years (on how to manage and bring under control the vast land and its diverse people) and economic policies were confused: on attitude toward foreign capital, on nationalization, on industrialization vs. rural development, on how to handle the entrepreneurial Chinese middle class, etc. Not surprisingly, there were no immediate land reforms that could have made more productive assets available to the rural poor, neither did the state intervene directly in the operations of the Dutch (who were still present in large numbers and in control of the financial sector) or the Chinese. It is safe to assume that there were few changes in within-group inequalities. Perhaps there was a slight decline in between-group inequalities (as a result of the diminished presence of the colonial elite), but not enough to significantly influence the overall levels of social inequality.

The patterns revealed in India's and Indonesia's transition to independence from colonization are repeated in country after country in Asia and Africa (Nigeria and Kenya, for example, followed the steps outlined here). The key features of these transitions are as follows:

Independence comes after a long struggle against a colonial power. The leaders are social reformers and insiders even if the colonizers view them as terrorists and revolutionaries. The dominant ideology is centered on the struggle, it is anti-colonial, anti-Western, and socialist to some degree. The new nation's primary task is to create a new national identity. The state handles the indigenous capitalist and middle classes carefully, unwilling to disaffect its potential financiers. Redistribution is not among the important items on the early agenda. The departure of the Europeans results in some decline in between-group inequality levels, but the levels of social and national income inequality do not undergo any dramatic change. Later, a decade or more after independence, many nations try to redistribute land, usually with little success. By then the nation has settled into a pattern of social and income inequality, and little change is seen over several decades.

Socialism and Post-Socialism

Some of the most important institutional transitions of the twentieth century have been to socialism (in the Soviet Union in 1917, its Eastern European satellites after World War II, and China in 1949), and, at the end of the century, to post-socialist market democracies of different forms in Russia and Eastern Europe. A very significant feature of these transitions has been the distributional impact—to more egalitarian distributions with the socialist transition, and, as shown in Chapter 2, to varying degrees of increased inequality with the post-socialist transition. Much is known about the conditions and policies that characterized these transitions and I will attempt no more than the briefest of summaries. I will look at the Soviet and Chinese transitions to socialism and the post-socialist transitions in the Soviet Union and its satellite countries to identify the key elements that have impacted the conditions of social inequality.

The socialist transitions were all ideological invasions. In Eastern Europe they were also physical invasions. In each case a group of revolutionaries took control of the state and radically altered the laws impacting income generation and distribution. Their ostensible goal was to create classless worker utopias and the primary method of doing so was to eliminate private ownership of the means of production, i.e., land and capital. In the Soviet Union and China the early post-revolutionary years were difficult ones. In both countries there was armed resistance to the revolutionaries, and much energy in those early years was expended on gaining a firm grip on the state using widespread violence. Lenin, the leader of the Bolsheviks in the Soviet Union, first adopted war communism (1918–1920) during which agricultural surpluses were taken by force after large landlords were stripped of their property, followed by the New Economic Policy (1921–28) during which limited markets for agricultural surpluses were allowed to exist. The state controlled the "commanding heights" of the economy by having complete ownership of the industrial sector. With the beginning of the five-year plans and Stalin's ascension, even more radical changes took place in the agriculture sector, which was collectivized and all traces of the market were removed. While the land reforms undoubtedly lowered both within- and between-group inequality levels significantly, by the time of Stalin's death in 1953, the rise of the *nomenklatura* (the Communist Party members who controlled all aspects of Soviet life and its economy), with their luxurious lifestyles, had created new divergences in between-group inequality levels (Dobson 1977). Social and income inequality levels declined thereafter, but by the early 1970s there was little difference between the distribution patterns of the Soviet Union and a market democracy like the United Kingdom (Bergson 1984). A good fraction of these relatively high inequalities were actually a result of geographic inequality (see Fuchs and Demko 1979), a theme that is alluded to but largely neglected in the economic and sociological literature, and one that I will take up in the next chapter.

At the time of Russia's revolution 80 percent of Russians worked in agriculture. In China, the proportion of agriculturalists was even higher, and the actions of the new socialist leadership were targeted toward removal of class differences in this sector. There is some dispute among China scholars on how deep rural or land inequalities were and whether they were growing in the pre-revolutionary period (Brandt and Sands 1990), but there is no question that by 1952, after the first phase of land reforms, landlords (who made up less than four percent of rural households but owned 30 percent of land) had been virtually eliminated while rich and middle-class peasants who actually worked their land were allowed to keep it (Khan 1977). These acts not only reduced between-group inequalities (refer to the sharp drop in income inequality reported in Chapter 2) but also raised agricultural productivity. However, between 1956 and 1958, agriculture was collectivized. This policy resulted in neither less inequality nor higher productivity, and was gradually abandoned starting with the Deng reforms in the late 1970s.

[handwritten margin notes: "(stand) change agents taking over the state?"]

The market-oriented reforms in China began a gradual move toward significantly higher inequality levels (I will discuss this in detail in Chapter 6). But the collapse of the socialist system in Soviet Union and its Eastern European satellites in 1989–91 was cataclysmic in its rapidity and distributional impacts. Faced with the economic pressure of the arms race, rising ethno-nationalism in the union's far flung republics after Gorbachev's *glasnost* allowed open dissent for the first time in decades, and the dramatic dismantling of the Berlin Wall by East Germans, things fell apart. The center could not hold, and the Soviet Union dissolved into a number of independent nations, while Eastern European nations too declared independence. The Cold War had ended without a shot being fired.

The new nations embarked on an unprecedented transition to markets and democratic politics using a wide range of transition policies and speeds. The first decade of the transition has seen a large-scale retreat of the state, accompanied by small to very large increases in income inequality, widespread recession, and unemployment and poverty levels unknown in recent decades in the region. The sharpest inequality changes have taken place in some post-Soviet nations in the Commonwealth of Independent States (CIS). Although inequality levels in most of the transition economies is still low by world standards—lower on average than in Latin America certainly, and in Africa—in some countries there has been an alarming increase in inequality. In Russia, Ukraine, and the Kyrgyz Republic, the Gini coefficients have doubled (from the mid 20s to the high 40s and 50s), in the Baltic states (Estonia, Latvia, Lithuania) the Ginis have increased by more than 50 percent.

The World Bank's (2000) comprehensive study of poverty and inequality in these official transition economies identifies the following causes behind the increase in inequality: (1) An increased inequality in labor earnings or a dispersion in wages everywhere, accompanied by an increased reliance on self-employment. (2) Rising returns to education, especially at the beginning of the transition and in Central Europe, but with little effect in CIS. (3) The emergence of an entrepreneurial class whose effect is particularly strong in Russia. (4) Enterprise privatization, housing privatization, and asset transfers. (5) Land privatization and land reform, which have had mixed effects because the implementation has varied widely. In terms of our framework, the market transition in Eastern Europe and Russia has led to significant changes in within-group and between-group inequalities. These changes are not uniform across the region (inequalities have increased much more in some places than in others), nor do the factors associated with the inequality increase have similar effects (state transfers are progressive in some countries, regressive in others; the elderly have benefited in some countries but not in others). Later in this chapter I will look at the question of why similar transitions have different distributional impacts.

Non-Socialist Revolutions

Not all twentieth-century revolutions have been socialistic in origin. In this section I discuss one example each of two types of non-socialist revolutions: peasant revolutions exemplified by the one in Bolivia in 1952–53 and theocratic revolutions exemplified by the Islamic revolution in Iran in 1978–79.

The insurrection in Bolivia began in La Paz as a protest and rebellion by a coalition of socialist parties and labor unions (the MNR) against the government.[15] But its urban impact was soon overshadowed, in this predominantly agricultural country, by a peasant uprising that went far beyond the intentions of the MNR, so much so that this event is known as a peasant revolution rather than a socialist one. At the time of the revolution the Bolivian peasantry struggled under the strictures of an onerous *hacienda* system dominated by large landlords of pure European descent—66 percent of the land was owned by 1.7 percent of landowners, while the poorest 83 percent of the peasants owned only 1.2 percent of the land. The peasants paid several taxes, the most burdensome one requiring them to work without compensation for three to four days every week on the large plantations. During the revolution, according to Kelley and Klein (1981, 123–4):

> Power was wrenched from the hands of a small exploitative elite which had held it for centuries; the army was destroyed and worker and peasant unions became the dominant armed power in the land; landlords were forcibly dispossessed, labor taxes abolished, and land turned over to the peasants who worked it...Within the year, the *hacendados* had been driven from the land, the work records burned, and peasants took effective ownership of the land.

These were permanent changes. The large landlord class appears to have been eliminated for good and the Bolivian peasant continues to have a very strong voice in national politics. The welfare consequences of the much improved income distribution pattern were, however, lessened by the fact that post-revolutionary productivity (in farming and mining) declined significantly, recovering to the pre-revolutionary levels only after a decade or more. Kelley and Klein (1981) also argue that the inequality decline after revolutions (in general) cannot be sustained because new forms of human capital-based inequality soon begin to become important. In Bolivia there is some evidence that inequality increased in the second decade after the revolution, but it is not clear that it was inevitable, nor that this increase can be separated from Bolivia's Latin American location, history, and norms.

Iran's Islamic revolution is well known in the West, not so much for what interests us here, but for the anti-Western rhetoric used by the revolutionary leaders then, through the Salman Rushdie *fatwa*, and now, and the matching rhetorical belligerence that has continued to emanate from Washington. The revolution itself officially began with a declaration in 1978 and was accomplished in 1979; it was a mass uprising of the lower and middle classes led by Islamic clerics and the Ayatollah Khomeini against the expropriating authoritarian regime of Reza Pahlavi, a staunch American ally. This was a redistributive transition. The new leadership had nothing in common with the deposed one; the individuals were different, their ideologies were different, their interests and constituencies were different. Not surprisingly, their policies were in stark contrast.

The Islamic regime nationalized big portions of the banking and manufacturing sectors.[16] The nationalization, which provided no compensation to shareholders, targeted wealthy individuals as well as sectors. By 1982, small and medium manufacturing firms that contributed 70 percent of value addition, and more than 95 percent of large firms had been nationalized. By early 1979, peasants started taking over large landholdings; by the time the authorities stopped the takeovers, 0.8 million hectares of prime agricultural land had been confiscated by peasants, in addition to one million hectares redistributed by the state. (Iran has 12 million hectares of agricultural land). The minimum wage was raised by a factor of 2.7 and wage ceilings were set for executives. The urban-expenditure Gini declined from 50 in 1977 to 40 in 1980, rising to 42 by 1984. The rural-expenditure Gini declined from 48 in 1979 to 41 in 1982. The returns to college education dropped sharply. Note that, despite these significant distributional changes, the Gini coefficient continued to remain moderately high. Plus, if we make the suggested correction to the expenditure Gini to make it comparable to the income Gini (because expenditure is generally more equitable than income), it is clear that, even after the revolution, income inequality in Iran continued to remain high. An explanation for this phenomenon comes from the reality of regional and ethnic differences in the country that the revolution did little to counteract. Aghajanian (1983) shows that ethnic Persians are more literate and urbanized and have much higher incomes and better amenities than the Baluchis, Kurds, and Turks. Hence, the Islamic revolution diminished one set of between-group inequalities (the acquired ones) but did little to bring regional balance or diminish the second significant set of between-group inequalities (the ascribed ones).

Reconstructions

Finally, let us look at a form of institutional transition that is less common (compared, say, with the socialist transition), but very important in developmental terms. This transition takes place when a country is occupied by a foreign power at the end of a major conflict; the foreign power deposes an older regime, becomes a transition authority for an extended period of several months to several years, and finally transfers authority to a new government that has, by definition, no relationship with the deposed power.[17] In fact, it is possible to think of reconstruction as two transitions: one to an occupying power (the U.S. in all the cases discussed here), and the other to a new state. At the end of World War II, such reconstruction transitions took place in several nations: in West Germany and Italy in Europe, and in Japan, South Korea and Taiwan in East Asia. Let us look at the latter cases in some detail.

These three East Asian countries are considered to be the most successful examples of market-led modernization and industrialization in the second half of the twentieth century.[18] They are paragons of virtuous development because they have shown that it is possible to achieve very rapid economic growth with equity. In fact, their low levels of inequality today (which have been sustained for the last three to five decades) were achieved in the duration of a few years, from earlier much higher levels, at the very beginning of the growth surge. Their achievements have forced development scholars to rethink some fundamental notions, other developing countries to question the wisdom of their own protective and inward-looking policies, and inequality theorists to rethink the so-called stylized fact of the Kuznets curve (see the discussion "Does Inequality Hinder Growth?" in Chapter 3). The foundations of these remarkable accomplishments, at least the ones pertaining to income distribution, were laid in the period after the end of World War II, during the U.S. occupation of these countries. As with most of the earlier cases discussed, land distribution was the key element in the distributional turnaround. Griffin, Khan, and Ickowitz (2001, 37) write: "The initial conditions were similar in all [three] countries, namely, extreme scarcity of land, a very large agricultural sector, high incidence of tenancy and an unequal distribution of landownership." Moreover, in South Korea and Taiwan, whose postwar growth performances have been truly remarkable, about 20 percent of the agricultural land had been expropriated by Japan, the imperial power in the region during and before the war. This land was directly available for redistribution after the war.

The basic methods used were the same in all three countries. Again, Griffin et al. write (2001, 38):

Land reform in Taiwan, South Korea and Japan was based on compulsory purchases of land by the government from those who had land in excess of a specified amount. The ceiling was set very low and the price paid by the government was well below a hypothetical market price. There was thus a substantial amount of confiscation. Land was distributed among tenants and landless households at a low price and payments by recipients was financed by granting them credit.

The rapid East Asian land reforms have led to the most equitable land distributions anywhere. Recent estimates of the Gini coefficient for land distribution are 47 for Taiwan, 39 for Japan, and 20 for South Korea. To put these figures in perspective, recall that in

Latin America the comparable numbers are generally above 85. Other than China (Gini = 21) the closest Gini coefficients are in Egypt (46) with disputed data, and Ethiopia (46), which has had forced villagization and collectivization. It is very likely that these equitable land distributions had cascading positive effects in the formation of social consensus (by creating opportunity and mobility possibilities for most individuals and all groups in society) and human capital. Land reforms in East Asia provided the foundation for future growth.

In Taiwan, these reforms were instituted between 1949 and 1953 by the Kuomintang government, which had lost the Chinese civil war to the communists and were unconnected to the landed elite of the island. They were backed by the power of the American army. In Korea, the land reform process started earlier, in 1945, introduced directly by the U.S. military government, which was then an occupying force. In Japan too, it was the U.S. military government that spearheaded the land reforms, beginning with the enforcement of a land ceiling act. Griffin et al. (2001) identify this factor—the presence of strong, radical governments that were unconnected to the local elite—as one of the keys to the permanence and success of the reforms. In our terms, these were invasions by revolutionaries who overhauled the laws that bore directly on income generation. The suggestion that East Asian growth with equity arose from Asian or traditional or Confucian or Buddhist values belies realities like the pre-socialist exploitation in China and Japanese imperialism and hierarchical social structure. Instead, the social norms in existence today owe a large debt to the autocratic egalitarianism of fifty years ago.

THE CRITICAL ISSUES

In this section I consider some of the critical questions and issues that relate to punctuated equilibria and social inequality. The case studies underline some of the main points of the theoretical framework, but some questions remain. I am not sure that I can answer all these questions in ways that are not superficial. Some issues, as we shall see, require us either to get to a deeper level of theory, or, as historians often do, summon explanations from the marginalia of luck and charisma. These are the questions we ponder here: Why do all institutional transitions not lead to distributional change? Why do similar transitions lead to different distributional outcomes? How do markets affect distributional transitions? Why does inequality not change between transitions?

Why do all Institutional Transitions not Lead to Distributional Change?

We have seen that all institutional transitions do not lead to changes in social- or income-inequality levels. All socialist, revolutionary and reconstruction transitions (discussed here) have led to lower levels of inequality, but the nationalist transitions generally have not led to any significant distributional change. Let us ignore the socialist and revolutionary transitions (which were meant to lower inequality) and consider only the nationalist and reconstruction transitions (in Taiwan and South Korea). In some respects, these transitions are similar. Both sets of transitions represent independence from a colonial power and took place around the same time. Both took place in largely agrarian countries with heavy population pressure and a highly skewed distribution of landholdings. All the countries involved were at similar levels of development measured by per capita income. In 1950, India and South Korea had almost identical per capita incomes. Yet the nationalists in India and Indonesia did not seriously intervene in the distribution of productive assets or the process of income generation, but the South Korean and Taiwanese states did so. Why?

The most direct explanation, the one I have offered throughout this chapter, is that the agents in charge of the state during and after the transition were fundamentally different. The nationalists were insiders, reformers; the reconstruction agents were outsiders, revolutionaries. Insiders generally cannot be revolutionaries because their insider status brings with it networks of trust and obligation. Their call for institutional change is presented and honed over years, garnering support, if their attempt is to be successful, from all (or most) groups and classes. Therefore, on assuming power, insiders cannot fundamentally change the structure of social and economic relations. It would be a violation of trust. Mohandas Gandhi, the indisputable leader of India's freedom movement, was close to the Birlas, a preeminent business family in India. The Birlas provided money for the nationalists' cause and were especially generous with time and money for Gandhi. How could he possibly nationalize the Birla factories? How could Nehru attack the large landowning class when many eminent members of his Congress party came from that class and he had to rely on their support to create a new pan-Indian national identity?

Outsiders and revolutionaries, on the other hand, are bound by no such networks of trust and obligation, especially with the older elite society. In fact, it may be in their best interest to demonstrate independence and create new popular alliances by radical acts of redistribution; the older elite, a potential threat, is removed, and a new relationship of allegiance with the masses is forged. The U.S. military establishment in Korea and Taiwan would stand to gain little from propping up the old landed aristocracy. They did not need the power of arms. They needed, instead, the power of popular support. Nothing could provide it more quickly than a radical redistribution of land.

History offers many examples of outsider revolutionaries.[19] In China, for instance, feudal exploitation resulted in periodic resistance from the peasants. From medieval times to the colonial era "most Chinese 'peasant movements' were led by such outsiders as monks, doctors, and professional criminals, or by petty officials and 'sophisticated but disaffected members of the literati class'" (Wakeman 1977, 204). Lenin, an outsider to the Russian ruling class, an exile all over Europe for many years before the 1917 revolution, was another such "disaffected member of the literati class."[20] The "shock therapy" advisors to Yeltsin in post-socialist Russia were outsiders, totally unconnected to Russian life or politics, and no less revolutionary in their policy prescriptions than the U.S. military government was in Korea, Taiwan, and Japan. Despite the reasons that outsiders should press for progressive distributional change in the societies over which they have power or influence, it does not always happen. What happens depends on the outsider's ideology. As I have shown earlier, expropriators such as colonizers and empire builders prefer to operate by creating or widening between-group inequality. Therefore, being an outsider to the existing power structure may be a necessary condition for revolutionary distributional change, but it is not a sufficient condition.

Why do Similar Transitions Have Different Distributional Outcomes?

The divergent distributional experience of the post-socialist states in the former Soviet Union and its satellites raises an important question: Why do similar transitions have different outcomes? I have shown (in Chapter 2 and earlier in this chapter) that most nations in Central Europe have experienced minimal to small increases in income inequality, while most Slavic and Central Asian nations have seen large to very large increases. The World Bank (2000) identifies the intensity of reforms—a combination of liberalizing and deregulating policies—as a major factor that explains the difference. According to Milanovic (1998, 47–48):

Is there a relationship between the type of adjustment ... and increases in the Gini coefficient? The only relationship that could be detected is that between the "populist" type of adjustment and low increases in inequality. The average Gini increase in the three "populist" adjustment countries (Poland, Hungary, Slovenia) was less than 2 Gini points.... Each movement toward "tougher adjustment" [as in Russia and Ukraine] was associated, on average, with a Gini increase of about 4 points.

The World Bank (2000) identifies corruption as a second major explanatory factor; the correlation between the Gini coefficient and Transparency International's Corruption Perception Index is 0.72 in the transition economies. Corruption includes the simple phenomenon of graft and insider deal-making in the private sphere, and the more damaging phenomenon of private firms' bribing the state to influence policy and the legal structure. The Russian oligarchs are well known. Their ability to acquire invaluable state assets at throwaway prices has also been widely publicized. Therefore, there is little doubt that reform intensity and corruption have had significant influences on the level of inequality. But the basic question still remains: Why have some nations experienced these problems while others have done so less intensely or not at all? Why have some states chosen "big-bang" or "shock-therapy" reforms? Why are some states less corrupt?

Let us consider the case of Poland (with moderate inequality increase) vs. Russia (with extreme inequality increase).[21] We can see that the insider/outsider effect worked here too. Poland was led into post-socialism by reformers/insiders while Russia was led by revolutionaries/outsiders, and, to some extent, it was possible to know *ex ante* that this was the situation. There is little doubt that Poland's transition was not sudden. The Solidarity movement led by Lech Walesa had already generated significant dissent, and by mutation and adaptation had already influenced the norms of civil society. In fact, in Poland, the communist state did not collapse (as it did in many other nations) but simply withered away in the face of popular non-communist union organization and a defeat in parliamentary elections. The leaders of Solidarity (who now assumed power) had reasonably well-thought-out ideas and plans and did not need to undergo shock therapy; their surplus-use ideology was oriented toward reinvestment and growth. Marketization has raised inequality levels to some degree (this is almost unavoidable),[22] but the state was helped no doubt by the fact that some proto-market elements already existed in Poland (especially in the farm sector).

Russia under Gorbachev was also moving toward mutation and adaptation out of communism through *perestroika* (restructuring); but the events of 1991—an unsuccessful coup against Gorbachev by communist hardliners—yielded Boris Yeltsin as the new leader with greater power. In many ways (but not completely) Yeltsin was an outsider to the reform process. His primary economic advisors were outsiders (international market-primacy ideologues); his close political advisors were family members and newly minted business oligarchs. Corruption in Russia started at the top, and, in the absence of any clear ideology to guide the transition process, the default ideology quickly became one of surplus expropriation. This situation was compounded by the deep and growing spatial inequalities in Russia, as we shall see in the next chapter.

Could these outcomes have been predicted? In the case of Poland, possibly. The Polish transition resembled the nationalist transitions in India and Indonesia. Much of the increased inequality resulted from marketization and recession, not because an expropriating state was enriching itself. Russia under Gorbachev would probably have had an outcome similar to Poland's, but Yeltsin was unpredictable. Nonetheless, a keen observer might have been able to foresee the distributive effects of the Yeltsin presidency. Hindsight is always better than foresight, but I suggest that the analytical framework presented here can be a good guide to understanding future inequality changes when the transition agents and their ideologies can be identified.

How do Markets Affect Distributional Transitions?

I have suggested earlier (and I am not alone in doing so) that belief in markets is an ideology that is manifested at the individual and institutional levels. The effects on income distribution may be somewhat different, depending on the analytical focus. Let us consider two principal issues derived from the two principal sources of social change: How do markets influence norms? How do markets influence laws?

The issues surrounding the relationship between markets and social norms are perhaps the most difficult ones. I have covered some of this territory before (in Chapter 4) but the questions, in many ways, defy resolution. To what degree are social norms (such as reciprocity and cooperation) that promote "niceness" and egalitarianism innate elements of human nature? To what degree are norms (such as unbridled self-interest and inter-group bias) that promote difference and power hierarchies innate to human nature? The answers are important because perfect markets, in theory, can take care of all fundamental interests, i.e., those interests that can affect individual survival. Markets can provide insurance and security (which are the two critical needs), and of course all necessary material goods and the means to acquire human capital. If this is true, then the "niceness" norms need not exist unless "niceness" is innately human. If the only purpose of "niceness" is to improve one's survival chances, and if perfect markets can serve that purpose, why be nice? I have suggested earlier that "niceness" is as innate as selfishness, hence reciprocity and cooperation would exist even if they served no direct evolutionary purpose. However, when markets provide insurance and security, the degree of individualism is likely to increase because individuals would be less reliant on social or group provisioning of these critical services. To that extent, "niceness" norms may be diluted. If that happens, within-group inequalities may increase. Can perfect markets eliminate groups and inter-group bias (tribalism)? As long as desired resources are scarce and individuals can often compete for these resources more effectively when they are organized into groups, there is little likelihood of eliminating groups. However, markets are likely to encourage trade and contact between groups, which in turn should lower between-group inequalities. Hence, with increasing marketization, the normative structure of society would remain essentially similar, perhaps with lower between-group and higher within-group inequalities.

This is pluralism. When within-group inequalities increase, the possibility of group fragmentation also increases. Remember that the defining characteristics of a group are its solidarity and ability to reach within-group consensus. If markets increase within-group inequalities (because of higher returns to skills and the general condition of increasing returns) and decrease between-group mobility barriers, the possibility of between-group mobility increases. As a result, it may be possible to see more groups formed around specific interests, rather than the basic ones of ascribed identity and acquired labor characteristics; it is also possible to see individuals becoming members of multiple groups.

The state in such a society is likely to depend for its existence on its ability to form coalitions of different groups. It will be difficult for such a state to be *overtly* expropriative or redistributive because it will be argued that both expropriation and redistribution hamper markets. Hence, with increasing market orientation, state ideology may increasingly be oriented toward reinvestment. Laws are oriented not toward expropriation nor toward redistribution, but toward growth. Revolutionary transitions become almost impossible, and therefore punctuations or rapid substantial changes in distribution patterns also become unlikely. Gradualism then becomes the only model of distributional change. These are important ideas, and in the final chapter I deal with them more fully.

Why does Inequality not Change Between Transitions?

This question also requires a fuller treatment later, after we have looked at the problem of spatial inequality. For now, let us proceed on the assumption that social inequality is the only cause of income inequality. The question then becomes: Why do between-transition social inequality levels not change? In one important way this is a misleading question, because I suggest that between-transition inequality levels do change, but not by much, and not at all rapidly. Later, I will argue (as I have done in the opening chapter) that, in many nations, social inequality and spatial inequality have moved in different directions, resulting in what appears to be a distributional equilibrium. Let us then briefly look at the reasons that social inequality changes little and changes slowly between transitions.

Let me begin with an assertion. In the second half of the twentieth century and thereafter, it has become difficult for states to enable conditions in which between-group inequalities can increase significantly. I have already shown (in Chapter 4) that income inequality levels are more sensitive to between-group inequality changes than within-group inequality changes. Therefore, when between-group inequalities do not increase, overall inequality levels are also less likely to increase. Now consider the bases of the assertion. There are two reasons that it is possible to assert that between-group inequalities have generally not increased in recent decades.

The first is directly connected to the discussion in the preceding section, where I argued that increasing marketization leads to situations of increasing within-group and declining between-group inequality. During the last 60 years, particularly the last 25 years, market orientation has become a common feature of state policy around the world. It already was the defining feature of the Western liberal democracies; now many developing nations are also adopting market orientation as a basic policy platform.[23] Therefore, marketization results in less divergence in between-group inequalities. In the developed world, where market orientation has been the standard for many decades, between-group inequalities have been declining. Racial inequalities are lower now than they have been for centuries. They continue to remain very high, but at the same time they are lower today than they were 25 or 50 years ago. Gender inequalities have declined. Class definitions have become diffuse. Groups have become fragmented, within-group inequalities have increased, but between-group inequalities are in decline.

Second, in the non-socialist developing nations, after independence, the social and economic policies adopted were constructed in a world of competing ideologies—market-oriented versus state-led. This ideological indecisiveness between market and command economies led to countervailing policies (mixed private- and public-sector industrialization, food-price subsidies and food-production supports, exchange rates and credit policies, etc.), which had distributional effects that negated each other. Neither did these states focus on direct redistribution. We have already seen why insiders/reformers cannot redistribute on a large scale. It may be useful to also consider theories of policy-making in pluralistic states for other explanatory approaches. Ashutosh Varshney (1999) has used the "median voter" theorem to analyze the relative failure of democracies in poverty removal. He shows why redistribution policies that are likely to be effective (such as land reform and investment in primary education) are rarely enacted in democracies, but populist, ineffective measures are.

The last two issues discussed here (on the effects of markets and why inequalities do not change between transitions) will need to be discussed again in the final chapter after a detailed discussion of spatial inequality. I argue that in the last half-century the general trend toward absence of distributional change is best understood as the outcome of compensating changes in social and spatial inequality. But first let us understand how changes in spatial inequality take place.

6

GRADUALISM AND SPATIAL INEQUALITY

Studies of the distribution of world income are published in important journals (Schultz 1998; Bourguignon and Morrison 2002; Milanovic 2002) and by high-quality publishers (Firebaugh 2003). The analytical approach in all these works is similar: to calculate world inequality as a combination of within-nation inequality (using distributions, where possible, or average incomes in groups of nations) and between-nation inequality (using average incomes). All these works conclude that the within-nation component contributes, at most, one-quarter to one-third of global income inequality; the between-nation component contributes the remainder.

We can easily transfer this approach to studies of within-nation inequality by decomposing it into a within-region component and a between-region component. Later in this chapter we will see several examples of studies that have done just that. These are all recent studies, partly because decomposable inequality measures were not available before the late 1960s, but more importantly because scholars (outside geography) have recognized the significance of the spatial component of inequality only recently. It is surprising that this is the case because even casual observers of global conditions can agree with Lant Pritchett (1997) that the story of development in the twentieth century is one of "divergence, big time." The point that is less obvious is that this divergence exists not only between countries but between regions within countries.[1] This regional difference in average income (or life chances) is called regional inequality. This chapter is devoted to an understanding of regional inequality and how it contributes to the gradualist model of changing income inequality.

The material is presented in five parts. I begin with a brief technical discussion on scale and measurement issues in geography. In the second part, I discuss the broad theoretical approaches to understanding interregional change in the long run. Included here is a discussion on the critical ideas in regional change: cumulative causation and increasing returns. In the third part, I discuss the role of institutions (primarily the state) in influencing regional change. We will see that the framework that was developed for analyzing institutional transitions in the previous chapter is also useful in understanding the relationship between institutions and regional change. The fourth part of the chapter details several case studies, namely Brazil, Mexico, India, Indonesia, China, Russia, Japan, and the U.S. The fifth part addresses some critical issues relating first to the increasing significance of increasing returns and second to the spatial impact of globalization.

The story that emerges is direct and powerful. The primary impact of technological change, trade, and the use of national power over the past three to five hundred years has been to fragment the world into small pieces that differ widely in terms of average income. Not only is the international system fragmented (this is well known and the subject of a vast literature; see Landes 1998), but nations are also fragmented. The principal instrument of this fragmentation is city formation and related metropolitanization (the formation of very large cities), and general urbanization. Because cities offer increasing returns to scale and proximity, a process of cumulative causation is generated, which leads to increasing population and income concentration in cities. This process can be managed (if not wholly suppressed) by the state. What the state actually does depends on its ideology. For some indeterminate length of time, cities offer increasing returns and the process of interregional divergence continues. This slow process is the primary source of gradual change (increase) in income inequality. Do generalized diminishing returns eventually offset the urban advantage? Do new cities and regions rise to challenge the existing urban order? They do, and result in more complex urban systems, but, with few exceptions, regional inequalities do not decline. Hence, regional inequality is a major source of income inequality in a nation. For most of modern history, and in most nations, regional inequalities have increased. Because regional inequalities usually change slowly, the impact on income inequality is gradual. Let us examine how these processes unfold in detail.

SOME TECHNICAL ISSUES

Scale

Before we can begin an examination of regional change, it is necessary to outline some general definition and measurement issues. Let us begin from a simple statement: a region is a spatial subdivision of a larger spatial unit where the latter is generally recognized to be an internally consistent unit along some dimension. The most obvious internally consistent unit is presumed to be the nation, and therefore, internal subdivisions of a nation, each also internally consistent along some dimension (not necessarily or usually the dimension that defines the nation), are typically considered regions. The reader will have noted the first problem with this approach to defining regions—i.e., if the national subdivisions are also internally consistent along some dimensions but inconsistent along others, why cannot they too be subdivided into regions? And if internal consistency is the basis on which a subdivision of a larger unit is identified, why cannot each such subdivision be also further subdivided until there are no more internally inconsistent units? This problem is solved, so to speak, by using administrative units as regions. This is not the best method, but since data are collected at the administrative unit level, it is a practical method.

There are three additional problems. The first, related to the discussion above, is referred to as the modifiable areal unit problem (MAUP) in geography. This is in recognition of the fact that administrative boundaries act like sharp edges (dividing clearly distinct material), whereas population variability is contoured as a continuous surface that does not have sharp edges. This problem can sometimes be mitigated, but only after much mathematical manipulation and technical dexterity employing geographical principles and tools (using nodes and networks, for instance). The second is what is known in segregation research as the "checkerboard problem" (White 1983; Chakravorty 1996). This arises because in most calculations of regional inequality (or racial segregation) the regions or parcels that make up the study area are assumed to exist in abstract space; that is, their spatial relationship to each other is not considered. Hence, an arrangement of parcels that is clustered into low- and high-income groups yields the same result as an arrangement where low- and high-income parcels exist side by side. (We will see later that this problem is of special significance in a country such as China, where regional inequality is driven by the inland–coast differential.) A third and similarly unresolved problem relates to the issue of the appropriate number of subdivisions—i.e., how many subdivisions are just right, how many are too few or too many? The literature appears to indicate that anything fewer than 15 may be too few, and any number greater than 50 (perhaps in deference to the U.S. behemoth) may be too many. (Note that these are old and well recognized problems in the geography literature; see, for instance, Odell 1974).

Consider some concrete examples from India. Generally, the political subdivision "state" is considered to be the appropriate unit representing a region. Yet Uttar Pradesh, with close to 140 million people in 1991 (before the state of Uttaranchal was recently carved out of it), is large enough to become the sixth-largest country in the world; Bihar, with more than 86 million people, would also be among the largest countries in the world—larger than any nation in Africa with the exception of Nigeria. At the same time, entire states in India (such as Arunachal Pradesh, Mizoram, Nagaland, Goa, etc.) are not only smaller than each of the metropolitan districts in the country (such as Greater Bombay and Calcutta) but are smaller even than most rural districts; for instance, the total population of Arunachal Pradesh or Mizoram is fewer than that of every district but five in Uttar Pradesh and every district but two in Bihar. This situation creates two sets of problems: first, when regional inequality within a nation is measured (or discussed), clearly non-comparable spatial units are used for comparison (as in the United Nations General Assembly, where Mauritius and India have equal voting rights). Second, when regional inequality between nations is considered, we have the incongruous situation of the Indian condition (where somewhere around 25 states are typically included) being compared with the Mauritian condition (where the latter, whose entire population of around one million would fit into a "region" of Calcutta district, is also subdivided into multiple regions). This comparison between incompatible scales, something quite commonly done, is a form of "ecological fallacy" (discussed in Chapter 4).

Often (as in India) the fact of comparing between states presumes that it is the most important or meaningful comparison; that is, the state is considered the most relevant spatial unit. The ratio of average incomes of Maharashtra and Bihar are considered important and deserving of policy intervention because that number is high, and has increased in the post-independence period from under 2.5 to over 3.5. Yet, within Bihar, it is possible that similar inegalitarian changes have taken place between the districts of, say, Purbi Singhbhum (where Jamshedpur, an urban-industrial center, is located) and Santal Parganas (a rural-tribal district); within Maharashtra similar changes have most likely taken place between Greater Bombay and Gadchiroli (for instance). But within Punjab (long the highest average income state in the nation), such inegalitarian changes have probably not taken place. This creates a very significant problem: the implicit normative presumption that linguistic differences (as the Indian states are constituted on the basis of linguistic consistency) are most meaningful has no ethical basis, and may feed identity-based sub-national movements; also, this presumption may violate a basic understanding of how inequality is perceived or felt (usually through proximate rather than distant events). As I pointed out earlier (in Chapter 4), relative deprivation is a local issue—an unskilled factory worker in Calcutta is rarely concerned about the profits of industrialists in Bombay, just as a landless laborer in Champaran is unlikely to care about the incomes of landlords in Latur.

Therefore, we can see that cross-country comparisons are very difficult, and following the same logic, intracountry–interregional comparisons are doable but difficult when the regions are of vastly different sizes. We can also see that, depending on the scale chosen for regional analysis, multiple outcomes are possible simultaneously—one can see increasing inequality between states of a nation, while there may be increasing inequality within some states and decreasing inequality within others, and altogether unexpected results may be seen if a nonpolitical unit such as a regular grid or lattice is used.

Measurement

In general, there are two approaches to measuring spatial inequality. Both can be used when the data available are so limited that only regional averages (of income or output) can be calculated. These averages can be used in different ways. They can be tabulated or mapped. Simple tabulation still remains the most common form of regional data display. In addition, researchers often use a summary measure of variance in the average incomes. The most commonly used measures are the coefficient of variation (CoV) and the Hirschman-Herfindahl Index (H). The MAU problem applies to both measures, but, more important, the "checkerboard problem" also applies. Some attempts at incorporating spatial information have been made (see the modified H Index in Yim 1989), but since economists rarely use spatial considerations, the use of spatial measures of regional inequality has not permeated the regional development literature.

The second approach to measuring regional inequality is more informative and is especially useful when micro data at the individual or household level are available. Following the work of Shorrocks (1980, 1984) it is possible to decompose regional inequality into its two constituent units: within-region inequality and between-region inequality. Of the various decomposable measures of inequality, the Theil index (Theil 1972), using concepts from information theory, appears to be the easiest to comprehend and is the most widely used. I will not go into the details of understanding the theoretical basis of the measure (see Coulter 1989 for a good discussion on the Theil measure). It does satisfy the Pigou-Dalton condition and is unaffected by proportional changes in all incomes. Its main drawback is that its upper limit is log(n), where n represents the number of enumeration units (i.e., the measure is not sample-size independent); hence it is not possible to make comparisons between samples of different sizes. I will shortly show why this drawback will not affect this section. The Theil measure can be written as follows:

$$T = \left[\sum_{g=1}^{G} Y_g * \log\left\{ \frac{Y_g}{n_g / n} \right\} \right] + \left[\sum_{g=1}^{G} Y_g * \left\{ \sum_{n=1}^{n_g} (Y_i / Y_g) * \log \frac{Y_i / Y_g}{1 / n_g} \right\} \right]$$

Where,

Y_g = Mean income of the gth group

Y_i = income of the ith member

n_g = sample size of the gth group

T = Theil index

This equation can also be written as,

$$T = T_b + \Sigma\, Y_g * T_w$$

where T_b denotes "between-group" inequality and T_w denotes "within-group" inequality. Note that when all groups have the same average income, T_b (the first term) vanishes. In such a case, the overall Theil inequality will equal the sum across groups of within-group inequality times the group mean income.

Hence, regional inequality in a system of regions can be measured using several metrics. We have the within- and between-group inequality levels of course, plus the sum of these two figures, which yields inequality in the system as a whole (this can be the Gini coefficient we are familiar with, but more usually it is a generalized entropy measure like the Theil coefficient discussed above), and the ratio of the two figures (between-group inequality/within-group inequality), which yields what Zhang and Kanbur (2001) call the Polarization index. As an illustration, consider the following example from Firebaugh (2003). The Theil measure of inequality among the world's nations in 1992 is 0.864; of this, 0.513 is from inequality between nations and 0.351 is from inequality within nations; the polarization index therefore works out to around 1.43.[2] This decomposable approach to measuring regional inequality has one major flaw in that an unnecessary and often arbitrary aggregation is necessary to create groups from smaller spatial units. It is useful when the groups thus constituted are relatively homogenous (i.e., there is little within-group inequality), otherwise the utility of this method may be limited. Other measures of polarization exist that may be better when regional groups cannot be easily defined. The Esteban and Ray (1994) measure can be made comparable to the Gini, and the Wolfson (1994) measure is based on the Gini of regional incomes. There are yet more approaches that do not measure spatial inequality directly, but estimate them from growth regressions (by calculating the rate at which average regional incomes may be converging; more on this soon).

REGIONAL DEVELOPMENT THEORY

If we assume that regions, however defined, are unequal in terms of average income (or average life chances for their residents) at some historical point, how do we understand what happens to regional inequality in the long run? This question has been considered from different epistemological and disciplinary approaches, but at the core, the question revolves around a single issue: Do regional incomes diverge or converge? Also, if they do converge, how long does the process take? When we consider the different theoretical approaches to the study of comparative regional development, we see that the supporters of the convergence thesis, economists generally, are solidly outnumbered by those who believe that regional divergence defines the modern period; the latter group includes economists, geographers, regional scientists, and sociologists. In this section I look at comparative regional development theory from these two theoretical perspectives.

Convergence

The dominant theoretical approach in neoclassical economics is one where regional development models are equilibrium- and convergence-seeking, are driven by export-driven growth and the economies and diseconomies of agglomeration in dynamic nodal regions, and where most regions derive long-term benefits from modernization and technical change (see Borts and Stein 1964; Richardson 1973; North

1975). On the question of what happens to comparative regional development (or regional inequality) over the long run, a number of different approaches are suggested in the mainstream economics literature. Perhaps the earliest (and certainly one of the most cited works) is Jeffrey Williamson's famous inverted-U curve of regional inequality (Williamson 1965). Williamson argued (following a line of reasoning made famous by Kuznets and his inverted-U curve of income inequality, covered in Chapter 3) that regional inequality increases during the early stages of development and declines during the later stages. His cross-sectional analysis of regional inequality in countries at different levels of development appeared to provide solid empirical support for his hypothesis (never mind that his calculations suffered seriously from the ecological fallacy, the MAU problem, and the checkerboard problem), and ever since, the "Williamson hypothesis" has become one of the cornerstones of the neoclassical regional-development literature. William Alonso (1980) went so far as to suggest that the Williamson curve is one of the five bell-shaped curves that almost invariably characterize the development process (see Chakravorty 1994 for a refutation).

The Williamson model of divergence followed by convergence, however, was a partial affirmation of the implications of the Solow growth model, where, due to constant returns to scale and diminishing returns to capital in the leading regions, convergence is the expected outcome. In other words, a region with low initial per capita income can be expected to grow faster than a region with higher initial average income (see Barro and Sala-i-Martin 1992). This idea was initially proposed in an international context, where low-income nations were expected to grow faster than high-income nations (see Abramovitz 1986 for an empirical critique). The Barro and Sala-i-Martin approach focuses on two types of convergence: ß-convergence (or absolute convergence) takes place when poorer regions start growing faster than high-income regions; σ-convergence (or relative convergence) takes place when the dispersion or variance between regions diminishes as a result of slower growth in the high income regions and/or faster growth in the low income ones. The latter can be interpreted to mean that complete convergence is not possible, but there are high and low income clubs *within* which convergence takes place. ß-convergence is a necessary and enabling condition for σ-convergence. Finally, Sala-i-Martin (1996) suggests the existence of conditional ß-convergence, whereby different groups of regions converge to their different steady states. In other words, poor nations/regions are not expected to converge to the income of rich nations/regions, but to their own steady states.[3] The regional data in a number of developed areas (the U.S., Japan, Europe, Canada, Australia) and a small number of developing nations appear to support the convergence hypothesis (see Sala-i-Martin 1996 for a survey). But the experience in almost all developing and socialist nations provides ample evidence to the contrary. Later in this chapter I will look at several case studies that comprehensively contradict the convergence hypothesis.

The question of when convergence can be expected to begin is a tricky one. If it is expected to begin as soon as one region gains an advantage (whereby other disadvantaged regions immediately become attractive) then the question remains: what happens to the reason that gave the advantaged region an advantage in the first place? In a theoretical world where information and investments flow instantaneously (in response to minor shifts in wages and productivity), sustained, or anything more than very temporary regional inequality is impossible. Analysts, however, recognize that capital investments are "sticky" (which suggests that history plays a role) and often "lumpy" (which suggests that scale economies and increasing returns are also important). Therefore, instantaneous adjustments are not possible. Nonetheless, the economic literature provides no guidance on the temporal question, and therefore must bear the accusation of being ahistorical.

Divergence

Increasing Returns   Urban and regional economists have long recognized that diminishing returns are not the only possible outcome in leading regions. Neoclassical pioneers such as Alfred Marshall, and institutional economists starting with Thorstein Veblen and continuing through Gunnar Myrdal and Albert Hirschman, have recognized for an even longer time that "increasing returns" are not only possible but likely in many situations. I argue that these increasing returns come about primarily as a result of spatial arrangements; this is because density is the principal source of increasing returns.

The most obvious form of increasing return is that to scale, and it is easy to see that increasing scale is possible only in a localized way. When a factory increases its scale of operation it grows larger in place, by addition; if it grows larger by multiplication, by opening new branch plants, it is not an increase in scale. Increasing the scale of certain operations, especially in industrial production and in transportation, leads, up to some point, to more efficient division of labor and use of inputs. This raises productivity (or in the case of transportation, increased throughput), average output, and wages. Increasing returns also arise from other kinds of density because of the increasing intensity of interaction, knowledge exchange and spillovers, and proximity to others firms and individuals in the same business (buyers, suppliers, and specialized labor). These are called economies of agglomeration, which, unlike increasing returns to scale, are external to the firm and therefore are also known as external economies (discussed below). Increasing returns have limits, of course, and these also arise because of density. An operation can get so dense that people get in each other's way, quick reactions to changing situations become difficult, and transactions costs and wages begin to increase. The primary reason for the existence and persistence of regional inequalities in the modern period (and we must remember, as I will show later, that regional inequality of the kind and intensity that exists today is a modern phenomenon) is increasing returns in urban and metropolitan regions.

One particular form of increasing returns has recently become the focus of some attention and is deserving of special notice. This refers to the increasing returns from industry clusters. The benefits of industry clustering were identified early by Marshall (1919) who suggested that these arise from localization economies: namely, the availability of common buyers and suppliers, the formation of a specialized/skilled labor pool, and the informal transfer of knowledge (on trade secrets, production processes, market agents, etc.). Krugman's work in economic geography (Krugman 1991, 1996) and Porter's work in business economics (Porter 1990, 1996) have drawn the interest of economists to the idea of increasing returns to proximity in the form of clusters (see Fujita, Krugman, and Venables 1999). The literature on industrial clustering and its causes (localization or urbanization economies, proximity to other firms or consumers) and effects (economic growth, unbalanced development, regional inequality, global industrial restructuring) continues to proliferate in journals of geography, economics, planning, and development (see Chakravorty 2000; Nadvi and Schmitz 1999; World Bank 1999).

In metropolitan regions there are contradictions between the economies of scale and agglomeration on the one hand (which imply increasing returns), and size-related congestion diseconomies or diminishing returns on the other (Wheaton and Shishido 1981; Petrakos 1992). In Paul Krugman's terms, there is tension between the "centripetal" forces of higher labor productivity, larger plant size, access to markets and products (backward and forward linkages), thick labor markets, knowledge spillovers, and the "centrifugal" forces of higher land rents, commuting costs, congestion and pollution, all leading to higher wages and taxes (see Krugman 1996).[4] Hence, for indeterminately long periods of time after industrial development begins, large cities offer increasing returns to capital and labor, and this increasingly causes divergence. Eventually, though, the costs of size-related congestion may rise to the extent that higher returns become possible in smaller urban centers.[5] In other words, the Williamson hypothesis of divergence followed by convergence may indeed be the appropriate model. It is clear, though, that many cities grow rapidly well beyond the supposed limit to city size, which may be nothing more than an average that cannot account for the outliers that truly drive regional and technological change. Therefore, it is necessary to know why convergence theory has relatively little empirical relevance in so much of the world, and why it appears to work in some countries but not others.

Political Economy   The convergence models operate in an abstract world where the state plays no role in influencing the allocation of resources or growth rates. The political–economic models discussed below pay serious attention to the role of the state (and to a lesser extent, the role of space or proximity). From the beginning of development practice and scholarship, political–economic approaches on regional development have been framed around the institutions of the state and the market: What are the possible outcomes for comparative regional development under free market conditions? What are the effects of state intervention on comparative regional development (the equity issue), and on the nation's growth prospects (the efficiency issue)?

The first political–economic perspectives on regional development came from pioneers in development economics: Gunnar Myrdal (1957) and Albert Hirschman (1958) suggested the *core-periphery* and *cumulative causation models* based on similar ideas about "polarization" or "backwash" (concentration of growth and resources in leading regions) and "trickle down" or "spread" (diffusion of growth and resources to lagging regions). Their ideas were somewhat influenced by the work of the French economist Francois Perroux (1950), and in turn influenced the work of Friedmann (1966, 1973), Boudeville (1966), Richardson (1980) and an entire generation of regional planners and economists.

In these models the core is typically a large metropolitan center, and the periphery, depending on the definition, is everything outside the core (some models include an intermediate category called a "transition" region). In this view, regional imbalances are likely to widen in the absence of state intervention because of a number of interrelated factors—mainly that industry is more productive than agriculture and can locate only where there is sufficient physical and social infrastructure (roads, power, telecommunication facilities, schools, hospitals, colleges, etc.), i.e., in the leading region/s. Hence, the infrastructure advantage of the leading region attracts more capital, which creates even greater advantages and initiates a process of cumulative or circular causation. The concept of cumulative causation—virtuous cycles in well-endowed regions, vicious cycles in poorly endowed ones—can be related to the concepts of habit and habitus outlined in Chapter 4.

Because regional divergence cannot easily be mitigated by market forces, which, in fact, contribute to increasing divergence, state intervention is politically necessary and inevitable, and actually improves the distribution of welfare. The more hopeful approach, that of Friedmann and Hirschman, is one where the core is the locus of change, where new ideas, technology, and capital intersect to generate economic and cultural dynamism, while the non-metropolitan periphery initially falls behind in relative, and sometimes absolute terms. Eventually, expanding markets and urbanization, the spatial diffusion of innovations and culture, and political demands from the periphery (mediated by state actions) should lead to some narrowing of the core–periphery gap. Friedmann has since rejected many elements of his normative model, but its relevance to regional development practice is evident in the very large scholarship on and real investments in growth poles and growth centers (see Darwent 1975). Myrdal, in particular, was much less sanguine about the prospects of the lagging regions. He argued that growth in one region would have negative or "backwash" effects on other lagging regions. He wrote:

> It is easy to see how expansion in one locality has "backwash effects" on other localities. More specifically the movements of labour, capital, goods, and services do not by themselves counteract the natural tendency to regional inequality. By themselves, migration, capital movements, and trade are rather the media through which the cumulative process evolves—upwards in the lucky regions and downwards in the unlucky ones. In general, if they have positive effects for the former, their effects on the latter are negative. (Quoted in Higgins and Savoie, 1995: 86).

The idea of a benevolent state that is primarily concerned with the welfare of its citizens is one that is also increasingly criticized. Public choice theorists such as Buchanan and Tullock (1962) have argued that the state, too, is a self-interested entity and takes actions to perpetuate its existence, seeks rent where possible, and thereby distorts the market and resource allocation process. The best known regional/spatial manifestation of this approach is Michael Lipton's "urban bias" thesis (Lipton

1976; Bradshaw 1987).[6] Lipton argues that the natural advantages of metropolitan regions are heightened by a series of policies on the exchange rate (which makes the import of industrial machinery cheaper while making the export of agricultural commodities dearer), trade, food pricing, etc., creating urban and metropolitan bias. This, of course, results in lagging agricultural regions' falling even further behind. Bates' (1983) work on agricultural development in sub-Saharan Africa, especially the functioning of the continent's agricultural marketing boards, clearly shows that the state machinery is actively engaged in transferring the rural surplus to the leading urban regions, using a complex array of producer price supports, purchasing and storage monopolies, and urban price subsidies.

But, without question, the strongest criticisms of the bourgeois state have been presented in the *Neomarxist* models of regional development. At the forefront of the critique have been the Latin school dependency theorists (such as Baran 1957; Frank 1967; Timberlake 1987). This group of scholars has argued that the spatial impress of modernization is manifested in deepening class polarization and geographical inequality. The interests of the international "metropole" drive not only the policies of the industrialized West, but are also incorporated in the policy framework of the third world through its *compradore "rajas."* In this view, intranational uneven development is less important than (and merely a continuation of the spectrum of) uneven development between nations. The dependent-periphery state elite assist the capital owners from the developed core to extract surplus, and the underdevelopment of the regional and international periphery is a necessary condition for the development of the core.

More recently, deindustrialization in the developed nations has been theorized under the perspectives of "post-Fordism" or "flexible accumulation" (see Piore and Sabel 1984; Scott 1988), where the emphasis is on "the character of technological change, the form and organization of firms and industries, (and) the creation and transformation of labor markets" in influencing regional change (Schoenberger 1989, 133). These theorists relate regional change to the periodic crises to which capitalism is prone, whereby every period of low growth is likely to be followed by a search for new technologies and new places/regions for investment. As a result, regional inequality will not follow any single, simple model, but is likely to be cyclical or episodic—convergence during low growth periods, divergence during capitalist expansion (see Harvey 1982; Dunford and Smith 2000). Some attempts to extend these ideas to the context of third-world development have also been made (Storper 1991; Diniz 1994). In all of the Neomarxist approaches, the state is implicated in acting as the handmaiden of international, first-world, and corporate interests in maintaining uneven development.

Hence, the current state of regional theory offers three distinct long-term outcomes. The polar positions, not surprisingly, are taken in the polar disciplines—one school of economists argues, relying on the principles of diminishing returns and factor mobility, that convergence is the inevitable outcome; divergence is, at most, a temporary phenomenon. Leftist historians and geographers, on the other hand, argue that economic principles are far less important than the political and ideological conditions under which the economic actions are undertaken; as a result, given the dependency of the third-world state on first-world interests, divergence (regionally and internationally) is the only possible outcome. In the middle lies a mix of beliefs and ideologies where, to begin with, divergence is to be expected, followed perhaps, depending on state action, by some convergence.

Many authors have noted a clear difference and contradiction between state action specifically geared to the mitigation of regional differences (let us call this "explicit" regional policy) and macroeconomic policies that apparently have no regional dimension but in reality have significant spatial implications (call this "implicit" regional policy; see Henderson, 1988). The "explicit" urban and regional policies aimed at regionally balanced growth—licensing control, location of public sector projects, promotion of industrial estates, tax and land acquisition incentives, etc., in favor of lagging regions—have often been subsumed by more powerful macroeconomic policies on development path, subsidies to industry relative to agriculture, monetary, exchange rate, and trade policies etc. (Henderson 1982; Mills 1987). Balanced regional development has received rhetorical support from policy makers, but the actual regional policies have been mere palliatives, which have been washed away by the policies geared toward enhancing growth or some other nationalist objective.[7]

So which one of these perspectives on the role of the state and regional inequality is the correct one? We have a Nobel laureate (Gunnar Myrdal) arguing that regional differences are likely to widen in the absence of state intervention, which, according to one of the most renowned regional planners (John Friedmann) is not necessarily a negative outcome; according to a preeminent economic historian (Jeffrey Williamson, who has argued elsewhere that open trade leads to international convergence) in the long run regional differences will decline anyway. State intervention is an inevitable and necessary aspect of the political process, argues one of the most original and respected institutional economists (Albert Hirschman); but, in the view of other original and maverick intellectuals, state intervention is biased toward urban areas (Michael Lipton) or developed nations (Andre Gunder Frank) or is inefficient or irrelevant. I suggest that we need not accept any single one of these perspectives because, following the analytical framework presented in the previous chapter (see Figure 5.1), the key variable is state ideology. Let us first look at the general relationship between ideology/institutions and regional change followed by a more detailed look at some specific cases to understand how and why regional inequality changes in the long run.

Institutions and Regional Change

Let us consider what the prospects for comparative regional development may be in the light of what has been discussed above and by avoiding the more obvious traps of simplification (economic modeling without political understanding) and generalization (where the experience of a specific place at a specific time may not be transferred to all places at all times). I suggest that regional differentiation (or differences between places in material terms) has long been the result of varying combinations of chance, trade, power differentials, technology, and state ideology. Ideology is perhaps the most important element in this framework. From Chapter 5: Ideology is a system of beliefs—on good and bad, right and wrong, justice and morality, and on human nature, rationality and spirituality, and race, gender, language, region, nation and identity. Moreover, ideology is also a set of desires, or sets of what should be desirable and what not. Therefore, it is useful for us to look at some of the significant ideological systems of the modern period and the regional consequences of their actions and institutions.

Let us begin by reiterating that the motive force behind regional differences is the process of city formation, and in the modern era, the process of metropolitanization. I do not mean to suggest that there are no differences between rural areas in terms of productivity or income today. In fact, worldwide, there are now very large differences in agricultural productivity. But historically, before the modern era, rural areas (where, even as late as 1800, more than 97 percent of the world's population still resided) were largely undifferentiated. Indeed, before the formation of the first cities in the Tigris-Euphrates valley about 6000 years ago, there is little reason to believe that material differences between any two places could come even close to approaching the vast differences that exist today. Gideon Sjoberg's (1960) analysis of the formation of the first cities is of interest here (readers can also refer to the discussion on the origins of inequality in Chapter 5). Sjoberg argues that the first cities came about as a result first of the agricultural revolution, which marked the transition from nomadism to settled agriculture; then, in fortunate places with the right ecological combination of good soil, water, and temperature, arose agricultural innovations such as the plow, irrigation, domestication of animals, and the use of storable grains (rice, wheat, maize, etc.). These led, for the first time, to the creation of an agricultural surplus, which simultaneously freed some individuals from agricultural labor, introduced barter and trade, and eventually led to social stratification and a rudimentary class system.

One can see that the availability of surplus was key to the formation of the first cities. Recall from Chapter 5 that I do not take a position on whether the state came first or the surplus; what is important here is to understand the spatial impacts of surplus creation. With further hardening of the class systems, more and more surplus was expropriated by the cities; often what was not surplus was also expropriated. The rise of large empires before the advent of Christendom is similarly linked to the expropriation of surplus. The largest cities in pre-modern times, Rome at the height of the Roman empire and Pataliputra at the height of the Gupta empire in India, both reached populations of one million people. These two cities were far wealthier, with far superior material standards than their smaller counterparts and the vast rural areas that they had subjugated. Rome and Pataliputra, of course, became much smaller when the empires fell (i.e., they could no longer grow by expropriating surplus from subjugated peoples). Rome had to wait till the rise of Mussolini to reach a million again, and Pataliputra (now Patna) had to wait for forty years after India's independence to reach that number. Please note again the two main points in this account: one, regional inequality has historically arisen due to city formation, and two, city formation has historically been linked to surplus expropriation.

I do not intend to sketch a history of urbanization here, but to move directly to the advent of colonialism. The state that existed in the pre-colonial regions before colonialism was too ephemeral and fragmentary, and the historical records too inadequate for us to be able to create a broad picture of regional inequality (see Chapter 5). The material and social conditions of life changed with the efficacy and generosity of the ruler of the day; prosperity, low taxes, and relative autonomy under one ruler, juxtaposed perhaps with want, deprivation, and oppression under another—or in the next kingdom or empire. The ruling class was small in number, there was virtually no middle class, and the vast majority of the population struggled with the land and nature as an undifferentiated mass (which, it is important to note, was much smaller in size than at present). The capital cities were relatively wealthy, and a few small trading cities, mostly inland, were better off than the countryside.

The colonialism period in Asia and Africa (roughly 1700 to 1945) was marked by radical alterations to the simplified picture presented above and by basic changes in the political, scientific, and economic principles governing Western societies. The idea of the "nation" was constructed; racial differentiation by perceived achievement capability was institutionalized; and Darwin's biological theory was reinterpreted in social and economic terms to justify Western superiority in ethics, morals, religion, institutions, behavior and culture. The economic logic of colonization, which was primarily to expropriate surplus and set favorable terms of trade (in other words, the desire to extract industrial raw material and agricultural commodities in as great quantities as cheaply as possible from subjugated peoples) led to events like the Berlin Conference of 1884 (for the division of Africa among colonial powers).

Colonization led to the withering away of traditional agricultural and handicraft production and of traditional inland trading routes and cities, and the establishment of coastal cities from sub-Saharan Africa to South, Southeast and East Asia. Mumbai, Kolkata, Chennai, Jakarta, Singapore, Manila, Nairobi, Dar-es-Salam, Cape Town, Johannesburg, Kinsasha, etc. are all colonial cities, as are virtually all the cities of the Americas, created by the colonialists to serve their political and economic purposes. Similarly, Hong Kong, Canton, and Shanghai, while not created by the colonialists, certainly grew to prominence under them following the Treaty of Nanjing in 1842. The rise of these coastal cities, in combination with restricted access to Western education, and the cooptation of the local large landowners and successful petty traders (the *compradore "rajas"*) led to widespread social and spatial differentiation and inequality. The "dual economy" was established at the large scale (between city and country), and at smaller scales such as the city (with the formal–informal employment dichotomy and segregated spatial structures). Interregional inequality, scarcely noteworthy in the past, was firmly established. For instance, Kolkata, which was a cluster of undistinguished (perhaps especially impoverished) villages before the arrival of the British traders, soon grew to be much richer than Murshidabad (the native capital of the Bengal region). Inevitably, intra- and interregional inequality increased. These were the inequalities that the newly independent nations inherited.

The nationalism period (roughly 1930 to 1980–85) followed almost directly from the ideological evolution of the West during the period of colonization. The nation-state became the basic territorial organizing device, whereas the great dialectic between communism and capitalism (as to which was the superior political–economic system) then being engaged in the West, carried over to the new nations. Social Darwinism and racism were rejected by the vast majority of intellectual leaders in conjunction with the liberal reconstruction of disciplines such as sociology and anthropology.[8] The idea of "development" emerged, and mainly from the economists of the West came some of the basic economic principles of the nationalism era—industrialization led modernization, the Rosenstain-Rodan "big push" theory, infant industry protection, import substitution, and self reliance.

In many cases, this package of programs created urban and metropolitan bias, turned the terms of trade in favor of urban areas and against rural areas, and deepened the urban and metropolitan focus of investments and development policy. Gigantic metropolitan areas emerged in the third world, larger than anything that had been seen in the first world. In 1950, there were just eight third-world metropolises in the list of the global top twenty-five; in 2000, nineteen third-world metropolises were on this list. Scholars expressed concern about "overurbanization" (in relation to the fact that the West had never attained these levels of urbanization at such low levels of industrialization) and "parasitic metropolitanization" (that was draining the agricultural regions of resources). Some countervailing actions were also taken—for example, subsidized food and anti-poverty programs, and regional development programs in lagging regions (also see "implicit" regional policies discussed earlier)—but the regional distribution patterns did not change fundamentally.[9] As I argued in Chapter 5, social inequality probably declined in most places and regional inequality grew or stayed stable, but the changes in most cases were not substantial.

As we know, when most of the third world was in its nationalist period, in many other nations the state ideology was socialism. Socialist rhetoric on regional inequality and social inequality were similar; that is, there was an ideological commitment to the reduction or elimination of urban–rural and interregional differences. However, socialist policies on regional inequality varied widely—from serious efforts at regional redistribution to more or less utter disregard. China exemplifies efforts to diminish regional and other forms of spatial inequality, whereas, in the Soviet Union, the few explicit spatial policies that were instituted were not oriented toward mitigating regional inequality, but, on the contrary, aimed to increase industrial efficiency and enhance military security. This is an interesting and stark point of difference. The Chinese efforts were successful in reducing regional inequalities substantially (except during brief periods) and were instrumental in reducing the overall level of income inequality. The Soviet efforts, such as they were, did not reduce regional inequalities; as a result, despite the fact that social inequalities had been lessened significantly, the overall level of income inequality remained moderate rather than low (remember that by the early 1970s income inequality in the Soviet Union was about the same as in capitalist United Kingdom). This is an important point, and I will discuss the details in the following section where case studies are presented.

CASE STUDIES

In this section I will look at the recent evidence on regional inequality in a number of large nations. It would have been useful to have regional income data for earlier periods, especially the colonial period when regional inequality most likely increased by very large amounts. But, like the income distribution data discussed in Chapter 2, regional data series are limited to the last half century generally, and in the odd case to the last century. The discussions below focus on Brazil and Mexico from Latin America, India and Indonesia from Asia, China and Russia from the (ex)socialist nations, and brief outlines of a number of other nations. While these discussions focus on what has happened to regional inequality over time (i.e., whether convergence or divergence has taken place), note also the absolute levels of regional inequality in the different nations. Often, as in the study of income inequality, the focus on change diverts attention from what may be the more important issue, which is the level or extent of regional inequality.

Brazil

Brazil is organized as a federation of 28 states aggregated into five regions. The country is so large, and the patterns of population distribution and development within it so clearly delineated, that the problem of overlapping regional definitions usually does not arise. One of the most significant and long-standing problems in Brazil is the north–south divide in development level. The important regions are the northeast and the southeast, which in 1996 contained about 29 and 45 percent of the total population respectively. In the southeast, the largest state is Sâo Paulo, containing 22 percent of the national population. Rio de Janeiro is another important state, more so after 1970 when the state of Guanabara was merged with it. In the northeast, the important states are Cearà, Pernambuco and Bahia, which together contain about 18 percent of the national population.

The bane of Brazilian development is generally perceived to be the extent and intransigence of regional inequality within the country; or, more accurately, the wide gulf in development standards and average incomes between the prosperous and populous southeast, and the impoverished northeast. Every recent administration in Brazil, autocratic or democratic, has sworn to uplift the northeast. The first formal attempt to attack the regional problem, which was much less severe then, came in 1909 with the creation of the National Inspectorate for Works against Droughts. In 1952, the Bank of the Northeast, headquartered in Fortaleza, was created to provide development assistance. In 1959, a council, which became the Superintendency for the Development of the Northeast (SUDENE) was established with a broad mandate to change the economic and social structure of the region. Despite these policies, in 1996 the richest state (Sâo Paulo) had a per capita income 6.2 times higher than that of the poorest state (Piauí), and the richest region, the southeast, had a per capita income three times that of the poorest region, the northeast (Azzoni 2001).

Chakravorty (1992) argues that there are three important points about regional inequality in Brazil: (1) The gap in average regional incomes has been declining from 1950 onward. Azzoni's (2001) more detailed analysis shows that there has been oscillating ß–convergence and divergence between 1939 and 1995, with some periods of convergence and some of divergence; he shows divergence in the mid 1990s, the latest period in his data. Between 1960 and 1970 there was a marginal increase in inequality, caused probably by the drought year of 1970 and the resulting poor agricultural performance of the northeast. (2) The variation among the economically active population (EAP) is considerably less than the variation among individuals, and somewhat less than among individuals. This indicates that there is substantial underemployment and unemployment in the low-income regions. (3) Despite the overall decline in regional inequality, the target region, the northeast, has apparently not gained at all. In fact, its 1980 normalized average of 410 (relative to 1000 for all of Brazil) is less than its 1960 average of 445, and just about equal to its 1950 average of 408. Much of the decline in regional inequality can be attributed to the improved performance of the center-west region (probably due to the creation and growth of Brasilia), and, to a lesser extent, to the gains made by the barely populated north region. Regional and income inequality in Brazil have followed similar tracks. Both are at very high levels, and over the last 40 years the changes in both have been minor.

Mexico

Mexico is divided into 32 states that can be aggregated into different clusters of meta regions. Researchers have generally distinguished between the following: The north region (with the Maquiladora or border region often considered a separate unit) which, in terms of average income, is broadly the most advanced of the meta regions; The center region (with the Federal District or Mexico City usually considered as a separate unit), which has wide intraregional disparities as a result of the presence of the urban giant; the south region, which is primarily agricultural and has long been the most impoverished of the regions and includes some of the lowest-income states, such as the neighbors Chiapas and Oaxaca. Mexico has a dualistic economy—with the coexistence of large industrial and traditional agricultural sectors —that is also regionally distinct. The north region has a significant industrial base (as does the Federal District), while the south has little industry. In addition, there are states like Campeche and Tabasco (also in the poor south) whose average incomes are significantly inflated by the presence of the oil sector.

Regional inequality has been a serious problem in Mexico for some time. In the middle third of the twentieth century, regional inequality increased largely as a result of the rapid growth and high income of Mexico City. Then, for a brief period between about 1970 and 1985, regional inequality declined (there was ß–convergence) because growth in Mexico City slowed down, the Maquiladora states on the U.S. border began industrializing and growing, and agricultural income increased in the southern states. However, the period of convergence proved short-lived. Beginning with the structural reforms initiated in 1985 and continuing after the initiation of NAFTA (the North American Free Trade Agreement) in 1994, the convergence momentum was lost and divergence became the norm again (Bouillon, Legovini, and Lustig 2003). According to Cikurel (2002, 1):

> [T]he winners from the structural change were those states initially endowed with, or able to attract, higher levels of human and industrial capital and better infrastructure. This was especially true for the northern states of the country, which benefited additionally from their proximity to the United States. In contrast, southern states … that have the greatest lags in human capital and infrastructure, are the losers from the policy shift undertaken during the mid-eighties.

In 1970, the per capita GDP in the Federal District was about 90 percent more than the national average; this condition remained more or less unchanged till 1980 and declined a bit to 1985 (at which point the average was only 81 percent higher), but by 1999 it was 251 percent higher.[10] Similar changes have taken place in relation to the poor southern states also. The ratio of per capita GDP between the Federal District and Oaxaca went from 5.4 in 1970, to 3.7 in 1985, and 5.7 in 1999. The same ratio with the state of Chiapas, a better-known case of regional inequality and consequent insurgence, went from 3.9 in 1970 to 2.2 in 1980, 2.7 in 1985 and 5.8 in 1999. In short, the current level of regional inequality in Mexico has probably reached or surpassed the earlier peak attained around 1970.

India

India is a large country divided into some 27 states and several union territories; these are further subdivided into about 500 districts. The number of states and districts is not constant. New districts are regularly carved out of old ones—three new states were created from old ones in 2000. The western region (made up of the industrial states of Maharashtra and Gujarat) is the economically leading region, followed in order by the southern region (where a large proportion of the much-discussed information technology firms are located), the northern region (where Punjab and Haryana are wealthy agricultural states), and the eastern region (where West Bengal, a state in decline, is the leader, and Bihar, the poorest state in the nation, continues to spiral further down).

Several studies of regional inequality in India have been made. Most cover the recent period, from about 1980 or 1990 onward, generally known as the reform period (structural reforms were instituted formally in 1991 and informally in 1985). Older data show that regional inequality may have been declining from the late 1960s to the late 1970s, not so much because of superior growth in lagging states but because the leading state in 1960 (West Bengal) had gone into precipitous decline (see Chakravorty 2000). However, between 1950 and 1989 (from just after independence to shortly before serious reforms were initiated), the CoV of average incomes increased from 0.26 to 0.34, and the population-weighted CoV increased from 0.92 to 0.99. The per capita income ratio between the richest state (Punjab) and the poorest (Bihar) increased from 2.45 to 3.31.

After the reforms there is little doubt that regional inequality has increased substantially. Noorbakhsh (2003) shows that the Gini of per capita net state domestic product increased from 28.1 in 1981–82 through 33.7 in 1991–92 to 43.3 in 1997–98. Polarization measures have also increased over the same period; the Esteban-Ray measure increased from 0.169 in 1981–82 through 0.271 in 1991–92 to 0.341 in 1997–98; the Wolfson index increased for the same years from 0.034 through 0.102 to 0.142. The Kanbur-Zhang measure shows very significant polarization increases in literacy, poverty, and urbanization. According to Milanovic (2004) the ratio of average incomes in the richest and poorest states has increased to 4.4. Sachs, Bajpai, and Ramiah (2002) have shown absolute divergence between 1980 and 1998. Rao, Shand, and Kalirajan (1999) have shown absolute and conditional divergence between 1965 and 1998, with increasing divergence in the 1990s, led by the location of private investment.[11] Almost identical conclusions are drawn by Ghosh, Marjit, and Neogi (1998), with data from 1965 to 1995. Singh et al. (2002) agree with these findings but suggest that divergence on other measures (such as human-development indices) is not as bad as the income data show. We should keep in mind that these substantial regional divergences have taken place during a period when income-inequality levels at the national or state level have hardly changed.

Indonesia

Indonesia is an archipelago of several large islands and hundreds of smaller ones. The land is divided into 27 provinces, which are usually aggregated into five regions: Sumatra, Java, Kalimantan, Sulawesi, and the outer islands. Java (which also includes the smaller island of Bali) constitutes less than seven percent of the land area but includes about 60 percent of the population and the country's largest cities, including Jakarta, an urban giant. The reduction of regional inequality is considered a very important goal in Indonesian policy, perhaps just behind promoting economic growth, and on par with poverty reduction.

Indonesia's macroeconomic performance, until the trauma of the Asian crisis of 1998, was generally described in positive terms—stable, egalitarian, prudent, wise—much as the early NICs have been described; in many ways, Indonesia's recent political economy resembled the pattern followed by the NICs, with similar virtuous cycles of development. Inequality levels have remained virtually unchanged (at a Gini of around 35 for expenditure) through more than three decades of significant economic change. The secondary data sources (Aswicahyono, Bird and Hill 1996; Akita and Lukman 1995) suggest that at the regional level too Indonesia's development has been stable, perhaps with some concentration of industrial and other investments in Java, especially Jakarta and west Java (the Jabotabek region). Investments in the oil sector, necessarily located near oil reserves, has had some effect on spatial dispersion (usually in Kalimantan), but the overall concentration of manufacturing in Java has increased during the reform period, mostly at the cost of losses in Sumatra. The summary data suggest that some deconcentration has taken place during the reform period in the secondary and tertiary sectors of the economy, while government consumption expenditure and fixed capital formation have become more concentrated (see Akita and Lukman 1995); Aswicahyono, Bird and Hill (1996: 356) note that "these aggregate groupings ... conceal important trends at the sub-regional level ... There has almost certainly been a rising concentration of industrial activity on the fringes of major urban concentrations, such as Jakarta and Surabaya."

One of the interesting features of regional inequality in Indonesia is the repeated finding that there are few differences in average income between broadly defined regions, but very substantial differences between provinces within regions and between regions. Consider the interregional scale first. At independence Java had the lowest average expenditure relative to the other big islands certainly and even to the outer smaller islands. By the mid 1980s these differences had virtually vanished, so that "there was no between-group inequality" (Bevan, Collier, and Gunning 1999, 293). Akita, Lukman, and Yamada (1999) estimate, using decomposable Theil measures, that in the early to mid 1990s between-region inequality accounted for only 15 to 19 percent of regional inequality. Akita (2003) estimates that in 1996 between-region differences accounted for 7.4 percent, while between-province differences accounted for 44.2 percent of regional inequality (measured by Theil). Consider the Java region as an illustration. In the mid 1990s the ratio of average income between Jakarta (the richest province) and Central Java (the poorest province in Java region) varied between 4.9 and 5.4. In the country as a whole, the ratio of income in Jakarta to the poorest province (East Nusa Tenggarra, in the outer islands) varied between 8.3 and 9.5. There are two points to note: one, the levels of interprovincial inequality are very high, and two, these levels have not been growing in recent years; if anything, they have declined.

Russia

"If it's bad in Moscow," said Nikita Khrushchev, "it's worse in the provinces." The Soviet system was built ideologically on the promise of egalitarianism, and, to a large extent, it delivered on that promise as far as class or social inequality was concerned. However, on spatial inequality generally and regional inequality specifically, the socialist system failed to deliver egalitarianism in the Soviet Union or its satellites. Large regional differences persisted well into the 1970s on variables such as income, housing quality and size, health outcomes and services, etc. For instance, per capita income in the richest republic (Estonia) was 2.5 times larger than in the poorest republic (Tadjikistan). Fuchs and Demko (1979) have complied a collection of such inequalities, arguing that the desire for military security and industrial efficiency trumped concerns about geographic inequality. Nevertheless, the level of regional inequality in the Soviet Union was relatively low for the country's size, especially when compared with large developing nations.

The Soviet Union is no more. In its place we have Russia, still physically the largest country in the world, with 21 republics and 55 administrative units called *krais* and *oblasts*. Fedorov (2000) uses these territorial divisions to provide the most detailed look at regional inequality and polarization in Russia after the demise of communism. His findings are unequivocal. Regional inequality has increased very significantly in Russia, as has regional polarization. He measures regional inequality using the Gini and Shorrocks' Generalized Entropy measures for income and expenditure between 1990 and 1999. Using either measure for either variable regional inequality has increased three- to six-fold during this period, with a peak in 1997 and a small decline thereafter. The Esteban-Ray measure of polarization shows a three-fold increase and the Wolfson measure shows a four-fold increase in this span, also with a peak in 1997 and a small decline from the peak thereafter. Using the Kanbur-Zhang index of polarization Fedorov shows that these results are best replicated when groups of regions are defined by size of capital city or by export share. That is, regional inequality and polarization are driven by concentration and growth of income in large cities which are also export-oriented or more globalized. The rapid increase in regional inequality is quite remarkable (mirroring the rapid rise in income inequality), and the primary causes are very revealing.

China

China, the world's most populous country, is divided into 30 provinces that are often aggregated into three meta regions (eastern, central, western) or two (coastal, inland). Dozens of studies of regional inequality in post-reform China are now published in an array of economics, geography, planning, sociology, and other journals. These paragraphs provide only a brief summary of the material, but because there is a consensus in the findings, it is possible to quickly identify the principal conclusions.

It is well established that inequality has increased in China in recent years. Income inequality levels began rising in the early to mid 1980s and had moved from Gini coefficients of around 25 to around 40 by the end of the 1990s. One of the curious aspects of China's post-reform data is that, using conventional summary measures of regional inequality (such as the CoV), it appears that the level of regional inequality actually declined from the mid 1970s to the early 1990s, despite clear expectations of the opposite (Wei 2000). Much of this finding is explained by the fact that in the first phase of reforms (1979–84) regional inequality did really decline. Some of this finding may be related to issues of scale and measurement, where significant changes arise from different ways of (dis)aggregating the three most important spatial units—the centrally administered municipalities of Beijing, Shanghai, and Tianjin. The data reported in different secondary sources (Fan 1995, Chai 1996, Wei and Ma 1996) point to the following empirical realities: First, the eastern coastal region has been the primary beneficiary of investment (FDI almost twenty times greater than in the western region, and total investment almost 2.3 times greater—both on a per capita basis, both differences increasing over time). Second, the per capita income gap between the eastern and western regions rose from under 1.5 to about 2.0 between 1978 and 1991, the gap between the richest province (Shanghai) and the poorest (Guizhou) rose from about a factor of 8 to more than 18. The decline in summary measures of regional inequality can be explained by the declining (but still preeminent) positions of Shanghai and Tianjin, while in the east, other provinces, such as Guangdong and Liaoning especially, have improved their positions primarily through infusions of foreign capital. Shanghai, Beijing, and Tianjin are still the wealthiest regions in China, but they have not grown as rapidly as most of the other, newly privileged fourteen "open coastal cities" (e.g., Natong, Ningbo, Fuzhou) and five "special economic zones" (e.g., Shenzen, Zhuhai, Shantou).

Kanbur and Zhang's (2001) study of fifty years of regional inequality in China shows that it is tied to major political economic phases: 1949–56 (revolution and land reform), 1957–61 (the great leap forward and the great famine), 1962–65 (post-famine recovery), 1966–78 (cultural revolution and transition to reform), 1979–84 (rural reform), and 1985 to present (decentralization and trade openness). Regional inequality measured by the Gini peaked during the great famine, fell steadily after that, rose during the mid 1970s, fell during rural reform, and has climbed ever since. Virtually identical results are reported using the Generalized Entropy measure. Polarization between urban and rural areas and between coastal and inland provinces began to increase rapidly starting in 1987–88 (right after the initiation of trade reforms), where the urban–rural gap is significantly higher than the coastal–inland gap (confirmed in Yang 1999). (Remember that, even during this period, urban and rural inequality in China continued to be low and relatively unchanged; see data in Appendix 1.) There is little doubt that regional inequality in China has widened during the reform period, by design and choice,[12] led by foreign investments in the privileged cities of its golden coastline.

Other Developing Nations

The case of Thailand is equally clear-cut. Income inequality in Thailand has been increasing steadily from the mid-1970s onward; in terms of the Gini coefficient, Thailand's income inequality had moved from the high 30s in the early 1970s to the low 50s by the end of the 1990s. Similarly, there is little doubt that regional inequality in Thailand, led by the explosive and concentrated growth of the Bangkok metropolitan region, has also been rapidly increasing from the mid-1970s (see Daniere 1996, Wongsuphasawat 1997). Ahuja et al. have suggested an explicit link between the two increasing inequalities. They write:

> There can be little doubt that the past two decades have seen a real increase in the dispersion of the Thai income distribution.... The urban or rural location of residence explains 17–18 percent of the inequality in 1975, and the region of residence explains 14–15 percent (and) the explanatory power of both variables increases substantially over time: in 1992 the location of residence explains 28–29 percent of the inequality and the region of residence explains between 25–27 percent ... this suggests that the spatial dimension of inequality is gaining importance in Thailand. (Ahuja et al. 1997, 38–42)

On the other hand, the Colombian economy, despite the problems of an insurgency and narcotics trafficking, was able to ride out the "lost decade" in Latin America with some economic growth and a marginal decline in inequality. The level of inequality is still very high (with a Gini higher than 50), and the extent of decline is not significant, yet it is noteworthy in terms of the general increases in the entire region. Simultaneously, there is a clear trend toward regional deconcentration. According to Cárdenas and Pontón (1995, 33):

> Conventional wisdom in Colombia states that interdepartmental differences in per capita income have become more acute in the postwar period .... [However] on the contrary, Colombia is a very successful story of regional convergence. In fact, the rate of ß

convergence is close to 4% per year, so that the catch-up rate (between poor and rich regions) is twice as fast as the one observed in industrial countries.... Income per capita in Bogotá was in 1950 10 times greater than that of Choco [the poorest territorial unit]. By 1989 the gap had narrowed to 2.7 times.

Japan

Most of the data (on population and income) in Japan are collected on the basis of political divisions called prefectures. There are 47 prefectures;[13] 42 of them are designated *ken*, Osaka and Kyoto are urban prefectures designated *fu*, and Tokyo is a metropolitan prefecture called *to*. Most Japanese regional researchers and all the official Japanese data sources appear to follow a standard regional aggregation of prefectures. According to Chakravorty (1992, Table 5.15) regional inequality (among all prefectures) reached a peak in the year 1960, and has been steadily declining ever since, except for a slight upsurge in the early 1980s. The share of the capital region (Kanto) has remained unchanged from 1975 on, while Kinki (the region centered around Osaka) has been steadily losing its income advantage since 1965. In fact, the convergence of per capita incomes since 1970 appears to have been achieved as much due to the declining relative averages in the leading regions as due to the rising averages of the lagging regions. It appears that, while greater numbers of people have moved into the leading regions from the lagging regions (indicating the superiority of investment and employment opportunities in these regions), the former have simultaneously lost the average income advantage they initially had over the latter. For instance, the average income ratio between Kanto and Okinawa declined from almost 2.0 in 1955 to just less than 1.5 in 1987. Since 1975, and particularly since 1982, the average incomes of most regions have hardly changed. It is necessary to note that several researchers have found that regional inequality measured by the CoV increased somewhat in Japan in the mid to late 1980s, but have fallen continuously through the 1990s (see Lee 2003).

It is possible to speculate, then, that the limit of regional income convergence may have been reached in Japan. The main reason for making this argument is that regional inequality is at such a low level that it is difficult to imagine that it could decline further to any significant extent. For instance, according to Abe (1997), in 1994 the income ratio between the highest-income region (Kanto) and the lowest-income region (Okinawa) was 1.65. However, Okinawa is a special case. If it is ignored, then the same ratio (with a different lowest-income region) becomes 1.35. The average income of Kanto was only 14 percent higher than the average of Japan as a whole, and the average income of Tokyo was merely 18 percent higher than the national average. We can see that, in Japan, regional and income inequality levels are complementary; both are at low to very low levels, and have changed little over the last 30 years.

Other Developed Nations

Empirical support for the theory of convergence comes primarily from developed nations, i.e., the United States and the European Union. When long-term U.S. data from about 1840 to 1990 at the state level are analyzed, there is little doubt that average incomes have converged to a significant degree. Much of this convergence has taken place after 1930 and before 1980. At the extremes, the income ratio of the richest to the poorest state has declined from just under four to around two. The richest states are still in the northeast and the west and the poorest states are still in the south, but the gap between their average incomes has declined. Barro and Sala-i-Martin (1992) show that over the period 1840–1988 the ß–convergence rate among U.S. states was 1.75 percent; a compelling graph plotting the per capita growth rate (for 1880–1988) against the 1880 per capita income shows a clear inverse relationship between the two variables. Sala-i-Martin (1996) estimates convergence rates of about 2 percent for U.S states between 1890 and 1990, 2.7 percent for Japanese prefectures between 1955 and 1990, and 2 percent for Europe (broken into 90 regions) between 1950 and 1990.

However, when data for the last two decades are analyzed, there is little or no evidence of ß or σ convergence. Tsionas (2000) uses U.S. state level data from 1977 to 1996 and finds no evidence of convergence. Sala-i-Martin's (1996) own estimates for Europe show that, between the mid 1970s and late 1980s, there was divergence, a condition that most likely continued into the 1990s. Some critics of the convergence thesis have suggested that conditional convergence is indistinguishable from club-convergence, in which there are distinct clubs or groups of nations/regions that may have within-club convergence but not between-club convergence. This is related to the critique that a region's growth cannot be separated from that of the larger national or international economy to which it belongs (Quah 1993). Others have pointed out that the clubs may be spatial clusters (e.g., Scandinavian countries are likely to exhibit similar growth characteristics, as are Balkan countries) whereby the growth regressions to estimate convergence may have spatial autocorrelation and thus may be econometrically flawed. Surely, looking for universal regional growth principles from 150 years of U.S. history would be difficult, for there are not many countries with its special feature of continental grab and settlement and slavery. Ultimately, we must conclude that, while real, significant regional convergence has taken place in developed nations, the recent decades have reversed some of those gains, and substantive north–south differences persist in many countries (the U.S., U.K., Italy, Portugal, Europe in general, etc.).

Summary of Findings

We can draw the following conclusions from the case studies:

- Every nation has the potential to experience both interregional convergence and divergence during its development history. Though we do not have the data to confirm it, the circumstantial evidence indicates that it is very likely that divergence has been the norm from the colonial period onward in most nations, and that convergence has been the twentieth century norm in most developed nations.[14]
- Convergence may follow divergence, but divergence may follow convergence too. In other words, the long-term trend is episodic rather than a Kuznets-like or Williamson-like inverted-U or bell-shaped curve. It is difficult to determine *a priori* how long an episode may last.
- Absolute convergence may never be possible. In most cases when growth in the leading regions slows down, it is the proximate or adjoining regions that benefit. Hence, convergence clubs, which are also geographically clustered, are prevalent and likely to become more so. Convergence clubs can be composed of nations or sub-national regional clusters.
- Very large regional differences persist even during periods of convergence. It is not uncommon to see average income ratios between rich and poor regions be fourfold and even higher. This point is ignored in the convergence literature, and, perhaps as a result the convergence thesis is discounted by radical and non-mainstream students of regional change.
- State actions have large impacts on comparative regional development. These actions can be directly redistributive with more success or less (as in Indonesia and Brazil respectively). But, more typically, implicit spatial policies have much bigger impacts. Examples include: openness to international trade (in post-reform Mexico, Russia, China and India, and in developed nations), military security (in the Soviet Union and pre-reform

China), land reform (during China's great leap forward and resultant famine), etc.

• The globalization period is associated with divergence almost universally. This is true of developing nations in Latin America (Brazil and Mexico), Asia (India and China), the transition economies (Russia), and developed economies (the U.S., the European Union). In many instances, divergence during the period of globalization or trade liberalization has followed a period of convergence or declining inequality (in the developed nations, China, India, Mexico, etc.).

THE CRITICAL ISSUES

The Impact of Globalization

Why, almost everywhere, should regional inequalities increase during globalization? Is globalization then the root cause of this increase? At several earlier points, I have discussed the fact that globalization is a multifaceted phenomenon; therefore, like the proverbial elephant being described by several blind men, there is a real danger of latching on to only one incomplete part of the reality. In keeping with the structure of the explanation thus far, I will focus on two key issues: return to capital (increasing, decreasing, or constant), and state policy. Let us begin with a few words on why globalization is important globally despite the fact that it is primarily a first-world phenomenon.

I suggest that it is not necessary to resolve the contrasting views of globalization to agree that, from a *policy* perspective, there is significant convergence. Economic globalization is driven by technological change (in communication and transportation) and is supported by an ideology and policy apparatus that was perhaps best enunciated in the tenets of the Washington Consensus. We know that cities are the engines of regional change and inequality. As far as cities are concerned, this policy apparatus includes support for markets and trade, democracy and decentralization, and "good governance" based on inclusion, transparency, and social justice. (I take up these themes in greater detail in the final chapter.) These ideological or policy elements of globalization are far more pervasive than economic globalization which, we know, has barely touched large parts of the developing world. The institutionalization of ideological globalization is an outcome of the perceived failures of the nationalist model and a combination of external forces: the success of the Asian tigers (in achieving remarkable levels of sustained equitable growth supposedly following liberal market principles), the failure of socialism in eastern Europe, and a period of debt crises or balance-of-payments crises in developing nations.

The standard or mainstream theoretical approach to understanding what happens to regional inequality as a result of the policy and technological shifts is to continue to think in terms of diminishing returns in the advanced regions. We already know that diminishing returns to capital and factor mobility are considered the key factors that are expected to lead to convergence. Variations on that basic argument are offered for these changing circumstances. For instance, Elizondo and Krugman (1992) suggest that post-reform regional development is likely to be more evenly balanced. They argue that the magnitude of internal trade is much larger than foreign trade in inward-looking trade regimes; "this leads to concentration of production and trading activities in large metropolitan cities ... an opening up of the economy is likely to break the monopoly power of these highly concentrated production and trading centers, weaken the traditional forward and backward linkages and lead to a more even distribution of economic activities across regions." (Das and Barua 1996, 365). Similarly, according to Gilbert (1993, 729), "the cities which benefited most from the previous development model [Lipton's urban bias model] have suddenly had an important prop to their growth removed" in the new model of liberalization and export orientation.

On the other hand, a serious case can be made for the increasing significance of increasing returns as a result of the policy changes. A significant factor influencing comparative regional growth and development is the location of new investment, which, I suggest, is partially a function of the source of investment (see Chakravorty 2003b). That is, state capital is likely to follow a location logic that is different from domestic private capital and even more different from the location logic of foreign capital. State capital (which is increasingly less available for productive purposes) is likely to try to meet some obligation toward regional balance by locating, to some degree, in lagging regions; domestic private capital is under no such social compulsion, and is likely to cluster where there are infrastructure advantages, such as on the edges of metropolitan areas; Foreign capital, as long as it is used to produce for the international market, will tend to locate at coastal points, perhaps near existing ports (this is also true for export-oriented domestic private capital).

There are numerous empirical confirmations of these arguments (discussed earlier). Let us compare what is happening in nations that are geographically non-comparable, say, China and Thailand. Both nations have been receiving large amounts of FDI, but China has a well developed urban hierarchy and a wide variety of urban centers to choose from, whereas Thailand has an urban system (where Bangkok is 50 times larger than the next largest city). China's FDI is coast oriented, with a focus on Guangdong province and the city of Shenzen (proximate to Hong Kong), but in general, the entire central eastern coast stretching up to Shanghai has benefited. In Thailand, unquestionably the overwhelming beneficiary has been the Bangkok metropolitan area, and the interior of the country has barely seen any improvement (Daniere 1996; Ahuja et al. 1997); but, given the economic geography of the country, could anything else have been expected? There is no doubt that in both countries the current regional conditions have been significantly shaped by the location of FDI.

How about India, which, despite liberalizing reforms has received little foreign investment? Here FDI plays virtually no role in shaping the regional development picture, and increasingly, domestic private capital is the determinant of comparative regional conditions. My research (Chakravorty 2000) shows that continued divergence is the reality of India—the lagging states (Bihar, Uttar Pradesh, West Bengal, and Kerala) are the losers, while the already advanced states (Maharashtra, Gujarat, Tamil Nadu, and Karnataka) are the winners; the private sector prefers coastal locations over inland locations (unlike state capital), and metropolitan locations over non-metropolitan ones (but much less so than in the pre-reform period). Investments are being deconcentrated, but within the leading regions rather than between them. In short, it is a situation of "concentrated decentralization."

In fact, it is possible to use economic theory to explain this turn of events in the developing and the developed world, where both have seen rising regional inequality in the last two decades. The Barro and Sala-i-Martin model of convergence is based on the assumption that, because of constant returns to scale and diminishing returns to capital in the leading (urban) regions, new capital formation (or investment) will take place in lagging regions *in the same country*. As long as the cost of transportation was high enough, this reasoning was arguably correct. However, with globalization, capital now has the opportunity to locate virtually anywhere in the world that has transportation links with the rest of the world. This condition gives rise to two outcomes. First, capital now seeks international locations (places with a good combination of skills and low wages), which happen to be the leading regions of developing nations. The wage differentials between leading and lagging regions inside specific countries of the developing world are not very consequential for the price of output. It is more important that there be sufficiently skilled labor and transportation infrastructure available. This leads to divergence in developing nations. Second, many of these new investments would have been made in the lagging regions of developed nations, had the choice of developing nations not been available. Therefore, many new investments that could have led to interregional convergence within developed nations are not made. Therefore, even without assuming that increasing returns actually make leading regions more attractive, it can be argued that the force of diminishing returns alone can lead to interregional divergence in developing and developed nations in a globalized world.

Regional Inequality and Income Inequality

In Chapter 4 we saw that high levels of regional inequality will lead to high levels of income inequality even when social inequality levels are low. In this chapter, we have seen that regional differences in average incomes can be very high; outside of developed nations, these levels can be as high as four-, ten- or even twentyfold. The literature seems to be entangled in the question of whether these differences are increasing or decreasing over time. This certainly is an important question and I will return to it in a moment. But we need to remember that the *structure* of income inequality in a country is determined to a very large extent by the *level* of regional inequality. If India were made up of only two states: Punjab and Bihar, or China were made up of only two provinces: Shanghai and Guizhou, the level of income inequality in India and China would be much higher than what is currently measured. The intraregional social structure could be unchanged, but the sheer magnitude of the interregional difference would make the level of income inequality very high.

The mainstream view among economists is that such large differences cannot persist for long. Because the returns to capital in the high-income region would diminish, and because the factors of non-agricultural production (capital and labor) are mobile, higher quantities of productive investment would flow into the low-income region and raise its growth rate beyond that of the high-income region. We have seen that this is indeed true for developed nations in the long run. Though the Italian or American south has not achieved (and perhaps will never achieve) the prosperity level of their respective norths, the gap has narrowed substantially. Therefore, though the decline in income inequality in these nations (especially the U.S.) is typically ascribed to other social causes (the rise of the middle class, improved educational attainment, lower gaps between the races, etc.), in reality a good proportion of the decline should be attributable to the decline in regional inequality. This has been a form of progressive gradualism.

In the rest of the world, however, the last two hundred years have been marked by regressive gradualism. We do not have the direct data that would allow us to calculate ßs or CoVs or polarization indices. But the circumstantial evidence—on urbanization rates, the process of metropolitanization, the variance in skill and education levels, etc. —allows us to argue strongly that, notwithstanding possible periods of convergence during this long span, regional inequality has been a primary and increasingly important component of income inequality. This gradual move toward higher levels of regional and therefore income inequality may have been slowed down or even marginally reversed during the nationalist or socialist phase in some countries. However, during the current globalization period, there is no doubt that gradual interregional divergence (and therefore increasing income inequality) is the dominant phenomenon—this geographical fragmentation is perhaps the defining feature of globalization.

7

WHERE WE STAND

In the end, I will reconcile the arguments and evidence and try to understand what the future holds. First, let us return to the basic questions listed at the beginning to see whether it is possible to provide concise answers. There are four basic questions: What explains the level of income inequality in a given nation? Why do income inequality levels vary so greatly worldwide? What causes the level of income inequality to change? What explains the diversity of trends in income inequality change? In the first section of this chapter I discuss the answers to these questions. The second section is speculative in the sense that I project our current understanding of social, spatial, and economic theory to suggest what distributional changes lie ahead. This prospective assessment is disappointing for those who desire more egalitarian societies, for I have to conclude that egalitarianism may not be possible in the foreseeable future.

BACK TO BASICS

What Explains the Level of Income Inequality in a Nation?

Let me begin by identifying one factor that does *not* explain the level of income inequality in a nation—the level of development as measured by per capita income. There is one indisputable association between these two variables: high-income nations do not have very high levels of inequality. However, the fact that every other combination of per capita income and inequality exists suggests that if there is a relationship between these two variables it is very weak. Some high-income nations have medium levels of inequality (the U.S., U.K., Australia), some medium-income nations have medium levels of inequality (Slovakia, Slovenia, Poland), and some low-income nations have medium levels of inequality (India, Indonesia). Some low-income nations have high inequality (several in Africa), and some medium-income nations have high inequality (in Latin America). And there are high-income nations with low inequality (in continental Western Europe), medium-income nations with low inequality (in East Asia), and low-income nations with low inequality (Bangladesh, China before the reforms).

Instead of looking at per capita income or economic growth as variables that explain inequality levels, I have focused on two major elements of national structure: social structure and geographical structure. I focused on changes in these structures in the earlier chapters and dealt less directly with the structures themselves. However, the main point is simple: social fragmentation and geographical fragmentation are associated with higher levels of inequality. Let us reexamine the main arguments.

Social Fragmentation How does social fragmentation make a difference, and why? Social fragmentation is a condition in which two or more distinct social groups coexist within a limited space. I have suggested earlier that groups are defined by interests and identity and maintained through consensus and solidarity, where consensus is easier to achieve when the groups are internally homogenous. When a population is racially and ethnically homogenous, two things happen. First, groups form on the basis of class, not race. Second, the differences between the groups are smaller. Hence, consensus formation within groups is easier, and inter-group bias and social inequality levels are lower. When there is social fragmentation the groups compete for scarce resources, and when there are significant power differences between the groups the stronger groups are able to deny the weaker ones many resources, especially those that are needed to build human capital (which is fundamental for building ability). Hence, social fragmentation is strongly associated with social inequality.

If we look for a relationship between per capita income and social inequality we find none. Some low social inequality nations have or have had very low incomes (China), others, such as Sweden and Japan, have very high incomes.[1] There are high-income, high-social-inequality nations (the

U.S., U.K., Australia), and medium-income, high-social-inequality nations (Brazil, Mexico). What is truly puzzling is the fact that all developed nations (which are all capitalist free-trading democracies) do not have similar levels of social inequality. I suggest that the answer lies in the differences in the social structures of these developed nations. The low-social-inequality countries (Sweden, Japan) are relatively homogenous by race and ethnicity, the high-social-inequality (Anglophone) countries have large ethnic minorities who are also the lower-income classes.

Alberto Alesina and Ed Glaeser (2004) provide solid support for the thesis that racial composition is the key difference between the political economic systems in the U.S. and Europe, where the latter have far more activist, redistributive, welfare states. Consider three views: the poor are trapped in poverty, the poor are lazy, and income is determined by luck. American public support for these propositions is 29, 60, and 30 percent, European public support is 60, 24, and 54 percent. In short, the views are diametrically opposite. Americans are more generous when they live among people of their race (as in Alaska) but far less so when they reside close to minorities (as in Alabama); welfare support per family is five times higher in the former than the latter. Note that the views on the poor are from all of Western Europe, despite the presence of the U.K., which, we have noted, has a fairly high level of social inequality. We can extend the same explanation to the U.K. (and Australia) also: it is the presence of a large racial minority that leads to high levels of social inequality; this condition is not mitigated by the state because state power is in the control of the wealthier group, which is unwilling to redistribute to the "other."

Does the mere existence of social heterogeneity lead to social inequality? Consider this question from the perspective of another set of countries: a relatively low-social-inequality pair made up of India and Indonesia and a pair made up of Brazil and Mexico with higher social inequality than the earlier pair. All are large countries. Earlier (in Chapter 5) we saw that the social structures of India and Indonesia differ from those of Mexico and Brazil because of the different colonial histories of the countries. The primary difference is that in the latter the social ladder has at its bottom the descendants of slaves and indentured servants, who were used to work the land and the mines, and the natives, who were clearly identified and treated as lower-class citizens. Therefore, the Latin American nations entered and passed through the twentieth century with deep social inequalities. India's traditional social hierarchy (the caste system) had many problems, but did not approach the intense division that a system of slavery brings.

In short, the social inequalities of given nations are historical legacies, sustained over long periods because they are based on social norms that we know to be durable. Two points are of note. First, I recognize the argument made by many that race is a social construction, but I leave open the strong possibility that it has sociobiological bases (as discussed in Chapter 4, where I discussed the evolutionary arguments for group formation), and suggest that even if there is no biological basis for group formation, groups remain potent organizational units. All social divisions are social constructions. The enduring ones are those that have been woven into the fabric of social life through myth, symbol, narrative, and power. Second, despite the durability of social norms they are, nonetheless, malleable. In Chapter 5 I discussed in detail how this is possible through reforms undertaken by insiders (by mutation and adaptation). A grand theme of post-World War II social history in many countries is the narrowing of group differences: in the U.S., in Brazil, in India, etc. The differences have not vanished by any means, because the systematic human capital deficits of the weaker groups that have accumulated over centuries cannot wash away in decades.[2]

Geographical Fragmentation Just as social heterogeneity creates cleavages in society, so does geographical heterogeneity. I do not mean that physical geography makes a major difference, but that the economic geography of a nation can be so fractured (based sometimes on physical geography features) that its citizens in different regions do not have access to the same opportunities or life chances. We know why these cleavages exist: industry is more productive than agriculture, modern sectors are more productive than traditional ones. The modern sectors cluster in cities. Hence, cities have higher average incomes than villages, urban regions have higher average incomes than rural ones. We also know that these geographical differences can be very large. It is possible to make two generalizations about these differences. First, the smaller the geographical unit of comparison, the larger is the difference between units. Second, geographical inequalities are lower in developed nations. Let us consider these facts in detail.

First: if a country is composed of several regions, each of which can be disaggregated into provinces, each of which can be disaggregated into districts, then the largest differences will be between districts and the smallest between regions. At every higher level of geographical aggregation there is less variance. Therefore, the inequalities typically calculated and analyzed (as in Chapter 6) are the smallest geographical inequalities in a nation. What does this mean for income inequality? Certainly the level of inequality is higher when there is more geographical heterogeneity. But just as important is the idea that these inequalities are likely to be reproduced and even magnified between generations when many of the essential inputs for human capital formation are provided with local resources.

Take the case of a low-regional-inequality country such as the U.S. Depending on how the state constitution is written, public schools may be funded using different combinations of local and state money. Where I live, in the Philadelphia region in the state of Pennsylvania on the U.S. east coast, public schools are generally funded with local taxes. The Philadelphia metropolitan region is broken into more than 300 smaller localities, most with their own public school systems. The spending per student in the wealthiest municipalities is twice as high as in the poorest. That is, within the metropolitan region itself, there are vast differences in the distribution of resources for human capital formation. If one considers the whole nation, spending per student in the wealthiest municipalities is up to 10 times as much as in the poorest municipalities, where teachers are paid less and have inferior credentials, libraries and laboratories have fewer and inferior resources, and there are few if any extramural programs. As a result, it is simply not possible for persons of equal genetic "ability" to reach anywhere close to the same levels of human capital acquisition in these very unequal public schools. And because wealthier schools are in desirable municipalities, their property values increase, enabling them to invest even higher amounts in their schools and to make them more desirable. The wealthy municipalities are in a virtuous cycle of cumulative causation, the poor ones are in a vicious cycle. Remember that this is the story in a nation with low regional inequality. It is easy to imagine that there are very large differences between good urban schools and poor village schools in a high-regional-inequality country such as India (see Drèze and Sen 1998).

Second, at almost any scale we consider the data, developed nations have less geographical inequality than developing nations. One of the obvious findings from Chapter 6 is that all the countries with low levels of regional inequality are high-income countries (even if regional inequalities have increased there in the last two decades), and all the countries with high regional inequality are low- and medium-income countries. It is apparent that country size does not matter. The U.S. and

Japan are large countries (the latter by population) with low levels of regional inequality. The countries with high levels of regional inequality (Brazil, Mexico, Russia, China, India, Indonesia) are all also large. It is clear that the level of economic development plays a role in determining the extent of geographical heterogeneity in a nation. Let us consider why.

We know from earlier discussions that sooner or later there should be diminishing returns to capital in a leading region. If the factors of production are mobile, then new investments should flow to lagging regions where the returns to capital should be higher, and labor from lagging regions should move to leading regions where wages are higher. This should raise productivity and income in the lagging regions, lower wages in the leading regions, and close the average income gap. This has happened in developed nations to a much greater extent than it has happened in developing nations. Why? I suggest two reasons. Following the discussions in earlier chapters, especially Chapter 6, we can look to the state and state ideology, which, whether based on expropriation or reinvestment, has favored cities to maximize growth. Even redistributive states (such as the Soviet Union) have favored urban industrialization in leading regions.[3] As a result, growth in advantaged regions has been propped up by state investments, in infrastructure at a minimum, and by state policies on industrialization, agriculture, exports, etc. Second, it is possible that the factors of production are not as mobile in developing nations. Capital is less mobile because there are significant scale and agglomeration economies to be realized in urban settings. Labor is less mobile, especially in ethnically heterogeneous states, because of the problems associated with out-group bias; migrants face group hostility at their destinations, which acts as a deterrent for potential migrants.

Why Do Income Inequality Levels Vary So Greatly Worldwide?

The levels of income inequality in different nations of the world today are the results of two major influences: first, historical legacies that date back several decades, even centuries, which suggests that the level of inequality at any given point is path dependent; and second, increasing returns in social systems and spatial structures. We can identify three specific ways in which the past continues to influence the distribution patterns of the present, and two ways in which increasing returns are important. Let us look at the role of history first.

Path Dependence   First, we have to consider the social formation of each territorial unit. Each nation is made up of a particular combination of population groups. We know that when these groups are internally consistent and when one group dominates another in paired situations, social inequality is the outcome. These inequalities persist for very long periods. Though, in many countries, developed and developing, these inequalities have declined over the last half century—for instance, racial inequalities have declined in the U.S., Brazil, and South Africa, caste inequalities have declined in India, and ethnic inequalities have declined in Malaysia—the inequality levels continue to be either quite high (as in Brazil) or very high (as in South Africa).[4]

Thus, the historical circumstances that have brought unequally powered groups together have planted the seeds of persistent social inequality. Wherever there has been slavery, or wherever there has been colonization (without subsequent decolonization), we can see that social inequality between races and ethnic groups is a serious issue. The worst situations are those where there have been both slavery and colonization. The weaker groups (descendants of slaves and colonized peoples) continue to have less capital, less education, less land, less opportunity, less voice, less influence, less income. Nations differ in their group formations as a result of the varieties of migration streams, wars, expulsions, invasions, alliances, and colonial and imperial enterprises. In general, when clearly demarcated dominant and dominated groups coexist, social inequality is a common outcome.

Second, we must recognize that inter-group bias becomes part of the social structure through the creation of social norms that are very durable. This is the principal reason for the persistence of differences between groups. The extreme cases of out-group derogation are seen in white/black situations. Slavery as an institution was legal less than 150 years ago in the U.S. Less than 100 years ago, Africans were exhibited along with animals in circuses. Less than 40 years ago, blacks could not eat, drink, or sleep where whites did. A decade ago, a policy bestseller sought to prove, with the approval and admiration of many, that blacks simply did not have the intelligence of other races and were effectively not educable to their standards (Herrnstein and Murray 1994). Myths of racial or ethnic superiority are commonplace in world history. Victorious groups have generally presumed that their victories have come from superior intelligence, culture, and values that are intrinsic to the group. The privileges of victorious or more powerful groups are institutionalized, given legal foundation, and enforced using the power of the state. These institutions too are durable. When durable norms form the basis of durable institutions it is very difficult for weaker groups to have equal access to the resources that generate human capital. Nations differ in the norms and institutions that promote inter-group bias and in the reforms that have mitigated these biases.

Third, national histories are marked by different punctuation points, which are state transitions that have significantly altered inter-group relations. I discussed the issue of punctuations extensively in Chapter 5 and showed that fundamental distributional changes have resulted from specific types of transitions. It is useful to remember that many of these transitions did not seek to alter inter-ethnic differences as much as they transformed inter-class differences.[5] Nevertheless, these transitions have radically changed some norms and most institutions that bear on inheritance and human capital formation. Would anyone question the assertion that, had South Korea and Taiwan not been occupied by the Americans at the end of World War II, whereby fundamental changes to the land ownership system were instituted, the levels of income inequality in those countries would have been very different from what they are now? Different nations have different punctuations. Some have had several (Russia, China) and some none at all (the Scandinavian nations, for example). Each punctuation has altered the narrative of inequality.

Increasing Returns Nations also differ in the extent of increasing returns. Two forms of increasing returns have significance for income generation. There are intergenerational increasing returns and geographical increasing returns. The former refers to the idea that individuals with higher levels of property and capital inheritance are able to invest more in acquiring human capital. Intergenerational increasing returns are also possible through social norms that encourage or dictate marriage between status equals, a process known as homogamy or assortative mating. Norms and laws on miscegenation were created to ensure marriage between status equals in the same race, ethnic group, or caste in order to maintain inter-group differences. It is easy to see that when both marriage partners have land they are able to bequeath more to their offspring than when only one partner has land or neither do. Not only does non-genetic inheritance have the potential to generate income directly (through rent and interest), but by providing better access to human capital resources, this form of inheritance further advantages the already well-endowed individuals. Hence, asset or property inequalities increase between generations, not only for individuals but for groups. Nations differ in the extent to which they tax property and capital inheritance. Welfare states in Europe tax inheritance quite heavily; several developing nations states also do so, but several developed nations (such as the U.S.) and most developing nations tax inheritance minimally.

Geographical increasing returns affect income distribution in two ways. As discussed in Chapter 6, proximity and density improve firm level productivity by improving inter-firm transactions, knowledge pooling and spillovers, and access to labor markets. These increasing returns provide advantages to spatially clustered firms over spatially isolated firms. Hence, firms cluster, and where they cluster, large cities emerge. Aside from pure market forces, clustering processes are aided by state actions that provide some elements of the necessary infrastructure only in cities, and by state policies that encourage urban over agricultural production. Nations differ in the extent to which state action abets urbanization and metropolitanization.

The second type of geographical increasing returns comes, as discussed earlier in this chapter, from the fact that the essential elements of human capital are made available at local scales. The quality of schools and access to them depend on local incomes and local social structure. Because localities differ enormously in per capita income (remember that income variance is inversely proportional to the size of unit of analysis), it follows that localities have very large differences in the quality of schooling. Moreover, low-income localities may have stronger barriers between groups that may diminish access by low-income groups. As shown earlier, these differences between localities have exponential effects, creating virtuous cycles in some and vicious cycles in others. Nations differ in the extent of geographical fragmentation and the resultant advantages for some individuals and groups.

What Causes The Level of Income Inequality to Change?

Following the argument that income inequality in a nation is a function of social inequality (or fragmentation) and geographical inequality (or fragmentation), it follows that changes in income inequality take place as a result of changes to social and/or spatial inequality. I have dealt with this argument in detail in the preceding chapters. Let me reiterate some of the key elements.

Consider changes to social inequality first. I have suggested that these changes can happen in two ways: as a result of gradualism (incremental changes over long periods of time) or punctuations (sudden, rapid, fundamental changes). In Chapter 5 I focused on the latter. I showed how distributional change in general can be understood as the outcome of the actions of change agents with specific ideologies, and how punctuations are changes brought about by outsiders/revolutionaries and gradual changes are reforms led by insiders. Distributional punctuations are rapid changes during state transition; the old ruling structure is replaced virtually overnight, productive assets are redistributed from powerful groups to weaker ones (or vice versa), and the legal structure is changed to support the new ideology and system of distribution. There are several examples of punctuated distributional change including revolutionary socialism, theocratic and peasant revolutions, and postwar reconstructions.

Gradualist distributional changes are slow, operating over several decades, initiated by social reformers who question the existing norms and social structure. Because insiders cannot and will not introduce revolutionary distributional change, the only possible form of distributional change when state transitions do not take place is gradualism. Therefore, stable states (usually democracies) experience gradual changes in social inequality. In many instances, these changes result in the creation of new groups (pluralism) because markets and individualism increase within-group inequalities. The creation of new groups may cause between-group inequalities to decline. Because between-group inequalities are more important in creating social inequality, the overall effect of gradualism, in many countries, is for social inequality to decline. This is a good case scenario. There are bad cases where between-group inequalities increase or are exacerbated to the point where groups seek violent resolution using riots, ethnic cleansing, or genocide.

The other source of inequality change is from changes in spatial inequality. These changes can only be gradual because changes in spatial inequality are slow. It takes many years for a city to grow, and decades for its income to become high enough that it must then be considered a geographical fragment. Similarly, it takes time for other cities to rise and challenge the economic domination of the leading cities. Therefore, whichever way spatial inequality goes, it goes slowly. The last two hundred years have seen the rise of many new cities, most of which are in the developing world. These cities have fragmented the national space into chunks of low-income agricultural regions and slivers of high-income urban and metropolitan regions. In much of the world, these have been years of increasing regional inequality.

What Explains the Diversity of Trends in Income Inequality Change?

I began this book with the argument, backed up by evidence in the preceding chapters, that three forms of inequality change are possible —increase, decrease, or none at all—and that each country has the potential to experience all three forms of inequality change over the long run. Let me now reconcile this reality with the argument that social inequality and spatial inequality are the two sources of income inequality change. There are four possible combinations of social and spatial inequality change: both can increase (in which case income inequality increases), both can decrease (in which case income inequality decreases), or two combinations where one can increase while the other decreases (in which case the impact on income inequality becomes indeterminate). Let us look at what we can deduce from the evidence offered in the earlier chapters.

I discussed the possibility that social and spatial inequality have actually changed in different directions in the last half century in many, perhaps most, developing nations. Social inequalities have declined while spatial inequalities have increased. There is a fair amount of evidence that the latter half of the statement is true (some of which has been documented in Chapter 6). There is less direct evidence that social inequalities (especially at the local level) have declined, though in many cases (the U.S., India, Malaysia, China), there is such evidence at the national or regional scale. I suggest that there is enough guidance from theory (discussed in Chapters 4 and 5), and enough circumstantial evidence to argue that, in the post-1950 period, social inequalities have declined and spatial inequalities have increased in most nations. It is difficult to be sure of the magnitude of change, but it is possible that the most common trend in distributional change—which is the absence of change—is explained by the fact that these two variables have moved in opposite directions. This is an important point whose implications are discussed later in this section.

What about the other possibility: that social inequalities have increased and spatial inequalities decreased? This is an unlikely scenario. First, spatial inequalities have decreased only in developed nations (a process that has been arrested and even reversed in the last two decades) where social inequalities have declined dramatically over the same period. There is no evidence of sustained declines in spatial inequality anywhere in the developing world. Moreover, it is difficult to think of conditions under which such a combination would be possible. Hence, I conclude that *a stylized fact of modern economic development is the combined long-term trend of declining social inequality with increasing spatial inequality.*

The diversity of trends in income inequality change can, therefore, be explained in terms of the relative movements of spatial and social inequality. Income inequality has increased in those countries where both social and spatial inequalities have increased (Russia in the 1990s is a good example of this phenomenon), or where the effect of spatial inequality increases have had stronger overall effects than social inequality declines; that is, where geographical fragmentation has had a more dominant effect on the distribution of income. We can think of China from the mid-1980s as a prime example of this type of change. In places where income inequalities have declined, it is likely that both social and spatial inequality have declined. It is possible for only one variable to have declined (usually that would be social inequality) and have had a stronger effect on overall distribution. Many developed nations during the middle third of the twentieth century belong in this group.

Finally, the most common phenomenon, that of the absence of distributional change, can be attributed to the fact that social and spatial inequality have changed in different directions. This argument makes it possible to understand the common phenomenon where the level of income inequality appears to oscillate around a steady mean, as we have seen in high-inequality nations such as Brazil and medium-inequality nations such as India. The disturbances to the mean are caused by short-term changes (such as droughts in parts of the country) that temporarily change either social or spatial inequality in such ways that one change dominates the other. However, these oscillations do not alter the long-term trends in social or spatial inequality, which is why the level of income inequality tends back toward the mean.

GLOBALIZATION AND THE FUTURE OF INCOME INEQUALITY

Is it possible to predict how income inequality in specific nations or groups of nations will change in the future, say over the next one to two decades? If the theoretical approach used here is more or less correct, it should be possible to at least identify the factors that can be expected to have a bearing on the shape of income inequality. We need to begin by agreeing that any discussion of the near future of inequality has to take place in the context of globalization. Earlier, in Chapter 3, I argued that globalization is not merely the integration of global markets through trade. It is that, but it is more. Globalization also encompasses a large number of other changes with significance for income distribution, which, in terms of the analysis done here, can be subsumed under a single category: ideology. Let us see why that is:

- In principle, globalization is a process involving international trade and technological change. What distinguishes it from past decades, during which both trade and technological change took place, is the volume or intensity. Today there is more trade and more technological change (especially in communication) at greater speeds than ever before. Let us call this process techno-economic globalization.
- The intensity of techno-economic globalization is very uneven worldwide. Some regions within some nations are actively and deeply involved in it, some regions are marginally involved, other regions in the same nations and entire other nations are not at all involved. Chapter 3 detailed the differences among nations, Chapter 6 detailed the differences among regions within nations.
- Aside from techno-economic globalization, there exists a more widespread phenomenon that we can call ideological globalization. This includes the ideas on markets, trade, democracy, and governance that underlie economic globalization. Ideological globalization is of great significance everywhere, but in cities and regions that are relatively untouched by techno-economic globalization, it may be of more consequence.
- To understand the impact of globalization on inequality it is therefore necessary to consider the joint effect of techno-economic and ideological globalization on social and spatial inequality.

Ideology and Social Change

Let me begin by maintaining the distinction, first reported in Chapter 3, between developed and developing nations as far as globalization is concerned. Techno-economic globalization is a far stronger phenomenon in the former than the latter. But, for either set of countries, it is difficult to make the case that globalization is an institutional transition on the scale of colonialism or independence; certainly we cannot compare the direct distributional effects of techno-economic globalization with that of revolution or war and its aftermath. In the official "transition" economies of Eastern Europe and the post-Soviet countries, a significant transition has taken place during the same period, but there the distributional outcomes have depended on history and ideology rather than the economics of globalization. Neither are the effects of techno-economic globalization similar in countries where, a priori, we could expect them to be. For instance, some globalizing nations (such as France) have reduced inequality at the same time that other globalizing nations (such as the U.K.) have had significant increases.

It is not my intention to suggest a one-size-fits-all answer to a question that many good scholars have grappled with without reaching consensus. Let me instead, in this speculative mode, think of the problem in terms of what we already know. Progressive social change involves two elements: the narrowing of within-group inequalities, and, more important, the narrowing of between-group differences. We know that most ideologies that have directly or indirectly sought distributional change have done so by changing between-group differences. We know that social fragmentation is an artifact of histories of inter-group domination and subjugation which makes progressive change difficult even today; we also know that invasive ideologies often lead to distributional transitions. Keeping these facts in mind, we can begin framing the key question on globalization and social change: How do the most important elements of the new governance paradigm—which are market-orientation for resource allocation and democracy for identifying the rulers—affect income distribution?

Market orientation is an article of faith of ideological globalization. Do markets, by themselves, increase inequalities (as is alleged by any number of analysts)? It is actually impossible to answer this question without knowing what came before. If markets are something new, they must be replacing something old. If that something old was a system of deep social inequalities (clear group identities and large between-group differences), then marketization is likely to have an equalizing effect. It is difficult to imagine that the existing strong groups, especially if they are numerical minorities, would be able to capture even more of the income-producing resources under a market system than they did under a system of expropriation. If, on the other hand, markets are introduced in places where there are few social differences (there is social homogeneity, easy consensus formation, reciprocity and redistribution), then there is a strong possibility that income inequalities will increase. Hence, markets alone do not necessarily increase inequality. Rather, markets can enable new and different group formations, which result in different forms of social inequality. As discussed in Chapter 5, when some of the most fundamental human needs—security and insurance—are met through market institutions, the need for groups to provide these essential services diminishes. There is less reciprocity and redistribution within groups, more status-seeking behavior, and an increase in within-group inequalities to the extent that some group identities can wither away. When group identities are tenuous, inter-group bias is also less severe, as a result of which between-group inequalities should decline. In short, under these conditions, identity-based differences are supplanted by class-based differences.

The overall effect of these changes is unclear and many questions remain. Do between-group inequalities decline more or do within-group inequalities increase more? Is it really possible for markets to wash away fundamental ideas about identity? Can class trump race and ethnicity? Can organization on the basis of class be as effective as that based on ascribed identity? Can lower-income classes organize as effectively as upper-income classes, especially when the possibility of class mobility exists?

I expect there are no single answers to these questions, rather that every society works out a relatively stable formation based on its social composition and history. Hence, social and income inequality may increase or decrease as a result of marketization, but whatever happens, the process is slow. Fundamental identities are not lost or gained overnight. In fact, in the short run at least, identity politics and spatially based inter-group conflict may be the defining feature of distributional politics (I take up this idea in more detail in the next section). The experience of the developed nations suggests that, over the long run, social inequalities do decline in market economies. We do not know how much of this decline is due to the existence of markets, how much due to successful bargaining by weaker groups, and how much due to ideological mutation and adaptation within stronger groups. (I find it difficult to imagine that a powerful group would voluntarily give up any advantage without some mutation and norm change.) Therefore, if globalization introduces markets in largely non-market societies, it is possible that, in the long run, social inequalities will decline, not necessarily directly because of markets, but possibly because of the indirect effects of markets. In the short run, however, any outcome is possible.

The second major plank of ideological globalization is to rely on democratic politics for identifying the rulers and the rules of decision-making. Democracies, for all their merits, are unable to change social or class differences quickly. This is good in one sense because social inequalities are unlikely to increase rapidly in democracies, but they are unlikely to decline rapidly either. The actions necessary to quickly move to progressive distribution patterns are well known—take income-producing resources from groups and classes who hoard them and redistribute to those groups and classes that do not have them. These actions are also bound to create significant social unrest as the resource hoarders are unlikely to give them up without a fight. Democracies tend to avoid unrest. They choose the soft options, populist measures such as subsidized electricity, or rice, or drinking water, where the subsidies, more often than not, are disproportionately captured by the well-to-do. Nevertheless, under democratic systems, it is possible for social inequalities to decrease slowly, usually using affirmative-action policies that gradually provide better access to education and employment to weaker, but often more populous groups. Rapid changes are not possible, but progressive incrementalism is possible and likely.

Ideology and Spatial Change

We have to be very careful about prognosticating on the future of social inequality, but much less so when we consider the future of spatial inequality during globalization. As shown earlier (in Chapter 6), in the last two decades regional inequalities have increased in almost every country and region we have considered, from the U.S. and Europe to China, Russia, India, Brazil, and Mexico. Some of this increasing regional divergence and fragmentation is caused directly by techno-economic globalization (due to uneven global flows of capital and technology). I suggest that ideological globalization simply adds to this process of divergence. Let me explain.

Ideological globalization has three tenets that have spatial significance (these derive basically from the "markets" and "democracy" arguments considered above). First, trade and markets are considered good: cities are natural locations of trade; therefore cities must be encouraged. Markets allocate resources efficiently; hence cities must become more market-oriented. Second, decentralization is considered good, it encourages local decision-making and democratic processes; hence, governments must decentralize money and power to local bodies (municipalities). Third, good governance (just, inclusive, transparent government) can cushion the shocks of openness while making cities more attractive for investment; good governance must be the goal of local governing bodies. On the surface, these are laudable principles indeed, but their implications for lagging regions are not quite positive.

Consider the emphasis on trade and markets first. To trade, a city or region must produce something that others (cities and regions) want —whether it is plastics or metals or information or entertainment, there must be some exportable good or service that can be sold at some market (a global market if possible, or at least a national or regional market). The problem of the lagging cities and regions is essentially this: they receive little new productive investment, therefore they can- *unequal* not competitively produce for global markets, and often the regional *exchange* markets are so impoverished that they cannot absorb new products with new technologies built in. These cities are very far down in the value chains of manufacturing, whereby the value added per unit of labor or capital is very low (Kaplinski 2001). Not only are these cities virtually absent from global systems of production and exchange, if by some unusual circumstance some of these cities were to become part of the global trade in manufactured goods, the value added would be too low to move these cities out of the periphery. This at a time when the leading cities and regions continue to strengthen their global trading links and keep moving up the value chain. It seems inevitable that opening markets and relying on global trade will increase productivity and incomes in the leading cities relative to lagging ones.[6]

Now consider decentralization. Decentralization calls for devolution of revenue and authority to local government bodies, which then increasingly become responsible for local services and planning. In theory, this would have the advantage of increased democratization and public participation and curb the influence of large cities and other traditional centers of authority. In practice, however, decentralization creates a new set of problems that work once again to the detriment of the peripheral cities and regions. For decentralization to be effective, it is necessary to have supportive institutions and human capital at the local level. Such institutions and human capital are not readily available even in many of the large cities of the developing world (where formal urban planning as opposed to urban public works or services began as late as in the 1960s); urban planners are not available, urban planning schools do not exist (or where they do exist they tend to be technocratic institutions), and infrastructure finance institutions are virtually unheard of.

In such situations what kind of municipal planning and development can small and medium-sized cities undertake? What happens and is likely to happen (see the case of Bolivia in Kohl 2002, or China in Kanbur and Zhang 2003) is that the larger cities, despite having to share resources, are better able to take advantage of decentralization and devolution as a result of a freer hand in local decision-making and revenue generation. (See World Bank 2000, Tables D4 and D5, on large-city advantages in terms of size of local government and revenues raised by it.) It is possible to identify exceptions to this statement (in Brazil, China, and India for instance), to identify specific medium-sized cities that have done well in terms of economic growth, but in most cases, their successes have arisen from locational advantages (usually by being on the coast) and, in rare cases, from inspired leadership. In the general case, decentralization leads to further marginalization of the already disadvantaged, nowhere more so than in the small and medium-sized cities in inland regions.

Finally, the push to institutionalize inclusive governance raises a particularly problematic issue: that identity-based politics can lead to serious social divisions. In multi-ethnic societies the ethnic composition of cities tends to change quite rapidly as a result of growth. New migrants from different ethnic groups move there for work; this changes the composition of the population and may result in political struggles over control of state resources. In some scenarios, these struggles sporadically flare up into ethnic violence (in India, Pakistan, Indonesia, Nigeria, Kenya), and in worse scenarios, they result in all-out civil war (in several nations of Africa). The bigger problem is in the cities that are not growing; there the perceived absence of opportunity and relative ethnic homogeneity leads to parochial regional politics —identity-based politics that morphs into ethnic nationalism, tribalism, separatism, and violence. It is necessary to recognize that one of the ideological counterpoints to economic globalization is identity politics. It is possible for corporate theorists to declare the end of the nation state, and to promote the birth of a neo-utopian "true global marketplace" (Ohmae 1995). But when the GNP of China is US$317 while that of Shenzen in China is US$5,695 (Ohmae's figures) is it irrational to expect parochialism and jingoism under the banner of that other global invention of the nineteenth century—nationalism? China's social homogeneity (combined with its autocratic police regime) may keep the lid on demands for change, but in other less homogenous or soft states such stark divisions are likely to lead to serious conflicts.

I do not suggest that the principles of "good governance" necessarily work against the prospects of lagging cities and regions. Indeed, urban violence is very much in evidence in many regional leaders too (Mumbai, Ahmedabad, Jakarta). What is worrisome is the possibility of rejection of good governance principles, along with a rejection of globalization in the lagging cities. In these relatively static, growth-deprived places, there are few internal challenges spurred by inter-ethnic competition. Instead, we tend to see the continuation of power oligarchies and entrenched interests, which often coalesce into regional ethnic identity politics. Governance takes a backseat to regional mobilization, and in the eyes of investors, foreign and domestic alike, these places appear to be anachronisms. It is not the nation-state per se that appears tired, old, and outdated (as many have suggested, see Rohlen 2002), but the state in lagging cities and regions that appears tired, old, and unable to keep up with the flashy globalizers. Albert Hirschman's words (1973, 49) on the "tunnel effect" now have renewed urgency:

> One might conclude that the tunnel effect will always come into being as, within each social class, those who are not advancing empathize initially with those who are. But this need not happen if each class is composed of ethnic or religious groups that are differentially involved in the growth process.... If, in segmented societies, economic advance becomes identified with one particular ethnic or language group or with members of one particular religion or region, then those who are left out or behind are unlikely to experience the tunnel effect: they will be convinced almost from the start of the process that the advancing group is achieving an unfair exploitative advantage over them.

Therefore, the geographical dimension of inequality is very important. The existence and proliferation of "spatial poverty traps" (see Jalan and Ravallion 1997) in many rural areas of most developing nations has already been recognized in the literature. I have argued that the most direct impact of globalization may be in geographical restructuring resulting in increased regional inequality, which can often lead to increased income inequality. This suggests the existence of "regional poverty traps" such as Bihar in India. Paradoxically, these regions, which are virtually unconnected to global trade networks, may be more acutely affected by globalization than regions that actually are part of global trade. The low average income of these regions is in all likelihood the critical element driving inequality indices upward at the national level. The arguments and evidence presented here make a strong case for focusing analysis and policy at the regional level.

Is Egalitarianism Feasible?

I have to end on a pessimistic note. If my arguments are correct, then globalization holds the promise of delivering lower levels of social inequality along with the threat of higher levels of spatial inequality. However, the latter is very much more certain than is the former. There is no surety that social inequalities will decline in most places, whereas it seems quite definite that spatial inequalities will increase. I have already discussed the main reasons that this is the likely scenario in the short and medium term. If true, this would continue the trend of the last two decades all over the world. The pessimism arises from the details of these general trends:

- First, the effect of increasing spatial inequality seems to be stronger than the effect of decreasing social inequality. Certainly there is a limit to how low social inequality can go (at best, all groups will have equal average incomes) but there is no limit, in theory, to how high spatial inequalities can become.
- Second, the possibility of egalitarian transitions do not appear to exist any longer; socialism is defunct, even serious land reform is not considered a major policy alternative anywhere.
- Third, the only transitions that have recently taken place are inegalitarian ones. Russia probably has a higher income inequality today than at anytime in its history, including the reigns of the most deplorable czars.
- Fourth, the differences between places on a global scale are truly staggering. It is difficult to imagine that the residents of New York City's Upper East Side and the millions who reside in the impoverished hand-to-mouth villages of north Bihar or Sudan share the same planet. These differences too are greater than they have ever been, despite this being a time when people have more information about each other than ever before.
- Fifth, in many countries there appears to be a recent hardening of attitudes toward minorities and weaker groups, an increased tendency to claim individual authorship of financial success, a rejection of the critical role of the public sphere, and a growth of rhetoric extolling the virtues of self-interest and unfettered markets.

Perhaps it is my personal location in two countries (India and the U.S.) with these characteristics that has biased my perception. Perhaps the antidote for this pessimism is not to look at the national picture, but at the local level. It is possible that the positive potential of globalization lies in the long run and at the small scale, and by focusing on the short run (a decade or two) and the large scale (the nation) the negatives appear to outweigh the positives. This is another way of saying that we should pay more attention to poverty reduction and less to income distribution. Without doubt, one of the most important challenges facing the world is the reduction and elimination of absolute poverty. But, it is necessary not to lose sight of the other important challenge of our time, the promise of equal opportunity.

NOTES

Chapter 1

1. These numbers are reported in the World Bank's World Development Reports of different years. Much more detailed data are presented in Chapter 2.

2. This is true not only in the normative sense that economic growth should be fair and inclusive, but also in a pragmatic sense because poverty alleviation is jointly influenced by both growth and distribution.

3. There are strong and growing dissident movements in economics. These so-called "non-autistic" approaches are far more successful in incorporating social reality into their theoretical framework. This book can be read as a contribution to this non-autistic literature.

4. Following Gerhard Lenski (1972) it is possible to use another metaphor to explain why this critique may not always apply. Think of water being boiled in a container. It is possible to predict with great accuracy what the effect of heat will be on volume and pressure, yet have little idea about how individuals water molecules behave from moment to moment. The water molecules are like individuals, the volume of water is like a system. One cannot exactly tell what happens at the individual level while having a pretty good idea about what happens at the systemic level.

Chapter 2

1. See for instance, Sen (1992) who in a footnote on inequality measurement cited over one hundred references.

2. See http://www.worldbank.org/poverty/inequal/methods/.

3. See also approaches and measures based on people's views on distributional comparisons or fairness, first identified by van Praag (1968) and summarized recently in Amiel (1998).

4. Earlier United Nations compilations (1981, 1985) were not as substantial as these three.

5. I am deeply indebted to WIDER for having created and provided public access to this resource. This part of the book would have been much impoverished without these data. After this book was written WIDER released a new beta version of a data set that includes more current estimates of inequality. Very few of these estimates are brand new and most are not yet "certified" by WIDER. With few exceptions, I have avoided using these newest data. I am also indebted to the Luxembourg Income Study (LIS) that is undertaking a serious effort to generate inequality data comparable over time and space. The LIS Working Paper series is also an excellent resource for current economic thinking and analysis on inequality in developed nations.

6. A dissenting view, that in the 1990s inequality in Canada has increased, along with globalization, can be found in Breau (2002). Indeed, the argument that globalization has led to increasing inequality virtually everywhere is commonplace; it is one of the basic planks of anti-globalization. I will discuss this argument in detail in Chapters 3, 6, and 7.

7. Economic historians have been able to compile some very interesting estimates on inequality in the U.K. over the last 300 years. Jackson (1994) reports (from the work of others) that in the mid nineteenth century the Gini index of England and Wales was more than 50, and by 1913 inequality was around the same or slightly lower level.

8. Milanovic quotes a study of the of the OECD countries where inequality increased most rapidly in the 1980s: the U.K., the U.S., etc. The Ginis in these OECD countries grew by about 0.5 points per year; in contrast, in the transition economies the Ginis grew by about 1.5 points per year.

Chapter 3

1. For instance, "political theory has...a "split mind"...On the one hand are the cold, spare, formalistic, rationalistic glass-and-steel constructions of liberal political theory; on the other, the warm, rich, substantive, emotive, and possibly suffocating ancestral dwellings (real or imagined) of communitarian theory" (Goerner and Thompson 1996, 620).

2. It is easy to imagine that a villager in north Bihar in India can be born with extraordinary musical or mathematical ability; yet, because he does not receive adequate education and/ or training, or lacks the necessary "cultural capital," he may live life as a semi-literate farmer earning a fraction of what his talent would have commanded in a world of perfect information and mobility.

3. Many analysts find the idea ludicrous that individuals can make lifetime calculations with absolute foreknowledge of interest rates; but this line of theorizing is widely accepted among mainstream economists.

4. At the center of the standard neoclassical model of growth (Solow 1956) also is a similar link with savings. In a recent survey of the empirical evidence on the savings-inequality link Schmidt-Hebbel and Servén (2000, 417) conclude that there is "no support for the notion that income inequality has any systematic effect on aggregate saving." This is not necessarily the last word on the subject because, as with the growth-inequality relationship, the findings and conclusions depend substantially on definitions and the scale of the studies.

5. According to Alesina and Rodrik (1994): "... any government is likely to be responsive to the wishes of the majority when key distributional issues are at stake ... even in a dictatorship distributional issues affecting the majority of the population will influence policy decisions. Hence, distributive struggles harmful to growth are more likely to take place when resources are distributed unevenly."

6. For instance, in one of the most recent of these studies (Forbes 2000), to make the Gini coefficients based on income consistent with those based on expenditure, the author follows Deininger and Squire's "suggestion" and adds 6.6 to the Gini coefficient of the latter. This number is nothing but a very general approximation, and the adjustment, in my view, does little to make the data consistent; in fact, this addition probably introduces serious distortions.

7. It is necessary to point out that Temple finds reasons to support cross-sectional growth analysis, despite the many problems he identifies.

8. The equality-to-growth theorization presumes that more equal distributions *directly* lead to better growth performances instead of taking the more reasonable line that a particular set of social and ideological conditions produce both more equal distributions and superior growth performance. The former argument suggests that "initial conditions," however created, guide subsequent situations; similar initial conditions, therefore, produce similar end conditions. I suggest that it is more important to know how the

initial conditions were produced; subsequent situations are likely to be influenced at least as much by how the initial conditions were produced.

9. In fact, the anti-globalization protests are themselves seen to be part of globalization (Sen 2002) and can be interpreted to suggest that the U.S. is the most anti-global nation (Robertson 2002).

10. There is debate over whether globalization is led by technological change in transportation and communication, or by policy changes that have allowed trade to flourish. Paul Krugman (1995, 328) argues that "the growth of trade [has] essentially political causes, seeing its great expansion after World War II largely as a result of the removal of the protectionist measures that had constricted world markets since 1913."

11. I am not even considering questions on the relative importance of international trade compared with domestic policy changes in these countries (see Mulé, 2001, on the significance of public policy in developed nations).

12. A question that has not been addressed in the literature gives one pause: What would have been the distributional impact of technological change without trade liberalization? If plastic goods were still made in the U.S. instead of being imported from China, would the U.S. and Chinese income distributions be more equal, given that all other technological changes in production and distribution would have continued unabated? It is possible to reasonably argue that it would have led to more inequality in the U.S., primarily as a result of the even higher skill premium at the technological leading edge. On the other hand, if plastic production is the leading edge in China, less of it would probably lead to less unequal distributions.

13. This argument has been suggested by dependency theorists, who argue that inequality in a country varies in proportion to the extent of multinational corporation (MNC) penetration in it. Again cross-country regressions are used to show that this relationship is empirically verified (Bornschier and Ballmer-Cao 1979; also see Alderson and Nielsen 1999). The usual methodological critique applies.

14. The "natural resource curse" idea, which was central to much-derided early deterministic models in anthropology and geography, has made a comeback of sorts in the economics literature. The link between natural resources and inequality in a recent model by Leamer at al. (1999) is expected to work through human capital accumulation. It is argued that resource-rich countries shift from non-industrial production straight to capital-intensive manufacturing with dire consequences for human capital accumulation and income inequality.

15. The material in this and the following paragraph are taken almost verbatim from Chakravorty (2003, 3-5).

Chapter 4

1. Similar results are seen in other distribution games like the "Public Goods" game and the "Dictator" game (see Bowles 1998 for a summary).

2. It is odd to note that the most ardent supporters of the self-interest thesis in America, individuals to the far right of the political spectrum, also are very uncomfortable with the idea of biological evolution, little recognizing or pretending not to recognize that the two are intimately interconnected.

3. There is a basic misunderstanding about whether the "strongest" or the "fittest" survive. Evolutionary theory actually suggests that it is the latter—adaptability and fitness in given environments is the key to survival. This opens up a fascinating question as to whether people try to create environments in which the most self-interested prosper (i.e., they attempt to adapt the social environment to their strength rather than adapting to the environment). Let us leave that juicy question open for some other venue.

4. In fact, without the altruism and sacrifice of some individuals, society would not have benefited from many of the vital scientific breakthroughs and political freedoms that

are taken for granted today. Some of the most important advances in human history—including scientific discoveries such as the heliocentric solar system and radioactivity, and political milestones such as emancipation, suffrage, and anti-colonial liberation—came not from the dogged pursuit of self-interest but from the enlightened pursuit of the interests of family, community, humanity, and abstract ideas like honor, duty, and professionalism.

5. The significant theoretical problem, one that has plagued analysts from Darwin onward, is that acquired characteristics cannot be inherited or passed on genetically. Social Darwinists of the nineteenth and early twentieth centuries used this argument to deny education to minorities and to sterilize people with mental and physical handicaps. The current consensus is that altruism and sacrifice are part of our genetic makeup.

6. The "Prisoner's Dilemma" and its variant "Altruist's Dilemma" games used in economics and sociology explore the possibility of group cooperation and solidarity. These games show that selfish behavior leads to irrational or sub-optimal outcomes; cooperative behavior leads to optimal outcomes (see Heckathorn 1991; Bowles 2004).

7. Among the stranger phenomena reported by psychologists is the emergence of intergroup hostility when group identities are randomly assigned, for example by tossing a coin (Tajfel 1981).

8. Also see Beckert's (1996) analysis of the "perfect information" thesis when individuals face uncertainty and are socially and institutionally embedded.

9. With minor variations this approach can be called Durkheimian in the sense that individual actions follow certain regularities (a "nomological core") but are constrained by social structures. Echoes of this perspective are also found in the "moral economy" theories of contemporary scholars like political scientist and anthropologist James Scott (1976, 1986) and anthropologist Eric Wolf (1982).

10. "Old" institutionalism has to be distinguished from the "new" institutionalism of Oliver Williamson (1975) and Douglass North (1990), in which rational self-interested individuals create institutions to facilitate markets, which precede all other forms of human interaction.

11. Take for instance the work of Max Weber. In his magisterial three-volume compilation *Economy and Society* (1968), power and domination occupy a focal position. Chapter III (The Types of Legitimate Domination), covers one-quarter of volume 1. About one-fifth of volume 3 is also dedicated to power and domination.

12. Remember from Chapter 3 (Lichbach 1996) that high levels of inequality do not automatically lead to unrest or revolution, but the potential for unrest or at least passive resistance becomes higher.

13. To take an Indian example: a small farmer in Aurangabad district in the state of Bihar is probably unaware of and certainly indifferent to the incomes earned by small or large landowners in Aurangabad district in the state of Maharashtra; his reference group is local, any intragroup redistribution among small farmers happens locally, and any intergroup redistribution (through gifts, feasts, small public works) or predation from large farmers to small also takes place locally.

14. Assortative mating norms are prevalent even in modern societies like the U.K. or South Korea, where the correlation levels for education and parents' social class between marriage partners are very high.

15. In the social science literature on labor market constraints in the developed world this is referred to as "the intersection of race, class, and gender."

Chapter 5

1. As shown in Chapter 1, this more familiar language is borrowed from the physical sciences. Physics is the natural science that most often provides metaphors for social science, especially economics. Evolutionary economists, on the other hand, argue that

biology is the natural science that provides the best metaphors for social formation and social change. Stephen Jay Gould, the evolutionary biologist who pioneered the punctuated equilibrium argument, thought that biology should take its metaphors from history (Gould 2002). Interestingly, biological metaphors have long been commonplace in studies of growth (especially urban growth and organic models of cities), but till the advent of evolutionary economics, they have been absent in mainstream economics.

2. These are, of course, very well known terms in the social justice and policy literature (see Roemer 1998). The basic policy debate on distribution is often framed in terms of the equality of opportunities versus the equality of outcome.

3. The term I use here—mobility gap—is similar to the concept of *social distance* used in sociology. Social distance emerges because different groups have different life chances and thus form specific conceptions of themselves and their societies. Individuals who view themselves as "equals" interact closely and distinguish themselves from others who they view as "superior" through deference behavior and those they view as "inferior" with status symbols (see Goffman 1959).

4. For instance, Goody (1971) and Haller (1981) argue that the absence of homogamy is perhaps the most important reason that many African societies did not produce "relatively enduring, culturally distinct social strata."

5. It may be useful for some readers to view this in terms of the tension between structure (norms and laws) and agency.

6. Insiders do attempt to change between-group norms, but rarely. Later we will see why.

7. In anthropology there is a long-standing debate, inspired by Evans-Pritchard's work on the Nuer of southern Sudan and subsequent work by others on the Somali, the Bedouin, the Maasai, etc., on whether pastoralists were egalitarian or hierarchical, and the meaning of these terms in societies that are very unlike modern societies (see Flanagan 1989; Salzman 1999).

8. Colonization was an invasion in South Asia too, yet, as we shall see, the distributional outcome in the Americas and South Asia were fundamentally different.

9. The North American system was not very different ideologically, and it is possible that, despite the fact that the population of natives and slaves was a smaller proportion of the total population, the extent of inequality was not much lower than in Latin America. Shammas (1993) estimates that, in colonial America, the wealthiest one percent owned between 18 and 28 percent, the wealthiest five percent owned between 41 and 63 percent, and the top quintile owned between 74 and 95 percent of all wealth. These inequalities were not limited to the U.S. South, where the vast majority of the slaves were located, but also in New England, which relied on large numbers of indentured servants for labor.

10. Banerjee and Iyer (2001) show that more than fifty years after the abolishment of the *zamindari* system, its institutional legacy is manifested in lower agricultural yields and poorer educational infrastructure and human capital formation compared with places where the *zamindari* system was not used.

11. These land inequalities are most likely lower than what existed during the colonial period. Land reform was enacted in post-colonial South Asia to some degree; as a result, by the early 1970s, land was more equally distributed than before. For instance, in India, the Gini coefficient of land inequality was down to 58.4 by the early 1960s.

12. Percival Spear (1965, 106), analyzing India's colonization by the British, writes: When we consider that it took less than eighty years for a foreign mercantile body from a distant country to gain control over a whole sub-continent containing an ancient civilization of its own and a rival alien culture with imperial traditions and a rich store of political, military, and cultural experience there is indeed matter for surprise and reflection.... The theory that pleased nineteenth-century Europeans was the intrinsic superiority of the west over the east, to which the late-century imperialists added the

rider of the exceptional qualities of the Anglo-Saxon race. What could an Asian do against a Clive or a Hastings, a Lawrence or a Nicholson?

13. There are many sources of Indian social, political, and economic history. Sumit Sarkar's (1999) account is an excellent one.

14. The urban bias thesis proposed by Michael Lipton (1977) has been widely discussed (and discussed again in Chapter 6). His primary case was India, but there is some debate on whether urban bias actually exists there.

15. The material in this section comes from a detailed study of the Bolivian revolution by Kelley and Klein (1981).

16. The data in this paragraph are from Behdad (1989).

17. At the moment of writing, Iraq is undergoing a reconstruction transition. Unlike the egalitarian transitions discussed in this section, it is possible that the Iraq transition will have no discernible or possibly even unequalizing distributional consequences. Again, unlike previous reconstructions, which installed strong states in an era when development was best thought to be state-led, this reconstruction is market-oriented. The consequences of this ideology are discussed later in this and the final chapter.

18. How much of the success of these states is due to market orientation and how much is due to state intervention is hotly debated (see Wade 1990).

19. As does popular culture. Movies abound with iconic outsider heroes who rescue or liberate powerless peasants from the depredations of ruthless exploiters. See *The Seven Samurai, The Good the Bad and the Ugly, Sholay* (Hindi).

20. "Disaffected" members are individuals who have undergone mutation (in terms of the analytical framework described earlier in this chapter); for whatever reason, they have spontaneously decided to question the social norms and order into which they were born. If many others begin to share their disaffection (as a result of organization, mobilization, or other means), social change takes place by adaptation. When the disaffected individuals capture power and change the legal structure, social change takes place by invasion.

21. To be more accurate, income inequality did not increase in Poland during the initial transition. It may actually have fallen somewhat. The increase came later, after the mid-1990s (see Podkaminer 2003; Keane and Prasad 2001).

22. The primary reason, *ceteris paribus*, for inequality increase from marketization after socialism is that returns to education increase. These differences are typically held down under socialism but cannot be state managed as directly in market regimes.

23. See John Williamson's (1990) "Washington Consensus" thesis.

Chapter 6

1. The reader can Google the phrase "there are many ..." and fill in the blank with Chinas or Indias or Russias or Brazils or Mexicos.

2. This is an increase from around 0.15 in the early nineteenth century. The opening paragraph of this chapter refers to this increasing polarization, which is "divergence, big time."

3. See Martin and Sunley (1998) for a geographical perspective on "convergence."

4. Krugman's truly interesting contribution is to link interregional convergence (industrial dispersion) and divergence (industrial concentration) to transportation costs. He shows that, when transportation costs are high, there is little trade, and industry is dispersed. When transportation costs start falling, industry begins to concentrate up to a point. Further declines in transportation costs result in industrial dispersal again. In other words, if transportation cost is the only factor in firm location, over the long run we can expect to see divergence followed by convergence.

5. This literature is also closely related to the notion of optimal city size, where it is suggested that efficiencies related to agglomeration may reach a peak at urban sizes between three and seven million (Sveikauskas 1975; Shukla 1984; Carlino 1985; Montgomery 1988).

6. Note that Lipton himself may be uncomfortable in the company of public choice theorists, who have often been associated with right-wing and conservative causes.

7. Take the case of India, the archetype large import-substituting country till 1991 and the advent of structural reforms. "Indian planning ... has been limited to (the) allocation of investments over time, sectors and sub-sectors, whereas there is no explicit spatial dimension in the formal planning models" (Awasthi 1991, 27). The policy makers, led by the Planning Commission and Soviet-inspired input–output macroeconomic models, concentrated on the factors of production to the exclusion of any spatial context. Johnson (1970, 167–69) has argued that in addition there were three extenuating factors: a belief in the "redemptive mystique" of large industry, wherever it may be located; two, the emulative desire to attain the demographic patterns of more developed countries"; and three, what Lewis (1995) calls a "village fetish." Lewis adds two more factors that were particularly important: one, that "any implementation of a positive spatial strategy would cost a lot of money," and that "the spatial dimension (of development) was most obviously and blatantly political" (Lewis 1995, 224). The Freight Equalization Policy of 1956, a clearly political regulation, which eroded the comparative advantage of the eastern states, is the most famous example of misguided (perhaps malevolent) regional policy that led to greater regional inequality.

8. Carlos Ramirez-Faria (1991, 79) writes: "The First World War, which left Western civilization exhausted and disillusioned about itself, effectively claimed social Darwinism as one of its casualties. By the time that another world conflagration was becoming imminent, the superior/inferior dichotomy was wearing thin."

9. The spatial and social structures inherited from colonialism were exaggerated but not fundamentally altered during the nationalist phase. The primary colonial cities grew very large while very few new cities were created—Brasilia, Islamabad, and Chandigarh are the exceptions, which, incidentally, have all failed to become "counter-magnets" to the giant metropolises. The "growth pole" strategy—of concentrating industrial investments in a few strategically chosen locations, so that these would spur modernism and economic dynamism in their proximate regions—has largely failed. Rather than being spurs to growth in the chosen regions, these places have become small high-income enclaves, largely disconnected from the local economies.

10. The data in this paragraph are calculated from Table B-12 in Maddison and Associates (1992) and Table 2 in Cikurel (2002).

11. Chakravorty (2003b) makes the same point about regional inequality's being driven by the location of private investment, which is efficiency-oriented and hence seeks already advantaged regions in developing nation settings.

12. See Griffin and Renwei (1993) on how the ideology has shifted toward a desire for greater inequality after "too long" a period when "the people have eaten from one large pot."

13. Up to 1972 there were 46 prefectures. That year, Okinawa came back under Japanese authority. All the data to be presented next have been derived with the population and income of Okinawa included, even for years earlier than 1972.

14. Several interesting studies in economic history provide suggestive but inconclusive support for the thesis that regional inequalities were declining well before the beginning of the twentieth century in parts of Europe (England, the Habsburg empire) and the U.S. (see Hunt 1986; Good 1986).

Chapter 7

1. How do we know what the level of *local* social inequality is in a nation? Remember from Chapter 3 that we usually do not have data on social inequality at the local level. Therefore, we have to surmise the level of social inequality from what we know about overall income inequality and spatial inequality, and use information on social inequality in the nation as a whole and in its sub-national units to make assumptions about social

inequality at the local level. Consider China for instance. We know that income inequality in China is moderate and spatial inequality is high. We also know that intra-urban and intra-rural inequality levels at the national scale and within individual provinces is low. Therefore, we can surmise that the level of local social inequality in China must be low. Similar deductive exercises are necessary for each of the country cases listed here.

2. On a darker note: though social reform processes are ongoing in most countries, catastrophic inter-group violence has been seen in many conflicts (for example, in Bosnia, Rwanda, and Sudan in the last decade). Less destructive but potentially ruinous violence is possible in several nations where there is little serious social reform and a resurgence of identity-based politics. It is possible to argue that, as a political organizing principle, class has turned out to be a temporary device, ascribed identity seems more permanent.

3. Did the Soviet Union's unwillingness to mitigate regional differences have to do with the fact that the lagging regions were also minority dominated? This is an intriguing question. I suggest that one of the principal reasons that communist China and the Soviet Union took radically different approaches to regional development is because they had different social structures.

4. I have not found space to consider the case of Malaysia, where, following ethnic riots in the mid 1960s, the state began an aggressive policy of affirmative action. The Malay natives (the Bhumiputeras), the numerical majority, were substantially poorer on average than the ethnic Chinese, the entrepreneurial class. Using policies of reservations in education, employment, and business, the Bhumiputeras substantially reduced the average gap with the Chinese between 1970 and the early 1990s (see Lucas and Verry 1996). The overall level of income inequality declined somewhat (prompting calls that this was a case of Kuznets affirmed; see Bowman 1997 for a critique), but they continue to remain high, probably because of increasing regional divergence and the domination of Kuala Lumpur.

5. It is also useful to remember that the distributional punctuations have been successful precisely where there is little identity fragmentation. Had Taiwan, for instance, been a multiethnic society with deep divisions before the U.S. intervention, would the intervention have been as successful in redistributing land? There are enough examples from history to suggest that such redistributive endeavors would have run into significant resistance.

6. I will not revisit the arguments against convergence detailed in Chapter 6. The reader can refer to the concluding section of that chapter where I make the argument that, even under conditions of diminishing returns in the leading cities in developed nations, it is possible to see interregional divergence within both developed and developing nations.

REFERENCES

Abe, H. 1997. Changing Regional Disparities and Policy Issues under the Globalization of Japanese Economy. 4th International Congress of Asian Planning School Association, Bandung, Indonesia.

Abercrombie, N. and B. S. Turner. 1978. The Dominant Ideology Thesis. *British Journal of Sociology* 29:149–70.

Abramovitz, M. 1986. Catching up, Forging Ahead, and Falling Behind. *Journal of Economic History* 46:385–406.

Acemoglu, D. 2002. Technical Change, Inequality, and the Labor Market. *Journal of Economic Literature* 40:7–73.

Acemoglu, D., S. Johnson, and J. A. Robinson. 2002. The Colonial Origins of Comparative Development: An Empirical Investigation. *American Economic Review* 91:1369–1401.

Adelman, I. and C. T. Morris. 1973. *Economic Growth and Social Equity In Developing Countries*. Stanford: Stanford University Press.

Adelman, I. and S. Robinson. 1989. Income Distribution and Development. In *Handbook of Development Economics. Vol. II.* H. B. Chenery and T. N. Srinivasan. Eds. Amsterdam: North Holland.

Aghajanian, A. 1983. Ethnic Inequality in Iran: An Overview. *International Journal of Middle East Studies* 15:211–24.

Aghion, P., E. Caroli. and C. Garcia-Penalosa. 1999. Inequality and Economic Growth: The Perspective of the New Growth Theories. *Journal of Economic Literature* 37:1615–60.

Ahluwalia, M. S. 1976. Income Distribution and Development: Some Stylized Facts. *American Economic Review* 66:128–35.

Ahluwalia, M. S. 1974. Income Inequality: Some Dimensions of the Problem. In *Redistribution with Growth.* H. B. Chenery et al. Eds. London: Oxford University Press.

Ahuja, V., B. Bidani, F. Ferreira, and M. Walton. 1997. *Everyone's Miracle? Revisiting Poverty and Inequality in East Asia.* Washington DC: World Bank.

Akita, T. 2003. Decomposing Regional Income Inequality in China and Indonesia using Two-stage Nested Theil Decomposition Method. *Annals of Regional Science* 37:55–77.

Akita, T., R. A. Lukman, and Y. Yamada. 1999. Inequality in the Distribution of Household Expenditures in Indonesia: A Theil Decomposition Analysis. *The Developing Economies* 37:197–221.

Akita, T. and R. A. Lukman. 1995. Interregional Inequalities in Indonesia: A Sectoral Decomposition Analysis for 1975–92, *Bulletin of Indonesian Economic Studies* 31: 61–81.

233

Alderson, A. S. and F. Nielsen. 1999. Income Inequality, Development, and Dependence: A Reconsideration. *American Sociological Review* 64:606–31.

Alesina, A. and E. Glaeser. 2004. *Fighting Poverty in the US and Europe: A World of Difference*. New York: Oxford University Press.

Alesina, A. and D. Rodrik. 1994. Distributive Politics and Economic Growth. *Quarterly Journal of Economics* 108:465–90.

Alesina, A. 1998. The Political Economy of Macroeconomic Stabilizations and Income Inequality: Myth and Reality. In *Income Distribution and High Quality Growth*. V. Tanzi and K. Chu Eds. Cambridge, MA: the MIT Press. pp. 299–326.

Alexeev, M. V. and C. G. Gaddy. 1993. Income Distribution in the U.S.S.R. in the 1980's. *Review of Income and Wealth* 39: 23–26.

Alonso, W. 1980. Five Bell Shapes in Development. *Papers of the Regional Science Association* 45:5–16.

Amiel, Y. 1998. *The Subjective Approach to the Measurement of Income Inequality*. Discussion paper no. DARP 38. Distributional Analysis Research Program. London: London School of Economics.

Anand, S. and S. M. R. Kanbur. 1993. The Kuznets Process and the Inequality-Development Relationship. *Journal of Development Economics* 40:25–52.

Angeles, L. 2004. Income Inequality and Colonialism: How Much Does History Matter? CEDIEM. Universidad Diego Portales. Mimeo.

Aspe, P. and J. Beristain. 1985. Toward a First Estimate of the Evolution of Inequality in Mexico, in *The Political Economy of Income Distribution in Mexico*, P. Aspe and P. E. Sigmund Eds., New York: Holmes and Meier.

Aswicahyono, H. H., K. Bird, and H. Hill. 1996. What Happens to Industrial Structure When Countries Liberalize? Indonesia Since the Mid-1980's. *Journal of Development Studies* 32:340–63.

Athanasopoulos, G. and F. Vahid. 2002. *Statistical Inference on Changes in Income Inequality in Australia*. Working Paper no. 9. Department of Economics and Business Statistics. Monash University.

Atkinson, A. B. 1970. On the Measurement of Inequality. *Journal of Economic Theory* 2:244–63.

Atkinson, A. B. 1983. *The Economics of Inequality*. 2nd ed. Oxford: Clarendon Press.

Atkinson, A. B. 1997. Bringing Income Distribution in From the Cold. *Economic Journal* 107:297–321.

Atkinson, A. B. and J. Micklewright. 1992. *Economic Transformation in Eastern Europe and the Distribution of Income*. Cambridge: Cambridge University Press.

Atkinson, A. B., L. Rainwater, and T. Smeeding. 1995. *Income Distribution in European Countries*. Working Paper Series, number 121, Luxembourg Income Study.

Attanasio, O., P. K. Goldberg, and N. Pavcnik. 2002. *Trade Reforms and Wage Inequality in Colombia*. Centre for the Evaluation of Development Policies. Institute for Fiscal Studies. Mimeo.

Australia. *Statistical Yearbook of Australia* (SYA). Various issues.

Awasthi. D. N. 1991. *Regional Patterns of Industrial Growth in India*. New Delhi: Concept Publishing.

Azzoni, C. R. 2001. Economic Growth and Regional Income Inequality in Brazil. *Annals of Regional Science* 35:133–52.

Banerjee, A. and L. Iyer. 2001. The Imperial Legacy: Colonial Land Tenure Systems and Independent India. MIT. Mimeo.

Bangladesh. *Statistical Yearbook of Bangladesh* (SYB). Various issues.

Baran, P. 1957. *The Political Economy of Growth*. New York: Monthly Review Press.

Barber, B. 1995. *Jihad vs. McWorld: How Globalism and Tribalism are Reshaping the World*. New York: Ballantine Books.

Barro, R. J. and X. Sala-i-Martin. 1992. Convergence. *Journal of Political Economy* 100:223–51.

Barro, R. J. and X. Sala-i-Martin. 1995. *Economic Growth*. New York: McGraw Hill.

Bates, R. H. 1983. *The Regulation of Rural Markets in Africa*. Washington D.C.: US. Agency for International Development.

Bazen, S. and P. Moyes. 2003. *International Comparisons of Income Distribution*. Working Paper no. 341. Luxembourg Income Study. Luxembourg.

Becker, G. S. 1962. Investment in Human Capital: A Theoretical Analysis. *Journal of Political Economy* 70:9–49.

Beckert, J. 1996. What is Sociological About Economic Sociology? Uncertainty and the Embeddedness of Economic Action. *Theory and Society* 25:803–40.

Behdad, S. 1989. Winners and Losers of the Iranian Revolution: A Study in Income Distribution. *International Journal of Middle East Studies* 21:327–58.

Behrman, J. and D. Rondinelli. 1992. The Cultural Imperatives of Globalization: Urban Economic Growth in the Twenty-first Century. *Economic Development Quarterly* 6:115–26.

Bellow, S. 1984. *Him with His Foot in His Mouth and Other Stories*. New York: Harper and Row.

Bénabou, R. 1996a. Equity and Efficiency in Human Capital Investment: The Local Connection. *Review of Economic Studies* 63:237–264.

Bénabou, R. 1996b. Inequality and Growth. *NBER Macroeconomics Annual* 11:11–74.

Bergson, A. 1984. Income Inequality Under Soviet Socialism. *Journal of Economic Literature* 22:1052–99.

Bergsman, J. 1980. *Income Distribution and Poverty in Mexico*. Staff Working Paper no. 395. World Bank.

Berreman, G. D. 1978. Scale and Social Relations. *Current Anthropology* 19:225–45.

Béteille, A. 1983. *The Idea of Natural Inequality and Other Essays*. New Delhi: Oxford University Press.

Bevan, D., P. Collier, and J. W. Gunning. 1999. *The Political Economy of Poverty, Equity, and Growth: Nigeria and Indonesia*. Published for the World Bank. New York: Oxford University Press.

Beyer, H., P. Rojas, and R. Vergara. 1999. Trade Liberalization and Wage Inequality. *Journal of Development Economics* 59:103–23.

Bhagwati, J. and V. H. Dehejia. 1994. Freer Trade and Wages of the Unskilled—is Marx Striking Again? In *Trade and Wages: Leveling Wages Down*. J. Bhagwati and M. H. Kosters, Eds. Washington D.C.: AEI Press. pp. 36–75.

Birdsall, N., D. Ross, and R. Sabot. 1995. Inequality and Growth Reconsidered: Lessons from East Asia. *World Bank Economic Review* (September):477–508.

Blau, P. M. 1964. *Exchange and Power in Social Life*. New York: Wiley.

Bollen, K. A. and B. D. Grandjean. 1981. The Dimension(s) of Democracy: Further Issues in the Measurement and Effects of Political Democracy. *American Sociological Review* 46:651–59.

Bollen, K. A. and R. W. Jackman. 1985. Political Democracy and the Size Distribution of Income. *American Sociological Review* 50:438–57.

Borjas, G. J. and V. A. Ramey. 1994. The Relationship Between Wage Inequality and International Trade. In *The Changing Distribution of Income in an Open U.S. Economy*. J. H. Bergstrand et al. Eds. Amsterdam: North Holland. pp. 217–42.

Bornschier, V. and T. H. Ballmer-Cao. 1979. Income Inequality: A Cross-National Study of the Relationships Between MNC Penetration, Dimensions of the Power Structure and Income Distribution. *American Sociological Review* 44:487–506.

Borts, G. H. and J. L. Stein. 1964. *Economic Growth in a Free Market*. New York: Columbia University Press.

Boudeville, J-R. 1966. *Problems of Regional Economic Planning*. Edinburgh: Edinburgh University Press.

Bouillon C. P., A. Legovini, and N. Lustig. 2003. Rising Inequality in Mexico: Household Characteristics and Regional Effects. *Journal of Development Studies* 39:112–133.

Bourdieu, P. 2002. Structures, Habitus, Practices. In *Contemporary Sociological Theory*. C. Calhoun et al. Eds. Oxford: Blackwell.

Bourguignon, F. 1998. Keynote Address: Inequality and Economic Growth. In *Poverty and Inequality*, S. J. Burki, S. Aiyer, and R. Hommes, Eds. Washington DC: World Bank.

Bourguignon, F. and C. Morrisson. 2002. Inequality Among World Citizens:1820–1992. *American Economic Review* 92:727–44.

Bowles, S. 1998. Endogenous Preferences: The Cultural Consequences of Markets and Other Economic Institutions. *Journal of Economic Literature* 36:75–111.

Bowles, S. and H. Gintis. 1973. IQ in the U.S. Class Structure. *Social Policy* 3:65–96.

Bowles, S. and H. Gintis. 2000. Walrasian Economics in Retrospect. *Quarterly Journal of Economics* 115:1411–39.

Bowman, K. S. 1997. Should the Kuznets Effect be Relied on to Induce Equalizing Growth? Evidence from Post-1950 Development. *World Development* 25:127–43.

Bradshaw, Y. W. 1987. Urbanization and Underdevelopment: A Global Study of Modernization, Urban Bias and Economic Dependency. *American Sociological Review* 52:224–39.

Brandolini, A. 1998a. The Personal Distribution of Incomes in Post-War Italy: Source Description, Data Quality, and the Time Pattern of Income Inequality. Mimeo.

Brandolini, A. 1998b. *A Bird's-Eye View of Long-Run Changes in Income Inequality*. Mimeo. Banca d'Italia, Research Department.

Brandolini, A. and N. Rossi. 1998. Income Distribution and Growth in Industrial Countries. In *Income Distribution and High Quality Growth*. V. Tanzi and K-Y Chu, Eds. Cambridge and London: MIT Press.

Brandolini, A. and G. D'Alessio. 2003. Household Structure and Income Inequality. In *Women's Work, the Family, and Social Policy: Focus on Italy in a European Perspective*. M. Repetto Alaia and D. del Boca, Eds. New York: Peter Lang.

Brandt, L. and B. Sands. 1990. Beyond Malthus and Ricardo: Economic Growth, Land Concentration, and Income Distribution in Early Twentieth-Century Rural China. *Journal of Economic History* 50:807–27.

Breau, S. 2002. *Globalization and Inequality in Canada: Trends in the 1990s*. Paper presented at the Graduate Conference on "Globalization: Governance and Inequality". Ventura, California.

Brooks, D. H. 1987. *Industrial Location and Decentralization Policies in Developing Countries*. Unpublished PhD dissertation. Brown University: Providence, Rhode Island.

Brown, C. and B. A. Campbell. 2002. The Impact of Technological Change on Work and Wages. *Industrial Relations* 41:1–33.

Bruton, H. J. and associates. 1992. *The Political Economy of Poverty, Equity, and Growth: Sri Lanka and Malaysia*. Published for the World Bank. New York: Oxford University Press.

Buchanan, J. M. and G. Tullock. 1962. *The Calculus of Consent: Logical Foundations of Constitutional Democracy*. Ann Arbor, Mich.: University of Michigan Press.

Burkhart, R. E. 1997. Comparative Democracy and Income Distribution: Shape and Direction of the Causal Arrow. *The Journal of Politics* 59:148–64.

Burki, S. J. 1988. Poverty in Pakistan: Myth or Reality? in *Rural Poverty in South Asia*. T. N. Srinivasan and P. K. Bardhan, Eds. Delhi: Oxford University Press.

Burtless, G. 1995. International Trade and the Rise in Earnings Inequality. *Journal of Economic Literature* 33:800–16.

Campano, F. and D. Salvatore. 1988. Economic Development. Income Distribution and the Kuznets Hypothesis. *Journal of Policy Modeling* 10:265–80.

Canada. *Income Distribution by Size in Canada.* Various issues. Household Survey Division, Statistics Canada.

Canada. Statistical Yearbook of Canada. Various issues.

Crdenas, M. and A. Pontön. 1995, Growth and Convergence in Colombia: 1950–1990. *Journal of Development Economics* 47:5–37.

Carlino, G. 1985. Declining City Productivity and the Growth of Rural Regions: A Test of Alternative Explanations. *Journal of Urban Economics* 18:11–27.

Carneiro, R. I. 1970. A Theory of the Origin of the State. *Science* 169:733–38.

Castello, A. and R. Doménech. 2002. Human Capital Inequality and Economic Growth: Some New Evidence. *The Economic Journal* 112:C187–200.

Central Bank of Ceylon. 1963. *Report on the Sample Survey of Consumer Finances,* Part I and II. Colombo.

Chai, J. C. H. 1996. Divergent Development and Regional Income Gap in China. *Journal of Contemporary Asia* 26:46–58.

Chakravorty, S. 1992. *Equity in the Urban System: A Study of Spatial Polarization Processes for Population and Income.* Unpublished PhD dissertation. Los Angeles: University of Southern California.

Chakravorty, S. 1994. Equity and the Big City. *Economic Geography* 70:1–22.

Chakravorty, S. 1996. A Measurement of Spatial Disparity: The Case of Income Inequality. *Urban Studies* 33:1671–86.

Chakravorty, S. 2000. How Does Structural Reform Affect Regional Development: Resolving Contradictory Theory with Evidence from India. *Economic Geography* 76:367–394.

Chakravorty, S. 2003a. Urban Development in the Global Periphery: The Consequences of Economic and Ideological Globalization. *Annals of Regional Science* 37:357–67.

Chakravorty, S. 2003b. Capital Source and the Location of Industrial Investment: A Tale of Divergence from Post-Reform India. *Journal of International Development* 15:365–83.

Chatterjee, P. 1986. *Nationalist Thought and the Colonial World: A Derivative Discourse?* Tokyo and London: Zed Books for the United Nations University.

Chen, S-H., G. Datt, and M. Ravallion. 1995. *Is Poverty Increasing in the Developing World?* Policy Research Department. The World Bank. Data Appendix.

Chenery, H. B. and M. Syrquin. 1975. *Patterns of Development:1950–1970.* New York: Oxford University Press.

Chiu, W. H. 1998. Income Inequality, Human Capital Accumulation and Economic Performance. *The Economic Journal* 108:44–59.

Choo, H. 1982. Estimation of Size Distribution of Income and its Sources of Changes in Korea, 1982. Working Paper 8515. Korea Development Institute.

Chu, C. Y. C. and L. Jiang. 1997. Demographic Transition, Family Structure, and Income Inequality. *The Review of Economics and Statistics* 79:665–69.

Cikurel, D. C. 2002. *Why Mexico's Regional Income Convergence Broke Down?* Paper presented at the WIDER conference on Spatial Inequality in Latin America. Mimeo.

Clarke, G. R. G. 1995. More Evidence on Income Distribution and Growth. *Journal of Development Economics* 47:403–27.

Cline, W. R. 1975. Distribution and Development: A Survey of Literature. *Journal of Development Economics* 1:359–400.

Coleman, J. S. 1974. Inequality, Sociology, and Moral Philosophy. *American Journal of Sociology* 80:739–64.

Cornia, G. A. 1994. Income Distribution, Poverty, and Welfare in Transitional Economies: A Comparison Between Eastern Europe and China. *Journal of International Development* 6.

Coulter, P. B. 1989. *Measuring Inequality: A Methodological Handbook.* Boulder: Westview Press.

Cowell, F. 1998. *Measurement of Inequality.* Discussion paper no. DARP 36. Distributional Analysis Research Program. London: London School of Economics.

Crane, J. 1991. The Epidemic Theory of Ghettos and Neighborhood Effects of Dropping Out and Teenage Childbearing. *American Journal of Sociology* 96:1226–1259.

Crenshaw, E. 1992. Cross-National Determinants of Income Inequality: A Replication and Extension Using Ecological-Evolutionary Theory. *Social Forces* 71:339–63.

Cromwell, J. 1977. The Size Distribution of Income: An International Comparison. *Review of Income and Wealth* 23:291–308.

DANE (Departamento Administrativo Nacional de Estadistica, Colombia). 1970. *Analisis Econometrico de Distribucion de Ingresos.* Bogotá.

Daniere, A. 1996. Growth, Inequality and Poverty in South-east Asia: The case of Thailand. *Third World Planning Review* 18:373–96.

Dahl, R. A. 1989. *Democracy and its Critics.* New Haven: Yale University Press.

Darwent, D. F. 1975. Growth Poles and Growth Centers in Regional Planning: A Review. In *Regional Policy: Readings in Theory and Applications,* J. Friedmann and W. Alonso, Eds. Cambridge, MA: The MIT Press.

Das, S. K. and A. Barua. 1996. Regional Inequalities, Economic Growth and Liberalisation: A Study of the Indian Economy. *The Journal of Development Studies* 32:364–390.

Datt, G. 1995. *Income Inequality in India.* Washington DC: The World Bank. Mimeo.

Datt, G. 1994. *Poverty in Sri Lanka: 1953 to 1986–87.* Washington DC: The World Bank. Mimeo.

Davis, K. and W. E. Moore. 1945. Some Principles of Stratification. *American Sociological Review* 10:242–49.

Dawkins, R. 1976. *The Selfish Gene.* Oxford: Oxford University Press.

Dawson, D. 1999. Evolutionary Theory and Group Selection: The Question of Warfare. *History and Theory* 38:79–100.

Deaton, A. S. and C. H. Paxson. 1997. The Effects of Economic and Population Growth on National Saving and Inequality. *Demography* 34:97–114.

Degler, C. 1991. *In Search of Human Nature: The Decline and Revival of Darwinism in American Social Thought.* New York: Oxford University Press.

Deininger, K. and L. Squire. 1998. New Ways of Looking at Old Issues: Inequality and Growth. *Journal of Development Economics* 57:259–87.

Deininger, K. and L. Squire. 1996. A New Dataset Measuring Income Inequality. *World Bank Economic Review* 10:565–91.

Denmark CSO. 1988. *Danmarks Statistik Ten-Year Review.*

Denmark. Various issues. *Danmarks Statistik Arbog.*

Diamond, J. 1997. *Guns, Germs, and Steel: The Fates of Human Societies.* New York and London: W. W. Norton.

Diniz, C. C. 1994. Polygonized Development in Brazil: Neither Decentralization nor Continued Polarization. *International Journal of Urban and Regional Research* 18: 293–314.

Dobson, R. B. 1977. Mobility and Stratification in the Soviet Union. *Annual Review of Sociology* 3:297–329.

Dowling, J. M. and D. Soo. 1983. Income Distribution and Economic Growth in Developing Asian Countries. Staff Paper, no. 15. Manila: Asian Development Bank.

Dequech, D. 2003. Cognitive and Cultural Embeddedness: Combining Institutional Economics and Economic Sociology. *Journal of Economic Issues* 37:461–70.

J. Drèze and A. K. Sen. 1998. *Indian Development: Selected Regional Perspectives.* New Delhi: Oxford University Press.

Duesenberry, J. 1960. Comment on "An Economic Analysis of Fertility". In *Demographic and Economic Change in Developed Countries.* NBER Ed. Princeton: Princeton University Press.

Dumont, L. 1972. *Homo Hierarchicus: The Caste System and its Implications*. London: Paladin.

Dunford, M. and A. Smith. 2000. Catching up or Falling Behind? Economic Performance and Regional Trajectories in the 'New Europe'. *Economic Geography* 76:169–95.

Eicher, T. S. and C. García-Peñalosa. 2001. Inequality and Growth: The Dual Role of Human Capital in Development. *Journal of Development Economics* 66:174–97.

Eldredge, N. and S. J. Gould. 1972. Punctuated Equilibria: An Alternative to Phyletic Gradualism. In *Models in Paleobiology*. T.J.M. Schopf Ed. San Francisco: Freeman, Cooper. pp. 82–115.

Elizondo, R. L. and P. Krugman. 1992. *Trade Policy and the Third World Metropolis*. NBER Working Paper No. 4238.

Elliott, J. E. 2000. Adam Smith's Conceptualization of Power, Markets, and Politics. *Review of Social Economy* 58:429–54.

Epstein, S. 1994. Integration of the Cognitive and Psychodynamic Unconscious. *American Psychologist* 49:709–24.

Esquivel, G. and J. A. Rodriguez-López. 2003. Technology, Trade, and Wage Inequality in Mexico Before and After NAFTA. *Journal of Development Economics* 72:543–65.

Esteban, J.-M. and D. Ray. 1994. On the Measurement of Polarization. *Econometrica* 62:819–51.

Estudillo, J. P. 1997. Income Inequality in the Philippines, 1961–91. *The Developing Economies* 1:68–95.

Fan, C. C. 1995. Of Belts and Ladders: State Policy and Uneven Regional Development in Post-Mao China. *Annals of the Association of American Geographers* 85:421–449.

Farne, S. 1994. Apertura Comercial y Distribucion de Ingreso: La Teoria y Las Experencias de Chile, Mexico, y Uruguay. Universitas Economica 9.

Favaro, E. and D. MacIsaac. 1995. *Who Benefited from Peru's Reform Program?* Washington DC: The World Bank. Mimeo.

Fedorov, L. 2002. Regional Inequality and Regional Polarization in Russia, 1990–1999. *World Development* 30:443–56.

Fehr, E. and U. Fischbacher. 2002. Why Social Preferences Matter—the Impact of Non-selfish Motives on Competition, Cooperation and Incentives. *Economic Journal* 112: C1–C33.

Fei, J. C. H., G. Ranis, and S. W. Y. Kuo. 1979. *Growth with Equity: The Taiwan case*. New York: Oxford University Press.

Feenstra, R. C. and G. H. Hanson. 1996. Globalization, Outsourcing, and Wage Inequality. *American Economic Review Papers and Proceedings* 86:240–45.

Felix, D. 1982. Income Distribution Trends in Mexico and the Kuznets Curves. In *Brazil and Mexico: Patterns in Late Development*. S. A. Hewlett and R. S. Weinert, Eds. Philadelphia: Institute for the Study of Human Issues.

Ferguson, C. E. and E. J. Nell. 1972. Two Books on the Theory of Income Distribution: A Review Article. *Journal of Economic Literature* 10:437–53.

Ferreira, L. 1996. *Poverty and Inequality During Structural Adjustment in Rural Tanzania*. Policy Research Working Paper No. 1641. The World Bank. Washington D.C.

Flanagan, J. G. 1989. Hierarchy in Simple "Egalitarian" Societies. *Annual Review of Anthropology* 18:245–66.

Fields, G. A. 1980. *Poverty, Inequality, and Development*. Cambridge: Cambridge University Press.

Fields, G. A. 1989. A Compendium of Data on Inequality and Poverty for the Developing World. Ithaca: Cornell University. Mimeo.

Fields, G. A. 2001. *Distribution and Development: A New Look at the Developing World*. Cambridge, MA: The MIT Press.

Fields, G. A. and G. H. Jakubson. 1994. *New Evidence on the Kuznets Curve*. Cornell University. Mimeo.

Fields, G. S. and S. Soares. 2002. *The Microeconomics of Changing Income Distribution in Malaysia*. The Inter-American Development Bank. Mimeo. http://www.iadb.org/sds/doc/POVMalaysiaE.pdf

Firebaugh, G. 2003. *The New Geography of Global Income Inequality*. Cambridge, MA: Harvard University Press.

Fishlow, A. 1972. Brazilian Size Distribution of Income. *American Economic Review* 62:391–402.

Finland. Various issues. *Statistical Yearbook of Finland*.

Forbes, K. J. 2000. A Reassessment of the Relationship between Inequality and Growth. *American Economic Review* 90:869–94.

Frank, A. G. 1967. *Capitalism and Underdevelopment in Latin America*. New York: Monthly Review Press.

Freeman, R. B. 1995. Are Your Wages Set in Beijing? *Journal of Economic Perspectives* 9:15–32.

Fried, M. H. 1967. *The Evolution of Political Society: An Essay in Political Anthropology*. New York: Random House.

Friedmann, J. 1966. *Regional Development Policy: A Case Study of Venezuela*. Cambridge, MA: MIT Press.

Friedmann, J. 1973. A Theory of Polarized Development. In *Urbanization, Planning and National Development*. Ed. J Friedmann. Beverly Hills: Sage. pp. 41–64.

Friedmann, T. L. 1999. *The Lexus and the Olive Tree: Understanding Globalization*. New York: Farrar, Strauss and Giroux.

Fuchs, R. J. and G. J. Demko. 1979. Geographic Inequality Under Socialism. *Annals of the Association of American Geographers* 69:304–18.

Fujita, M., P. Krugman, and A. Venables. 1999. *The Spatial Economy: Cities, Regions, and International Trade*. Cambridge, MA: MIT Press.

Galiani, S. and P. Sanguinetti. 2003. The Impact of Trade Liberalization on Wage Inequality: Evidence from Argentina. *Journal of Development Economics* 72:497–513.

Galor, O. and D. Tsiddon. 1997. The Distribution of Human Capital and Economic Growth. *Journal of Economic Growth* 2:93–124.

Ghosh, B., S. Marjit, and C. Neogi. 1998. Economic Growth and Regional Divergence in India: 1960 to 1995. *Economic and Political Weekly* 33:1623–30.

Gibrat, R. 1931. *Les Inégalités Economiques*. Paris: Recueil Sirey.

Gilbert, A. 1993. Third World Cities: The Changing National Settlement System. *Urban Studies* 30:721–740.

Glade, W. 1996. Institutions and Inequality in Latin America: Text and Subtext. *Journal of Interamerican Studies and World Affairs* 38:159–180.

Goerlich, F. J. and M. Mas. 2000. *The Measurement of Inequality: Contribution to a Regional Database*. Universitat de Valencia. Mimeo.

Goerner, E. A. and W. J. Thompson. 1996. Politics and Coercion. *Political Theory* 24:620–52.

Goffman, E. 1959. *The Presentation of Self in Everyday Life*. New York: Doubleday.

Goldberg, P. K. and N. Pavcnik. 2004. *Trade, Inequality, and Poverty: What do We Know? Empirical Evidence on the Relationship Between Trade Liberalization, Inequality, and Poverty*, National Bureau of Economic Research, working paper w10593, Cambridge, Ma.

Gonzalez, D. A. and T. McKinley. 1997. The Paradox of Narrowing Wage Differentials and Widening Wage Inequality in Mexico. *Development and Change* 28:505–30.

Good, D. F. 1986. Uneven Development in the Nineteenth Century: A Comparison of the Habsburg Empire and the United States. *Journal of Economic History* XLVI:137–51.

Goodman, A. and S. Webb. 1994. *For Richer, For Poorer: The Changing Distribution of Income in the United Kingdom, 1961–1991*. London: Institute for Fiscal Studies.

Goody, J. 1971. Class and Marriage in Africa and Eurasia. *American Journal of Sociology* 76:585–603.

Gottschalk, P., B. Gustafsson, and E. Palmer, Eds. 1997. *Changing Patterns in the Distribution of Economic Welfare: An International Perspective.* Cambridge: Cambridge University Press.

Gould, S. J. 1982. Darwinism and the Expansion of Evolutionary Theory. *Science* 216: 380–387.

Gould, S. J. 2002. *The Structure of Evolutionary Theory.* Cambridge, MA: Harvard University Press.

Grandjean, B. D. 1975. An Economic Analysis of the Davis-Moore Theory of Stratification. *Social Forces* 53:543–52.

Granovetter, M. 1985. Economic Action and Social Structure: The Problem of Embeddedness. *American Journal of Sociology* 91:481–510.

Grant, R. and J. R. Short (ed). 2002. *Globalization and the Margins.* Basingstoke, UK, and New York: Palgrave Macmillan.

Greenhalgh, S. 1985. Is Inequality Demographically Induced? The Family Cycle and the Distribution of Income in Taiwan. *American Anthropologist* 87:571–94.

Gregorio, J. and J-W Lee. 2002. Education and Income Inequality: New Evidence from Cross Country Data. *Review of Income and Wealth* 48:395–416.

Grenier, C. 1984. An Empirical Assessment of the Inequality-Development Relationship: An International Comparative Analysis. *International Journal of Contemporary Sociology* 21:83–98.

Griffin, K. and Z. Renwei. 1993. *The Distribution of Income in China.* London: St. Martin's Press.

Griffin, K., A. R. Khan, and A. Ickowitz. 2001. *Poverty and the Distribution of Land.* Department of Economics, University of California, Riverside. Mimeo.

Haas, A. 1993. Social inequality in Aboriginal North America: A Test of Lenski's Theory. *Social Forces* 72:295–313.

Hall, T. and P. Hubbard. 1998. *The Entrepreneurial City.* Chichester: Wiley.

Haller, M. 1981. Marriage, Women, and Social Stratification: A Theoretical Critique. *The American Journal of Sociology* 86:766–95.

Hansen, B. and S. Radwan. 1982. *Employment Opportunities and Equity in Egypt.* Geneva: International Labor Office.

Harding, A. and H. Greenwell. 2001. *Trends in Income and Expenditure Inequality in the 1980s and 1990s.* Discussion Paper no. 56. National Center for Social and Economic Modeling. Canberra: University of Canberra.

Harvey, D. 1982. *The Limits to Capital.* Oxford: Blackwell.

Hausman, R. and R. Rigobon, Editors. 1993. *Government Spending and Income Distribution in Latin America.* Washington DC: The Inter-American Development Bank.

Heckathorn, D. D. 1991. Extension's of the Prisoner's Dilemma Paradigm: The Altruist's Dilemma and Group Solidarity. *Sociological Theory* 9:34–52.

Henderson, J. V. 1982. The Impact of Government Policies on Urban Concentration. *Journal of Urban Economics* 9:64–71.

Herrnstein, R. and C. Murray. 1994. *The Bell Curve: Intelligence and Class Structure in American Life.* New York: The Free Press.

Henderson, J. V. 1988. *Urban Development: Theory, Fact and Illusion.* New York: Oxford University Press.

Hewstone, M., M. Rubin, and H. Willis. 2002. Intergroup Bias. *Annual Review of Psychology* 53:575–604.

Higgins, B. and D. J. Savoie. 1995. *Regional Development Theories and their Application.* London: Transaction Publishers.

Higgins, M. and J. G. Williamson. 2002. Explaining Inequality the World Round: Cohort Size, Kuznets Curves, and Openness. *Southeast Asian Studies* 40:268–302.

Hirschman, A. O. 1958. *The Strategy of Economic Development.* New Haven: Yale University Press.

Hirschman, A. O. 1973. The Changing Tolerance for Income Inequality in the Course of Economic Development. *Quarterly Journal of Economics* 87:544–65.

Hodgson, G. M. 1998. The Approach of Institutional Economics. *Journal of Economic Literature* 36:166–92.

Hung, R. 1996. The Great U-Turn in Taiwan: Economic Restructuring and a Surge in Inequality. *Journal of Contemporary Asia* 26:151–63.

Hunt, E. H. 1986. Industrialization and Regional Inequality: Wages in Britain, 1760–1914. *Journal of Economic History* XLVI: 935–66.

IADB (Integration and Regional Programs) website. http://www.iadb.org/sds/pov/site_16_e.htm

Ikemoto, Y. 1993. Income Distribution and Malnutrition in Thailand. *Chulalongkorn Journal of Economics* 5:136–60.

Ikemoto, Y. and K. Limskul. 1987. Income Inequality and Regional Disparity in Thailand, 1962–81. *The Developing Economies* 25:249–69.

Indonesia. Various issues. *Statistical Yearbook of Indonesia.*

Israeli Ministry of Finance. 1998. Annual State of Revenue Report for 1997.

Jackson, R. V. 1994. Inequality of Incomes and Lifespans in England Since 1688. *The Economic History Review* 47:508–24.

Jain, S. 1975. *Size Distribution of Income: A Compilation of Data.* Washington DC: The World Bank.

Jalan, J. and M. Ravallion. 1997. *Spatial Poverty Traps?* Development Research Group Working Paper # 1862. Washington D.C.: World Bank.

Jessop, B. 1972. *Social Order, Reform and Revolution: A Power, Exchange and Institutionalization Perspective.* New York: Herder and Herder.

Jha, R. 1999. Reducing Poverty and Inequality in India: Has Liberalization Helped? UNU/WIDER draft paper. Mimeo.

Jha, S. K. 1996. The Kuznets Curve: A Reassessment. *World Development* 24:773–80.

Johnson, E. A. J. 1970. *The Organization of Space in Developing Countries.* Cambridge, MA: Harvard University Press.

Kahneman, D. 2003. Maps of Bounded Rationality: Psychology for Behavioral Economics. *American Economic Review* 93:1449–75.

Kakwani, N. 1986. *Analyzing Redistribution Policies.* Cambridge: Cambridge University Press.

Kakwani, N. 1996. Income Inequality, Welfare, and Poverty in Ukraine. *Development and Change* 27:663–91.

Kaldor, N. 1956. Alternative Theories of Distribution. *Review of Economic Studies* 23:83–100.

Kaldor, N. 1957. A Model of Economic Growth. *The Economic Journal* 67:591–624.

Kamark, A. M. 1983. *Economics and the Real World.* Oxford: Blackwell.

Kamark, A. M. 2002. *Economics as a Social Science: An Approach to Nonautistic Theory.* Ann Arbor: University of Michigan Press.

Kanbur, R. and X. Zhang. 2003. Fifty Years of Regional Inequality in China: A Journey Through Central Planning, Reform and Openness. Paper presented at UNU WIDER Conference on Spatial inequality in Asia, March 2003. Downloaded on April 5, 2004 from http://www.wider.unu.edu/conference/conference-2003-1/conference2003-1.htm

Kaplinsky, R. 2001. Globalisation and Unequalisation: What Can be Learned from Value Chain Analysis. *Journal of Development Studies* 37:117–46.

Keane, M. P. and E. S. Prasad. 2001. Poland: Inequality, Transfers, and Growth in Transition. *Finance and Development.* March pp. 50–54.

Keister, L. 2000. *Wealth in America: Trends in Wealth Inequality.* Cambridge: Cambridge University Press.

Kelley, J. and H. S. Klein. 1981. *Revolution and the Rebirth of Inequality: A Theory Applied to the National Revolution in Bolivia.* Berkeley: The University of California Press.

Khan, A. R. 1977. The Distribution of Income in Rural China. In *Poverty and Landlessness in Rural Asia.* Geneva: ILO.

Khan, A. R. 1993. Structural Adjustment and Income Distribution: Issues and Experience. Geneva: International Labour Office.

Knight, J. B. and R. H. Sabot. 1983. Educational Attainment and the Kuznets Effect. *American Economic Review* 73:1132–6.

Kohl, B. 2002. Stabilizing Neoliberalism in Bolivia: Popular Participation and Privatization. *Political Geography* 21:449–72.

Kolm, S.-C. 1969. The Optimal Production of Social Justice. In *Public Economics.* J. Margolis and H. Guitton Eds. London: MacMillan. pp. 145–200.

Korea NBS (National Bureau of Statistics). Various issues. Social Indicators in Korea.

Kravis, I. G. 1960. International Differences in the Distribution of Income. *Review of Economics and Statistics* 42:408–16.

Krugman, P. 1991. Increasing Returns and Economic Geography. *Journal of Political Economy* 99:483–499.

Krugman, P. 1992. The Rich, the Right, and the Facts: Deconstructing the Income Distribution Debate. *The American Prospect.* Vol3, Issue 11. Online at http://www.prospect.org/print/V3/11/krugman-p.html

Krugman, P. 1995. Growing World Trade: Causes and Consequences. *Brookings Papers on Economic Activity* 25:327–77.

Krugman, P. 1996. Urban Concentration: The Role of Increasing Returns and Transport Costs. *International Regional Science Review* 19:5–30

Kuznets, S. 1955. Economic Growth and Income Inequality. *American Economic Review* 45:1–28.

Landes, D. S. 1998. *The Wealth and Poverty of Nations: Why Are Some So Rich and Some So Poor?* New York: Norton.

Lawrence, R. and M. Slaughter. 1993. Trade and US Wages: Giant Sucking Sound or Small Hiccup? *Brookings Papers on Economic Activity* 161–226.

Leamer, E. E. 1998. In Search of Stolper-Samuelson Linkages Between International Trade and Lower Wages. In *Imports, Exports, and the American Worker.* S. Collins, Ed. Washington D.C.: The Brookings Institution.

Leamer, E. E., H. Maul, S. Rodriguez, and P. K. Schott. 1999. Does Natural Resource Abundance Increase Latin American Income Inequality? *Journal of Development Economics* 59:3–42.

Lecaillon, J., F. Paukert, C. Morrisson, and D. Germidis. 1984. Income Distribution and Economic Development. Geneva: International Labour Office.

Lee, S-S. 2003. Spatial Dynamic Variations of Regional Inequality: The Cases of Korea and Japan. Paper presented at the RSAI meeting in Japan. Mimeo. Online at http://www.econ.tamacc.chuo-u.ac.jp/~kmasashi/DP54.pdf

Lenski, G. 1966. *Power and Privilege.* New York: McGraw-Hill.

Lenski, G. 1975. History and Social Change. *American Journal of Sociology* 82:548–564.

Leon, C. A. and H. Leon. 1979. Estructura y Niveles de Ingreso Familiar en el Peru. Universidad del Pacifico. Mimeo.

Lewis, J. P. 1995. *India's Political Economy: Governance and Reform.* New Delhi: Oxford University Press.

Lichbach, M. I. 1989. An Evaluation of "Does Inequality Breed Political Conflict" Studies. *World Politics* 41:431–70.

Lindert, P. H. and J. G. Williamson. 1985. Growth, Equality, and History. *Explorations In Economic History* 22:341–77.

Lipton, M. 1977. Why Poor People Stay Poor: Urban Bias and World Development. London: Temple Smith.

LIS Web. 2000. Luxembourg Income Study (LIS). http://www.aeaweb.org/RFE/Data/World/LIS.html.

Lucas, R. E. B. and D. W. Verry. 1996. Growth and Income Distribution in Malaysia. *International Labor Review* 35:553–75.

Lustig. N. Ed. 1995. *Coping with Austerity: Poverty and Inequality In Latin America.* Washington DC: World Bank.

Lustig, N. 1998. Comment on External Sector and Income Distribution. In *Income Distribution and High Quality Growth.* V. Tanzi and K. Chu Eds. Cambridge, MA: the MIT Press. pp. 291–294.

Lydall, H. 1977. *Income Distribution During the Process of Development.* Geneva: International Labor Office.

Maddison, A. and Associates. 1992. *The Political Economy of Poverty, Equity, and Growth: Brazil and Mexico.* New York: Oxford University Press (published for the World Bank).

Marjit, S. and R. Acharyya. 2003. *International Trade, Wage Inequality, and the Developing Economy: A General Equilibrium Approach.* Heidelburg: Physica-Verlag.

Marshall, A. 1919. *Industry and Trade.* London: Macmillan.

Martin, R. and P. Sunley. 1998. Slow Convergence? The New Endogenous Growth Theory and Regional Development. *Economic Geography* 74:201–227.

Meade, J. E. 1976. *The Just Economy. Vol. 4. Principles of Political Economy.* Albany: State University of New York Press.

Midlarsky, M. I. 1999. *The Evolution of Inequality: War, State Survival, and Democracy in Comparative Perspective.* Stanford, CA: Stanford University Press.

Milanovic, B. 1994. *Determinants of Cross-country Income Inequality: An Augmented Kuznets Hypothesis.* World Bank Policy Research Working Paper number 1246. Washington DC: The World Bank.

Milanovic, B. 1998. *Income, Inequality, and Poverty during the Transition from Planned to Market Economy.* Washington DC: World Bank.

Milanovic, B. 2002. True World Income Distribution, 1988 and 1993: First Calculation Based on Household Surveys Alone. *Economic Journal* 112:51–92.

Milanovic, B. 2004. *Half a World: Regional Inequality in Five Great Federations.* Mimeo.

Milanovic, B. and Y. Ying. 1996. *Notes on Income Distribution in Eastern Europe.* Washington DC: The World Bank.

Mills, E. S. 1987. Non-Urban Policies as Urban Policies. *Urban Studies* 24:245–254.

Mincer, J. 1974. *Schooling, Experience, and Earnings.* New York: National Bureau of Economic Research.

Mizoguichi, T. 1985. Economic Development Policy and Income Distribution: The Experience in East and Southeast Asia. *The Developing Economies* 23:307–24.

Mizoguchi, T. and N. Takayama. 1984. *Equity and Poverty Under Rapid Economic Growth: The Japanese Experience.* Tokyo: Kinokuniya.

Montgomery, M. 1988. How Large is Too Large? Implications of the City Size Literature for Population Policy and Research. *Economic Development and Cultural Change* 36:691–720.

Mookherjee, D. and D. Ray. 2003. Persistent Inequality. *Review of Economic Studies* 70:369–93.

Moore, B. Jr. 1966. *Social Origins of Dictatorship and Democracy.* Boston: Beacon.

Moore, B. Jr. 1978. *Injustice: The Social Bases of Obedience and Revolt.* White Plains, NY: Sharpe.

Mulé, R. 2001. *Political Parties, Games, and Redistribution.* Cambridge: Cambridge University Press.

Muller, E. N. 1988. Democracy, Economic Development, and Income Inequality. *American Sociological Review* 53:50–68.

Myrdal, G. 1957. *Economic Theory and Underdeveloped Regions.* London: Duckworth.

Nadvi, G. and H. Schmitz. 1999. Industrial Clusters in Developing Countries (special topic) *World Development* 27:1503–1704.

Netherlands CSO. 1995. Inkomen en Vermogen 1992–1994.

Netherlands. Various issues. *Statistical Yearbook of the Netherlands.*

New Zealand CSO. Household Economic Survey. www.stats.govt.nz/products-and-services/info-releases/hes-info-releases.htm

New Zealand. Various issues. *Official Yearbook (OYN).* Department of Statistics.

Ngwafon, J. 1995. Income Inequality in Nigeria. Washington DC: The World Bank.

Nisbet, R. 1969. *Social Change and History.* New York: Oxford Galaxy.

Noorbakhsh, F. 2003. *Spatial Inequality and Polarization in India.* CREDIT Research Paper no. 03/16. University of Nottingham. Mimeo.

North, D. C. 1975. Location Theory and Regional Economic Growth. In *Regional Policy: Readings in Theory and Application.* J. Friedmann and W. Alonso Eds. Cambridge, MA: MIT Press.

North, D. C. 1990. *Institutions, Institutional Change, and Economic Performance.* Cambridge: Cambridge University Press.

Norway. Various issues. *Statistical Yearbook of Norway.*

Nugent, J. B. 1983. An Alternative Source of Measurement Error as Explanation for the Inverted Hypothesis. *Economic Development and Cultural Change* 31:385–396.

Odell, P. R. 1974. The Problem of Geographical Scale in Approaching Regional Development Issues and Policies. In *Proceedings of the Commission on Regional Aspects of Development.* Toronto: Allister.

Ogwang, T. 1995. The Economic Development—Income Inequality Nexus: Further Evidence on Kuznets' U-Curve Hypothesis. *American Journal of Economics and Sociology* 54:217–29.

Ohmae, K. 1995. *The End of the Nation State: The Rise of Regional Economies.* New York: The Free Press.

Okun, A. M. 1975. *Equality and Efficiency: The Big Trade Off.* Washington, D.C.: The Brookings Institution.

Oshima, H. T. 1994. The Impact of Technological Transformation on Historical Trends in Income Distribution of Asia and the West. *The Developing Economies* 32: 237–55.

Oshima, H. T. 1962. The International Comparison of Size Distribution of Family Income with Special Reference to Asia. *Review of Economics and Statistics* 44:439–44.

Paige, J. M. 1983. Social Theory and Peasant Revolution in Vietnam and Guatemala. *Theory and Society* 12:699–737.

Pakistan. 1992. *Economic Survey 1990–91.* Karachi: Government of Pakistan.

Pakistan. Various issues. *Household Income and Expenditure Survey.* Karachi: Government of Pakistan.

Panama DEC. Censos Nacionales de 1980: Octavo Censo de Poblacion; Cuarto Censo de Vivienda. Panama City: Characteristicas Economicas.

Panuco-Laguette, H. and Szekely, M. 1996. Income Distribution and Poverty in Mexico. In *The New Economic Model in Latin America and its Impact on Income Distribution and Poverty.* V. Bulmer-Thomas, Ed. Institute for Latin American Studies. London: University of London.

Papanek, G. 1978. Economic Growth, Income Distribution, and the Political Process in Less Developed Countries. In *Income Distribution and Economic Inequality*, Griliches et al. Eds. New York: Halsted Press.

Papanek, G. and O. Kyn. 1986. The Effect on Income Distribution of Development, the Growth Rate, and Economic Strategy. *Journal of Development Economics* 23:55–65.

Pareto, V. 1897. *Cours d'Economie Politique*. Lausanne: Rouge.

Park, J-G. 1980. Data on the Distribution of Income in El Salvador. Division Working Paper no. 1980–7. Washington DC: The World Bank.

Parsa, M. 2000. *States, Ideologies, and Social Revolutions: A Comparative Analysis of Iran, Nicaragua, and the Philippines*. Cambridge: Cambridge University Press.

Pasinetti, L. L. 1962. The Rate of Profit and Income Distribution in Relation to the Rate of Economic Growth. *Review of Economic Studies* 29:267–79.

Paukert, F. 1973. Income Distribution at Different Levels of Development. *International Labor Review* 108:97–125.

Paynter, R. 1989. The Archaeology of Equality and Inequality. *Annual Review of Anthropology* 18:369–99.

Pen, J. 1971. *Income Distribution*. Hammondsworth: Allen Lane.

Perotti, R. 1993. Political Equilibrium, Income Distribution, and Growth. *Review of Economic Studies* 60:755–66.

Perroux, F. 1950. Economic Space: Theory and Applications. *Quarterly Journal of Economics* 64:89–104.

Persson, T. and G. Tabellini. 1994. Is Inequality Harmful for Growth? *American Economic Review* 84:600–21.

Peru. 1991. Annuario Estadico. Lima.

Perumal, M. 1989. Economic Growth and Income Inequality in Malaysia, 1957–1984. *Singapore Economic Review* 34:32–46.

Petrakos, G. C. 1992. Urban Concentration and Agglomeration: Re-Examining the Relationship. *Urban Studies* 29:1219–1230.

Philippines. Various issues. *Philippine Statistical Yearbook*. Manila.

Pigou, A. C. 1920 [1932]. *The Economics of Welfare*. Fourth Edition. London: Macmillan.

Piore, M., Sabel C. 1984. *The Second Industrial Divide*. New York: Basic Books.

Podder, N. 1972. Distribution of Household Income in Australia. *The Economic Record* 48:181–200.

Podkaminer, L. 2003. A Note on the Evolution of Inequality in Poland, 1992–99. *Cambridge Journal of Economics* 27:755–68.

Polanyi, K. *The Great Transformation*. New York: Rinehart.

Popkin, S. 1979. *The Rational Peasant*. Berkeley: The University of California Press.

Porter, M. 1990. *The Competitive Advantage of Nations*. London: Macmillan.

Porter, M. 1996. Competitive Advantage, Agglomeration Economies, and Regional Policy. *International Regional Science Review* 19:160–76

Pritchett, L. 1997. Divergence, Big Time. *Journal of Economic Perspectives* 11:3–17.

Psacharopoulos, G., S. Morley, A. Fiszbein, H. Lee, and B. Wood. 1992. Poverty and Income Distribution in Latin America: The Story of the 1980's. Technical Paper no. 351. Washington DC: The World Bank.

Psacharopoulos, G., S. Morley, A. Fiszbein, H. Lee, and W. C. Wood. 1995. Poverty and Income Inequality in Latin America During the 1980s. *Review of Income and Wealth* 41:245–64.

Quah, D. 1993. Empirical Cross Section Dynamics in Economic Growth. *European Economics* 37:35–46.

Ram, R.1988. Economic Development and Income Inequality: Further Evidence on the U Curve Hypothesis. *World Development* 16:1371–75.

Ramirez-Faria, C. 1991. *The Origins of Economic Inequality between Nations: A Critique on Western Theories of Development and Underdevelopment.* London: Unwin Hyman.

Ranis, G. 1996. Comment on Inequality, Poverty, and Growth: Where Do We Stand? by Albert Fishlow in *Annual World Bank Conference on Development Economics 1995*, M. Bruno and B. Pleskovic. Eds. Washington DC: The World Bank.

Rao, G. M., R. Shand, K. and P. Kalirajan. 1999. Convergence of Incomes Across Indian States: A Divergent View. *Economic and Political Weekly.* March 27.

Rao, V. V. B. 1989. Income Inequality and Poverty in East Asia: Trends and Implications. *Indian Economic Journal* 37.

Rawls, J. A. 1971. *A Theory of Justice.* Cambridge, MA: Harvard University Press.

Reynolds, L. G. 1996. Some Sources of Income Inequality in Latin America. *Journal of Interamerican Studies and World Affairs* 38:39–47.

Richardson, H. W. 1973. *Regional Growth Theory.* London: MacMillan.

Robertson, R. 1992. *Globalisation.* London: Sage.

Robertson, R. 2002. Opposition and Resistance to Globalization. In *Globalization and the Margins.* R. Grant and J. R. Short, Eds. Basingstoke, UK, and New York: Palgrave Macmillan.

Roemer, J. E. 1998. *Equality of Opportunity.* Cambridge, MA: Harvard University Press.

Rohlen, T. P. 2002. Cosmopolitan Cities and Nation States: Open Economics, Urban Dynamics, and Government in East Asia. Stanford: Asia/Pacific Research Center. Mimeo.

Rosser, J. B. Jr. 1999. On the Complexities of Complex Economic Dynamics. *Journal of Economic Perspectives* 13:169–92.

Russell, T. 1997. The Rationality Hypothesis in Economics: From Wall Street to Main Street. *Journal of Economic Methodology* 4:83–100.

Sachs, J. D., N. Bajpai, and A. Ramiah. 2002. Understanding Regional Economic Growth in India. CID Working Paper #88. Harvard University. Mimeo.

Sachs, J. and H. Shatz. 1994. Trade and Jobs in U.S. Manufacturing. *Brookings Papers on Economic Activity* 1–84.

Sahota, G. S. 1978. Theories of Personal Income Distribution: A Survey. *Journal of Economic Literature* 16:1–55.

Saith, A. 1983. Development and Distribution: A Critique of the Cross-Country U-Hypothesis. *Journal of Development Economics* 13:15–32.

Sala-i-Martin, X. 1996. Regional Cohesion: Evidence and Theories of Regional Growth and Convergence. *European Economic Review* 40:1325–52.

Saltz, I. S. 1995. Income Distribution in the Third World: Its Estimation via Proxy Data. *American Journal of Economics and Sociology* 54:15–31.

Salzman, P. C. 1999. Is Inequality Universal? *Current Anthropology* 40:31–61.

Sarkar, S. 1999. *Writing Social History.* Oxford and New Delhi: Oxford University Press.

Sastry, D. V. S. and U. R. Kelkar. 1994. Note on the Decomposition of Gini Inequality. *The Review of Economics and Statistics* 76:584–86.

Saunders, P. 1993. Longer Run Changes in the Distribution of Income in Australia. *The Economic Record* 69:353–66.

Schmidt-Hebbel, K. and L. Servén. 2000. Does Income Inequality Raise Aggregate Saving? *Journal of Development Economics* 61:417–46.

Schultz, T. P. 1998. Inequality in the Distribution of Personal Income in the World: How it is Changing and Why. *Journal of Population Economics* 11:307–44.

Schultz, T. W. 1960. Capital Formation by Education. *Journal of Political Economy* 68:571–83.

Schultz, T. W. 1971. *Investment in Human Capital.* New York: Free Press.

Schumpeter, J. 1951. *Imperialism and Social Classes.* New York: New American Library.

Scott, A. J. 1988. Flexible Production Systems and Regional Development: The Rise of New Industrial Spaces in North America and Western Europe. *International Journal of Urban and Regional Research* 12:171–185.

Scott, J. C. 1976. *The Moral Economy of the Peasant*. New Haven: Yale University Press.

Scott, J. C. 1986. *Weapons of the Weak: Everyday Forms of Peasant Resistance*. New Haven: Yale University Press.

Sen, A. K. 1973. *On Economic Inequality*. Oxford: Clarendon Press.

Sen, A. K. 1977. Rational Fools: A Critique of the Behavioral Foundations of Economic Theory. *Philosophy and Public Affairs* 6:317–44.

Sen, A. K. 1985. *Commodities and Capabilities*. Amsterdam: North Holland.

Sen, A. K. 1987. *On Ethics and Economics*. Oxford and New York: Blackwell.

Sen, A. K. 1992. *Inequality Reexamined*. New York and Oxford: Russell Sage Foundation and Clarendon Press.

Sen, A. K. 2002. Globalization, Inequality, and Global Protest. *Development* 45:11–16.

Shammas, C. 1993. A New Look at Long-Term Trends in Wealth Inequality in the United States. *American Historical Review* 98:418–35.

Shirahase, S. 2001. *Japanese Income Inequality by Household Types in Comparative Perspective*. Working Paper no. 268. Luxembourg Income Study. Luxembourg.

Shorrocks, A. F.1975. On Stochastic Models of Size Distributions. *Review of Economic Studies* 42:631–41.

Shorrocks, A. F. 1982. Inequality Decomposition by Factor Components. *Econometrica* 50:193–211.

Shorrocks, A. F. 1984. Inequality Decomposition by Population Subgroups. *Econometrica* 52:1369–85.

Shukla, V. 1984. The Productivity of Indian Cities and Some Implications for Development Policy. Unpublished Ph.D. thesis. Princeton, NJ: Princeton University.

Simon, H. A. 1955. A Behavioral Model of Rational Choice. *Quarterly Journal of Economics* 69:99–118.

Singh, N., L. Bhandari, A. Chen, and A. Khare. 2002. *Regional Inequality in India: A Fresh Look*. Mimeo.

Sjoberg, G. 1960. *The Pre-Industrial City*. Rotterdam: The Free Press.

Slovic, P., M. Finucane, E. Peters, and D.G. McGregor. 2002. The Affect Heuristic. In *Heuristics and Biases: The Psychology of Intuitive Thought*. T. Gilovich, D. Griffin, and D. Kahneman, Eds. New York: Cambridge University Press. pp. 397–420.

Smith, A. 1776. *An Inquiry into the Nature and Causes of the Wealth of Nations*. London: Routledge.

Sober, E. and D. S. Wilson. 1998. *Unto Others: The Evolution and Psychology of Unselfish Behavior*. Cambridge, MA: Harvard University Press.

Sokoloff, K. L. and S. L. Engerman. 2000. History Lessons Institutions, Factor Endowments, and Paths of Development in the New World. *Journal of Economic Perspectives* 14: 217–32.

Sollogoub, M. 1988. L'Inegalite des Revenus Primaires en France de 1962 a 1979. *Revue Economique*, No 3.

Solow, R. 1956. A Contribution to the Theory of Economic Growth. *Quarterly Journal of Economics* 70:65–94.

Spear, P. 1965. *A History of India. Volume Two*. New Delhi: Penguin Books.

Starrett, D. 1976. Social Institutions, Imperfect Information, and the Distribution of Income. *The Quarterly Journal of Economics* 90:261–84.

Stewart, F. and A. Berry. 2000. Globalization, Liberalization, and Inequality: Real Causes. *Challenge* 43:44–92.

Stiglitz, J. E. and L. Squire. 1998. International Development: Is it Possible? *Foreign Policy*. Spring: 138–51.

Storper, M. 1991. *Industrialization, Economic Development and the Regional Question in the Third World: From Import Substitution to Flexible Production.* London: Pion.

Sundrum, R. M. 1987. *Growth and Income Distribution in India: Policy and Performance Since Independence.* New Delhi, Newberry Park, and London: Sage.

Sveikauskas, L. 1975. The Productivity of Cities. *Quarterly Journal of Economics* 89:393–413.

Sweden. Various issues. *Statistical Abstract of Sweden* (SAS). Stockholm: Sveriges Office Statistik.

Szekely, M. and M. Hilgert. 1999. *What Is Behind the Inequality We Measure?* An Investigation Using Latin American Data. Working Paper no. 234. Luxembourg Income Study. Luxembourg.

Tachibanaki, T. 1998. *Nihon no Keizaikakusa* (Economic Inequality in Japan). Tokyo: Iwanami Shoten.

Taiwan. Directorate-General of Budget Accounts and Statistics. *Report on the Survey of Personal Income Distribution in Taiwan Area of the Republic of China* (SPIDT). Various Issues. The Executive Yuan. Taiwan.

Taubman, P. 1975. *Sources of Inequality of Earnings.* Amsterdam: North Holland.

Temple, J. 1999. The New Growth Evidence. *Journal of Economic Literature* 37:112–56.

Theil, H. 1972. *Statistical Decomposition Analysis.* Amsterdam: North Holland.

Thompson, E. P. 1963. *The Making of the English Working Class.* New York: Vintage Books.

Tilly, C. 1978. *From Mobilization to Revolution.* Reading, MA: Addison-Wesley.

Tilly, C. 1998. *Durable Inequality.* Berkeley: University of California Press.

Timberlake, M. 1987. World-System Theory and the Study of Comparative Urbanization. In *The Capitalist City: Global Restructuring and Community Politics.* M. P. Smith and J. R. Feagin Eds. London: Blackwell. pp. 37–65.

Tsionas, E. G. 2000. Regional Growth and Convergence: Evidence from the United States. *Regional Studies* 34:231–38.

Tunisia, Institut National de la Statistique (INS). 1993. *Enquete Nationale sur le Budget et la Consommation des Menages–1990,* Vol. A.

Turkey. Various issues. Statistical Yearbook of Turkey.

United Nations. 1981. *A Survey of National Sources of Income Distribution Statistics.* Statistical Papers, Series M, No. 72. New York:UN.

United Nations. 1985. *National Accounts Statistics: Compendium of Income Distribution Statistics.* Statistical Papers, Series M, No. 79. New York: UN.

US Bureau of the Census (USBCS). 1992 and 1984. *Current Population Reports,* Series P-60, No. 142 and No. 180.

Uusitalo, H. 1989. *Income Distribution in Finland.* Helsinki: Central Statistical Office of Finland.

van Ginneken, W. 1982. *Rural and Urban Income Inequalities in Indonesia, Mexico, Pakistan, Tanzania and Tunisia.* Geneva: International Labor Office

van Ginneken, W. and J-G Park. 1984. *Generating Internationally Comparable Income Distribution Estimates.* Geneva: International Labor Office.

Van Praag, B. M. S. 1968. *Individual Welfare Functions and Consumer Behavior.* Amsterdam: North Holland.

Varshney, A. 1999. *Democracy and Poverty.* Paper for the Conference on World Development Report 2000 (mimeo).

Wade, R. 1990. *Governing the Market.* Princeton: Princeton University Press.

Wakeman, F. 1977. Rebellion and Revolution: The Study of Popular Movements in Chinese History. *Journal of Asian Studies* 36:201–37.

Weber, M. 1968. *Economy and Society: An Outline of Interpretive Sociology.* Translated by G. Roth and C. Wittich. New York: Bedminster Press.

Weede, E. 1982. The Effects of Democracy and Socialist Strength on the Size Distribution of Income. *International Journal of Comparative Sociology* 23:151–65.

Wei, Y. D. 2000. *Regional Development in China: States, Globalization, and Inequality.* London and New York: Routledge.

Wei, Y. D. and L. J. C. Ma. 1996. Changing Patterns of Spatial Inequality in China, 1952–1990. *Third World Planning Review* 18:177–91.

Wheaton, W. C. and H. Shishido. 1981. Urban Concentration, Agglomeration Economies and the Levels of Economic Development. *Economic Development and Cultural Change* 30:17–30.

White, M. 1983. The Measurement of Spatial Segregation. *American Journal of Sociology* 88:1008–18.

Williamson, J. 1990. *Latin American Adjustment: How Much has Happened?* Washington DC: Institute of International Economics.

Williamson, J. 2000, What Should the World Bank Think about the Washington Consensus? *World Bank Research Observer* 15:251–64.

Williamson, J. G. 1965. Regional Inequality and the Process of National Development. *Economic Development and Cultural Change* 13:3–45.

Williamson, O. 1975. *Markets and Hierarchies, Analysis and Anti-trust Implications: A Study in the Economics of Internal Organization.* New York: Free Press.

Wolf, E. R. 1982. *Peasant Wars of the Twentieth Century.* New York: Harper and Row.

Wolff, E. N. 2000. *Recent Trends in Wealth Ownership, 1983–1998.* Working Paper no. 300. Jerome Levy Economics Institute.

Wolfson, M. C. 1994. When Inequalities Diverge. *American Economic Review* 84:353–58.

Wongshphasawat, L. 1997. The Extended Bangkok Metropolitan Region and Uneven Industrial Development in Thailand. In *Uneven Development in Southeast Asia*, C. Dixon and D. Drakakis-Smith Eds. Aldershot: Ashgate.

Wood, A. 1995. How Trade Hurts Unskilled Workers. *Journal of Economic Perspectives* 9:57–80.

Wood, A. 1997. Openness and Wage Inequality in Developing Countries: The Latin American Challenge to the East Asian Conventional Wisdom. *World Bank Economic Review* 11:33–57.

Wood, C. and J. Carvalho. 1988. *The Demography of Inequality in Brazil.* Cambridge: Cambridge University Press.

World Bank. 1994. *Colombia Poverty Assessment Report.* Report 12673. Washington DC: The World Bank.

World Bank. 1999. *Entering the 21st Century: World Development Report 1999/2000.* Washington, D.C.: The World Bank.

World Bank. 2000. *Making Transition Work for Everyone: Poverty and Inequality in Europe and Central Asia.* Washington D.C.: The World Bank.

World Bank. 2001. *World Development Indicators 2001.* Washington D.C.: The World Bank.

WIDER (World Institute for Development Economics Research). 2000. *World Income Inequality Database: User Guide and Data Sources.* Helsinki: United Nations University.

Yang, D. T. 1999. Urban-Biased Policies and Rising Income Inequality in China. *American Economic Review* (Papers and Proceedings) 89:306–10.

Yim, C-H. 1985. Spatial Population Concentration and Socio-spatial Inequality Changes in the Development Path: The Case of Korea. Unpublished Ph.D. dissertation. Harvard University.

Ying, W. Y. 1995. Income, Poverty, and Inequality in China during the Transition. Mimeo. Washington DC: The World Bank.

Zhang, X. and R. Kanbur. 2001. What Differences do Polarization Measures Make? An Application to China. *Journal of Development Studies* 37:85–98.

Zukin, S. and P. DiMaggio, Eds. 1990. Introduction. In *Structures of Capital.* Cambridge: Cambridge University Press.

INDEX

p 159/62 problem

who is outsider
change agent?

163-4 trade + gap
inequality vs unequal
exchange
(219)

Reg. devel.t (178-79)

Roemer models?

uneven devel.t?

evidential claim · 213-6

evolutionary theories